Alexander Allardyce

The City of Sunshine

Vol. I

Alexander Allardyce

The City of Sunshine
Vol. I

ISBN/EAN: 9783337040482

Printed in Europe, USA, Canada, Australia, Japan

Cover: Foto ©ninafisch / pixelio.de

More available books at **www.hansebooks.com**

THE CITY OF SUNSHINE

A NOVEL

BY

ALEXANDER ALLARDYCE

IN THREE VOLUMES

VOL. I.

WILLIAM BLACKWOOD AND SONS
EDINBURGH AND LONDON
MDCCCLXXVII

CONTENTS OF THE FIRST VOLUME.

CHAP.		PAGE
I.	THE LINGA OF DHUPNAGAR,	1
II.	THREE SHELLS, THE MAHAJAN,	17
III.	RADHA'S THREE LOVERS,	34
IV.	FATHER AND SON,	52
V.	THE COUNCIL OF FIVE,	72
VI.	THE PRIEST SCOTCHES A SNAKE,	89
VII.	SHAMSUDDEEN KHAN, THE SUBADAR,	100
VIII.	THREE SHELLS' CONVERSION,	123
IX.	THE PRIEST'S ZENANA,	141
X.	THE DIPTY CATCHES AN IDEA,	156
XI.	EVERSLEY SAHIB,	171
XII.	KRISHNA'S LETTERS,	187
XIII.	HUSBAND AND WIFE,	207
XIV.	A GIFT FROM THE GREEKS,	226
XV.	A MORNING AT RUTTON PAL'S,	243
XVI.	BEJOY, THE GHATAK,	260
XVII.	KRISHNA AGONISTES,	285

THE CITY OF SUNSHINE.

CHAPTER I.

THE LINGA OF DHUPNAGAR.

It was the morning after the Dewali Puja, the Hindoo "Feast of Lanterns," and though the sun was already high over head, not a soul was astir in the little village of Dhupnagar. The waters of the big tank where folks bathed the first thing of a morning, sparkled brightly in the dazzling rays, undisturbed except by the nocturnal cur that, encouraged by the unusual stillness, had ventured out of the jungle to drink. The bazaar was tenantless. Shops, with their wares temptingly exposed to any passing thief, stood open upon each side of the street; but the owners, worn out by last night's excitement, were still too sleepy to think of buying or selling. Even greedy Ram Lall, the oilman, who was generally the first to open his shop in the morning and the last to leave it at night, had not made his appearance, but was still probably dreaming of the profits that he had netted off last night's illuminations. The jackals were snuffing about the deserted streets, looking hungrily for garbage, and wondering what had become of the lords of the creation. All over the village there were signs of the festival. Each house had its row of tiny earthen lamps arranged upon the window-sill, or hung from a projecting bamboo sapling. Some of the wealthier had even gone so far in their devotion as to display candles in neat lanterns of coloured mica. And the morning air was loaded with a fetid smell of oil and burnt wick.

More than any of the other houses the great brick mansion of the Lahory family, blackened with age and crumbling into ruins, showed traces of Dewali splendour. The verandah was hung with festoons of party-coloured lanterns, and the walls were clothed from base to summit with a network of bamboos, upon which little earthen cressets—some of them still flickering faintly in the strong sunshine—had been set forth in countless numbers. In front of the house, a score of servants or hangers-on of the family were sleeping in the open air, each stretched upon a rectangular slip of matting, with his head pillowed upon his arm or upon a roll of clothing.

Pass inside and you will find the tenants and guests of Baboo Kristo Doss Lahory lying upon *charpais*, or rude four-legged couches, snatching a few hours' rest after the riot and excitement of last night's festival, before they should set out for their homes to resume the ordinary business of life. All was quiet; no breeze stirred the trees or ruffled the smooth surfaces of the tanks; there was not even a chattering parrot or a rattling woodpecker to break the silence. A stranger entering Dhupnagar, "the city of sunshine," that morning, might have been pardoned for thinking that he fallen into a Sleepy Hollow in the plains of Bengal.

But cross the village green from the house of Lahory—pass through the hedge of thorny bamboo, whose straight tapering stems and delicately-feathered branches form a fairer curtain for a holy place than the hand of art could have designed — enter the village temple, and you are sure to find the priest astir, and probably occupying his favourite seat in the porch or enjoying his morning smoke. The temple stands in a spacious courtyard or "compound," which is entered through an arched doorway, flanked on each side by a small turret, and by apartments for the porter and other servants of the shrine. The temple is on the summit of a little knoll, and is a small unpretentious building with arched door and pointed roof, devoid of all architectural show except a few simple mouldings upon the façade. Two or three stone steps lead up to the porch which the boughs of a sacred *peepul* tree, fast rooted in the temple wall above the entrance, had been trained to form; and here in the cool evenings the priest and those friends who were privileged to enjoy his society, would seat themselves upon the broad stone platform to smoke their hookhas, chat over the village gossip, and enjoy the still beauty of the scene.

Inside the temple a small antechamber led to a central room, where in a niche stood the guardian genius of the place, the palladium of Dhupnagar. It was not a three-headed god, or a ten-armed goddess, or any of the other monstrosities of the Hindoo mythology. It was simply a round pyramidal block of black polished stone, standing a foot and a half high, and with a slight projection at its base. This was the Linga, the symbol by which men have rudely expressed the creative attributes of the self-existent Siva, the second member of the Hindoo triad; and it is, moreover, the *phallus* of Grecian worship. But the Linga of Dhupnagar is not like other Lingas, as the priest and three-fourths of the district are ready to swear. The Linga of the neighbouring town of Gapshapganj, for instance, or that of Bhutpore, the *zilla*, or county, town, are, as everybody knows, nothing more than common black stones from the Patna district, which required a deal of chiselling to bring them into the sacred form. But not so the Linga of Dhupnagar. Three or four generations back, before miracles had ceased because of the red-coated infidels creeping over the land, this Linga had started up from the ground at the feet of Harrinath Gossain, ancestor of the present priest, as he journeyed homeward from a pilgrimage to Benares, where he had offered up ten thousand rupees at the Manikarnika temple, and had gorged to surfeit fifty of the poorest Brahmins that he could find in the holy city. Harrinath had accepted the portent as a suitable acknowledgment of his piety; and taking the Linga home with him, he built for it a temple and installed himself as its priest.

When this miracle was noised abroad, worshippers flocked in crowds to Dhupnagar, whose offerings speedily recouped Harrinath in ten-fold degree for the expenses of his pilgrimage. Priests of rival shrines began to look with dismay upon the popularity of the upstart temple. Some of them did not hesitate to assert that the miracle had existed only in Harrinath's imagination; while others professed themselves ready to swear that he had either purchased or stolen the stone on his way down country. But Harrinath treated such slanders with merited contempt. In vain did the priest of Bhutpore, whose shrine had hitherto been the most fashionable place of worship in the Gungaputra district, hire a mad devotee to undergo the *shora*, for the purpose of exposing the imposture. But though the enthusiast remained wrapped in prayer before the Linga for fifteen days and nights in red garments; though he repeated the thousand sacred names of Siva ten thousand times; though he walked round the Linga in the fashion of a triangle one thousand two hundred and sixty times, prostrating himself at full length each time he passed before the image;—though he did all this without omitting the minutest particular of the *shora*, yet did not the Linga break or even bow before him, as it must infallibly have done had there not been divinity in the stone. Equally vain was it for the priest of Gapshapganj to proclaim the miraculous cure of an elephant foot, effected under the auspices of *his* Linga. A woman, indeed, asserted that such a cure had been wrought upon her, but she came from a far part of the country, and nobody could be found to vouch either for her elephantiasis or her veracity.

The spite of these detractors only added to the prosperity of the Dhupnagar temple, and soon cures were reported about which there could be no possible doubt. A rich merchant of Calcutta, whose son was wasting away with disease, had sent the lad on a pilgrimage to Dhupnagar; and its sacred atmosphere, combined with the removal of the means of dissipation, soon wrought a favourable change in the young man's health. The grateful father made over to the shrine three houses in the wealthiest quarter of Calcutta; and there they stand at this hour to refute the sneers of the sceptical. A neighbouring landholder, who had been notorious as an oppressor of his tenantry, had set apart a portion of his estates for the service of the Dhupnagar temple that things might be made smoother for his entry into the next world, and ever after he had enjoyed peace of conscience in a remarkable degree. In short, the Dhupnagar temple speedily became one of the most flourishing concerns of the kind in Lower Bengal; and the income of Ramanath Gossain was to that of the majority of other priests as a bishop's salary is to a curate's stipend.

The present incumbent of Dhupnagar was a man considerably past the prime of life. Ramanath Gossain might perhaps be fifty, or even sixty years of age, but his figure was still erect and active, his countenance fresh, and his brow unwrinkled. He had led an easy, careless, prosperous life, knowing nothing of the struggles for existence that were going on in the outside world, and troubling himself little about other people's affairs, so long as they did not affect his own comfort. The crosses he had met with had been few and trifling; his circumstances had always been affluent; his priestly office and his own amiable character procured him reverence from all with whom he came in contact; and he had been happy in his family and his domestic relations. His only brother was dwelling at Benares in the odour of sanctity as guardian of one of the wealthiest shrines in the holy city; and being himself childless, he had adopted Ramanath's second son as his heir and successor. The priest's eldest son, and only other child, a young lad of great promise, was completing his studies in Calcutta, whither Ramanath with pardonable vanity of the boy's talents had been tempted to send him. It was not until the mother of his children died that Ramanath had availed himself of his countrymen's privilege to choose a second wife; for he well knew that when the wives of his bosom cast out, the husband cannot long remain neutral. The only female inmates of his house were his own wife—the Thakoorani or lady, as she was called—a young woman of little more than half Ramanath's age, and Chakwi, the wife of his absent son. In spite of her unlucky name—Chakwi signifies a goose—the daughter-in-law was a gentle and amiable girl, the sunshine of the priest's household. She was not pretty, for her face was chubby and her eyes small and weak; and she had not even that lithe graceful figure which is common to all Bengalee girls, but was plump, dumpy, and almost waistless. She had, however, two rows of pearly teeth, unstained by betel juice, which her laughing lips seldom concealed; and her hair was glossy black and of a great length, although she always wore it braided up into a simple knot at the back of her head. The Thakoorani was indolent and fond of dress; and her time was fully taken up in bathing, dressing, and perfuming her person, and in eating, sleeping, smoking her silver hookha, and chewing tobacco mixed with betel; so that all the duties of the household fell upon the industrious Chakwi. It was Chakwi who rose at the false dawn and brought the *ghi* (clarified butter) and oil for anointing the image to her father-in-law, as he was setting out for morning worship. It was Chakwi who went over the house every morning sprinkling the floors with cow-dung and water to cleanse the rooms from the presence of ghosts and demons and other spirits of evil that might have intruded in the night-time. It was Chakwi that had prepared the breakfast of rice and fresh milk, with his favourite sweetmeats to follow, when the priest came back hungry from the temple. In short, whatever was done in Ramanath's household was done by Chakwi's hands or by Chakwi's orders.

Chakwi was legally but not actually Ramanath's daughter-in-law. The marriage ceremonies had all been performed, but the young Krishna Chandra Gossain had never yet received his bride from the hands of his father. The marriage had been contracted while both were still infants, and Krishna had never seen his young mate until she was brought to Dhupnagar in the bridal procession, when he was just turned of fifteen, and Chakwi had little more than entered upon her teens. When Krishna first saw the girl arrayed in silks and embroidery, and glittering with jewels amid the blaze of torches and coloured lamps, she had seemed to his heated imagination beautiful as one of the Apsaras who dance before the elephant throne of the god Indra. But the bridal party had scarcely reached Dhupnagar before he had convinced himself that Chakwi was not only not beautiful, but that her features and figure were cast in the very homeliest mould. From the consequent disappointment sprang a feeling of positive dislike; and when Ramanath, observing the young man's aversion, had suggested that he might as well complete his education before the consummation of the marriage, Krishna joyfully accepted the reprieve and set off for Calcutta in high spirits. At every Durga Puja Krishna returned home, bringing with him a load of prizes and testimonials from his college, and congratulatory letters to his father from all their Calcutta friends; but though he was brought into constant contact with Chakwi, and he indeed treated her with quite a brotherly fondness, not a word had ever passed his lips regarding the future relationship in which they were to stand through life. Though merry and spirited as a young kitten, Chakwi was timid and retiring in the presence of her husband, scarcely daring to let her eyes light upon him, and never raising her voice above a whisper when he was beside her. The priest, who loved the girl as his own daughter, had pleaded ineffectually with Krishna to demean himself more affectionately towards one upon whom so much of his future happiness was to depend; but though the young man promised obedience, and before his father made a show of affection for Chakwi, it was evident to Ramanath that the marriage must turn out an ill-assorted one.

And this was not the only respect in which Ramanath had cause to be dissatisfied with his son. Although the priest was proud of Krishna's scholarly acquirements, and would never tire of telling his neighbours the flattering things that the Calcutta pundits had said of him, he had of late begun to entertain serious doubts of his son's religious opinions.

When he had first determined on sending Krishna to Calcutta there were two disasters which the priest sought to guard against: one—the danger of being contaminated by profligate associates—he had averted by boarding the young man with a high-caste Brahmin who followed the virtuous and ascetic habits of the Vedic sages; the other—the chance of imbibing heterodox opinions—was, as the father thought, fully removed, when he had shown his son how injurious heresy would be to his worldly prospects. But, though all agreed that Krishna's moral character was blameless, and that his conduct was an example to the whole of his fellow-students, the priest was far from satisfied that his son was sound in the faith. Ramanath was no bigot: he was punctual in the performance of his religious duties; he professed as much reverence and enthusiasm for the Linga of Dhupnagar as could be expected from its guardian; and he gave just as much alms and fed as many Brahmins as was proper for a man in his position; and he did no more. It is possible that he may have had his own views of the Linga's sanctity, but he kept them to himself, and if he could not be called a pious man, he at least was not a godless priest. He had made up his mind that Krishna should succeed him in the guardianship of the Linga; and however tolerant he was disposed to be himself, he dared not commit the shrine to the hands of a heretic.

But each time that Krishna returned home, his father was grieved to see some fresh and stronger symptoms of a wavering faith. He who as a little child had daily tottered in his father's hand to the temple and prostrated himself in awe-struck reverence before the idol while the ceremony of adoration was being performed, would now return to Calcutta after a visit to Dhupnagar without once setting a foot inside the shrine. More than that, he openly sneered at Siva, and at the fools who thought to win the god's favour by boring their tongues or casting themselves upon spikes, as pious fanatics were wont to do in the month Choitra. But what was worst of all, he had walked into the temple one day during his last vacation, and handling the Linga without prayer or prostration, had reviled it—the sacred stone! the palladium of Dhupnagar!—as an "aerolitic monolith;" of which blasphemous expression the horrified Ramanath never dared to inquire the import. Krishna's college career was, however, nearly completed; in a few months he would have taken his degree; and then when he had settled down at home, as had been arranged, his father did not doubt that his own influence and the society of the pious Chakwi, who held in devout awe the Linga of Dhupnagar, would soon banish such unprofitable vagaries from the lad's head.

On the morning after the Dewali Puja, worthy Ramanath Gossain was stirring long before any of his townsmen. He had himself seen that his dwelling-house and the temple were illuminated by a sufficient number of lamps; he had put forth a basketful of rice still in the ear that his household might adore it as the emblem of good fortune; he had given a small present to each of his servants, with an injunction to avoid the gambling and dissipation with which the Puja was generally wound up; and then he had gone off to bed with a clear conscience, leaving his townsmen to squander away their earnings at *pachisi* with cards, or to stupefy their senses by smoking *ganja*, an intoxicating preparation of hemp-leaves. Ramanath had risen in the morning with a sound head and a good stomach; had bathed and anointed the idol, crowned it with flowers, placed an offering of incense and sweetmeats before it; and then having prostrated himself for a few minutes in prayer, he came forth and sat down on the broad stone platform outside the door to indulge in a morning smoke before going home to breakfast. A *peepul* tree which had rooted itself among the broken masonry of the roof threw forward a canopy of green tendrils over the priest's head, screening him from the morning sun, and the aspen-like murmur of its leaves soothed him into a pleasant reverie. Away from the front of the temple the country fell with a gentle slope towards the banks of the Gungaputra; and far beyond, the eye could travel over a wide expanse where green jungle alternated with greener rice-fields, with here and there the white dome of a pagoda or the brown-thatched roof of a ryot's cottage to break the prevailing colour. Bounding the view rose a low line of hills clad with forest and crested with tall *sal* trees, the first step by which the alluvial plains rose into the stony wolds and rough mountains of the Bengal highlands. The range was split into five rocky peaks, which had procured it the name of Panch Pahar among the natives of the valley. The scene was one that might well have been familiar to Ramanath's eyes, for he had sat and smoked upon that stone platform at the same time every morning these forty years; and it could not be supposed that his mind would dwell much upon the calm beauty and picturesqueness of the landscape before him.

The crackling of the dry grass outside the temple compound told of the approach of a worshipper; and soon Tin Cowry, the village *mahajan*, or money-lender, made his appearance. Shuffling along in gaudily-embroidered slippers, which were as awkward to walk in as they were ornamental to look at, Tin Cowry, or "Three Shells," as his name is rendered, was a tall, thin person, almost a walking skeleton, with a countenance cadaverous enough to complete the ghostly allusion. In demeanour Three Shells was obsequious even to servility, flattering and fawning upon every one off whom there was a possibility of his making any money. His head was generally bent and his hands clasped in respectful homage to the person whom he was for the time addressing; but those who caught a glance of the twinkling eyes and hard cruel mouth of the money-lender could not help feeling that they were face to face with a tiger in human form; a man who would not scruple to devour them, flesh and blood and bones, if ever chance should yield them to him for a prey. But Three Shells passed for a pious man in the village of Dhupnagar; and indeed it was under the plea of religion and reverence for the Linga that he had taken up his residence there, for Three Shells was a stranger from a distant part of the country. His interest seldom exceeded fifty per cent, and he never foreclosed upon a client so long as anything was to be made out of him. A much-respected man was Three Shells, for wherever he went, "salaams" and bent heads greeted his presence. A reason for this doubtless was, that there were not twelve persons in Dhupnagar but were dipped to a greater or less extent in the mahajan's books; scarcely a shopkeeper in the village whose stock the mahajan could not at any moment have seized upon as his own; hardly a plough or an ox among any of the surrounding peasants that had not been mortgaged to defray the expenses of a daughter's marriage or a father's *shraad* (funeral rites). What though the poor wretches had redeemed their pledges ten or even a hundred times over? Three Shells never quitted the grasp of a client. But in every village of Bengal the rapacity of the usurer is insatiable as that of the horse-leech; and the folks of Dhupnagar had, on the whole, reason to be satisfied that they had fallen into the hands of so equitable a mahajan. Three Shells was, as has been said, a man of great religious pretensions. No one in the village was a more regular worshipper at the temple; and no one was more strict to mark all the observances laid down in the Brahminical books. With regard to his caste, doubts had been raised when he came to Dhupnagar six years ago; but as the villagers began to borrow of him their scruples vanished, and, with the exception of the priest and the Lahories, who had never yet deigned to drink or smoke with him—the acknowledgment of caste equality—there was no one in the district who could afford to treat the mahajan otherwise than as a high-caste Brahmin.

Such was the man who now came forward to the temple door, making many lowly salutations to Ramanath as he advanced.

CHAPTER II.

THREE SHELLS, THE MAHAJAN.

THREE SHELLS stood at the foot of the steps, his body bent forward and his right hand raised in salutation to his forehead. "Salaam, great king," he murmured in a meek, whining voice. "May your prayers of the morning, which are grateful to the gods as an offering of *amrit* (ambrosia), return upon your head in the shape of heavenly blessings! May your life be prolonged, O protector of the poor!" and the moneylender, as he spoke, made a motion as if he would embrace the priest's feet.

"Salaam, Three Shells," said the priest curtly, as he scarcely raised his hookha from his lips to greet the mahajan, and waved the new-comer with his left hand to a seat on the platform.

With much deference and affectation of humility, Three Shells sat down at a respectful distance from the priest. Ramanath smoked on in silence, for the difference of caste did not permit him to offer his hookha to the money-lender.

"It was a great festival last night in Dhupnagar," Three Shells at length ventured to observe. "The streets of the village were lighted up like the courts of Agni, the god of fire. Ah, what a comfort it is to live among respectable people who worship the gods so well!"

"You set them a good example, Three Shells," said Ramanath; "those coloured lanterns that adorned your verandah were not put there for pice. I'll warrant, now, that you had them from the *zilla* (county) town, for I don't think they make such things here in Dhupnagar."

"Unworthy of your notice," responded Three Shells. "They came from Calcutta, and were all that I could do to show that, though a poor man, I am not ungrateful for the favours the gods have sent me. But, maharajah, you should have seen the *jatra* (play) at Kristo Baboo's last night. No expense was spared; the young Rajah of Ghatghar's own band of music was there, and there were two female dancers that have been honoured by the highest noblemen in Bengal. Oh, they were lovely as Lakshmi, the goddess of prosperity, and their dancing was stately as the movements of the moon through the heavens! You were not there, maharajah?"

"No," grunted Ramanath. "I went to bed, which better became a respectable man than to sit gazing at the lascivious posturings of such wantons. I am glad that Kristo Baboo has money enough to squander upon play-acting and *nâtches*."

"He he!" sniggered the mahajan, casting a sharp glance with his keen little eyes upon the priest's stolid countenance; "not so much, perhaps, if every one had his own; who knows whose pockets supplied the cost of last night's entertainments! But the Lahories are a family of good caste, and it becomes Kristo Baboo to support the dignity of his house."

"Ay, if feeding all his friends and relations upon *ghi* (clarified butter) and sweetmeats for one month, and starving himself and his family upon parched rice and cold water for the other eleven, will keep up the dignity of any family, commend me to Kristo Baboo's way of doing it. He will have to put his hands in your coffers before long, I doubt, Three Shells; that daughter of his *must* be married some day. It is a disgrace to the village that a girl of her age should be without a husband. I wish good may come of it."

Ramanath smoked away in grave disapprobation of Kristo Baboo's laxity, for among the Hindoos nothing is considered more improper than to allow a woman to reach maturity before she has been provided with a husband. But in marrying his daughter, the Hindoo of high caste has two great difficulties to encounter. In the first place, the number of eligible husbands is restricted by the minute limitations of caste; and secondly, the terrible expenditure upon the marriage ceremonies, and the heavy dower expected with the bride, fall with great severity upon a poor and proud family. It is to these considerations, which extend as far as caste itself does, that the fearful progress of infanticide in Hindoo society is due; and it is these feelings that tempt the haughty Rajpoot father who could never afford to make a suitable settlement upon his daughter, to stretch forth his hand against the life of his own offspring.

"Kristo Baboo will not be easy to please with a son-in-law," said the money-lender; "he holds his head higher than all the Brahmins in the district, except the Rajah of Ghatghar, and the Rajah has two wives already."

"A good reason why he should take a third one, Three Shells," said the priest, sententiously. "When a man has only two wives, each calls upon him for aid against the other when they fall out; but when he gets a third, the other two turn against the new-comer and leave him at peace."

"Well done! a rare jest," sniggered the money-lender, torturing his pinched features into the fashion of a smile; "but were the Rajah to offer himself, Kristo Baboo could never afford to marry his daughter to so great a man. Why, the marriage expenses could not cost less than half a lakh of rupees. And yet it is a sad pity, for the girl's beauty is famed throughout Dhupnagar."

"It *is* a pity, and that is all that can be said about it, for no good comes of gossiping about other men's family matters," said Ramanath, becoming mindful that his own household was liable to objection as containing a virgin wife. "But let us hope that Kristo Baboo may get her off his hands as soon and as decently as possible."

"There is your great son, that ocean of learning, who is the instructor of all the sages in Calcutta," insinuated the money-lender. "Why should you not take the maiden for a bride to him, maharajah? Such a match would raise the head of Kristo Baboo among men again, for your caste is as noble as his own."

"My son is already mated," said Ramanath, curtly, as he applied himself to his hookha more vigorously than before.

"Which does not prevent him from being mated again," quietly observed the mahajan. "Idle people said, maharajah, that your son had cast loving eyes upon Kristo Baboo's daughter, and that he would rather have taken her to his bosom than the wife whom you had provided for him."

"Idle people should mind their own affairs," said Ramanath, angrily, as he started up to his feet. "Vishnu confound them! is there no other young man in the village, that my son must be made the talk of the bazaar? You should marry the girl yourself, Three Shells, since you take so much interest in her as to become her *ghatak*." *

---

* A *ghatak* is a professional go-between, who by dint of flattery and lying upon both sides arranges the marriages of Hindoos.

"Forgive me, maharajah," said Three Shells, affecting great concern. "I meant not that my mouth should speak irreverently of your honoured family; and, I pray you, couple not the maiden's name with my humbleness, lest her father should be displeased; for, as you know, I am not of quite so high a caste as the Lahories."

"Not quite," said Ramanath, drily; "but never mind, Three Shells, let Kristo Baboo once put his fingers in your purse and you will never hear of caste again. He will then hold out the hand of fellowship to you any day; and now, if you have got any offerings to make and prayers to say, go inside and have done with them, for I see my daughter Chakwi on the verandah beckoning me to breakfast."

Calling one of the servants to attend the mahajan throughout his devotions, Ramanath set out towards his house, while Three Shells entered the temple and prostrated himself before the idol. The attendant peeped in, but observing Three Shells bent in prayer, he decorously withdrew to the outside until the moneylender had finished, when he might reasonably expect that so prosperous a person would not suffer his little attentions to go unrewarded.

But there was little of prayer crossing Three Shells' lips. "It is all true that he says," he was muttering; "once let me get Kristo Baboo into my hands, and we shall see if I be longer a dog in his presence. The Mussulmans' Law says well:—

"'Short since I was a weaver,
I am a Shaikh this year,
And twelve months' time shall see me a Sayyid
If corn still keep dear.'

"Strong as their castes are, money is stronger, and there is nothing on earth which it may not purchase: even Kristo Baboo's daughter has her price. That slave is listening. · O Siva, the all-powerful one, the preserver of man and beast, the fountain of life, keep the head of thy suppliant! O thou who dwellest upon the hills, I salute thee! He is gone now," continued the mahajan, dropping the snuffling tone which he had assumed while the man was within earshot. "He will expect at least four annas, for yesterday was a great festival. It is an expensive thing this religion, and yet it pays one. I wonder, now, how much Ramanath makes in the year off this god of his: it cannot be much under a lakh of rupees between lands and temple-offerings. I shall never get my hands upon him, I suppose; but if I did——. However, there is the son, and no one can say what he may bring the property to with his extravagant Calcutta habits. There was the old Rajah of Ghatghar, the stingiest churl in the whole country, who would not have given away to a beggar the grain of rice that he could stow in his own stomach. Well, he starved himself, and ground down his ryots until the poor wretches could scarcely call their skins their own—and for what? Home comes his son from the Calcutta colleges, and what with feasting and dancing, play-acting and horse-racing, his wives and his concubines, he has to put his hands into my purse before he can keep the fifth anniversary of his father's death. And who is Rajah of Ghatghar now? Not that broken-down young bankrupt, an old man at five-and-twenty, with his fine house and gold-laced raiment. Ho, ho! here he kneels, plain Three Shells, the money-lender, he is the man for whom the Ghatghar ryots scrape their rents together. The slave again approaches—from which and from all other evils deliver me by thy might. O glorious Siva, conqueror of death, protect the humblest of thy servants in all his sojournings!"

Leaving Three Shells to complete his devotions after his own fashion, we may cross the village green and see what is going on at the house of the Lahories. It was a huge square brick building of almost palatial dimensions, but the walls were blackened with age, and had in several places crumbled into ruins, which the proprietor could never afford to repair. In front the upper storey opened out to a pillared balcony, hung with *chicks* of green bamboo to defend it from the sun's rays during the daytime. The windows opening to the outside, of which there were two rows, an upper and a lower, were all defended by wooden venetians, which served as well to secure the inmates from intrusive eyes as to shut out the fierce glare of noonday.

The house is by this time astir, and most of Kristo Baboo's many guests have gone to the great tank behind the mansion to bathe and pray, or they are bustling about preparing a hasty meal before they take leave of their entertainer, and return to their own homes. Entering through the wide doorway we come into a great quadrangle, round which, on the upper floor, are arranged the apartments of the family; and at the extreme end stands the idol - room or family chapel, cut off from observation by only a few pillars. Here old Digumbra, the family priest and pundit, is making the morning oblations to the guardian deities of the house of Lahory. The Lahories are highly orthodox people. No suspicion of scepticism has ever attached to any member of this family: no people were more strict in their observance of the Hindoo ritual: none fed more Brahmins, or gave a higher largess to the strolling devotee: none could observe festivals and ceremonies more carefully than Kristo Baboo and his family. Their zeal for religion had in fact sadly impaired the Lahories' substance. The Lahory domains had once been ample, including not only all Dhupnagar, but much of the surrounding district. But the Hindoo law of inheritance and the joint family system had wrought their usual effects. Instead of each son as he grew up to manhood taking his portion in money and going out into the world to seek a career for himself, he settled down upon the family property and in the family mansion, married and begot a family of his own, which in course of time became a still further charge upon the family lands. In a few generations, the rental which had supported only a single family became burdened with a little clan of Lahories; and then the head of the family, who had to maintain a position worthy of his dignity, and to contribute the largest portion of the expenditure upon the religious rites common to himself and his kinsmen, began to feel his circumstances straitened, and was obliged to cast about him for some means of increasing his income. His unfortunate tenants naturally first suggested themselves, and their rents were screwed and screwed until the poor wretches had scarcely left to them the wherewithal to keep soul and body together. Now, a portion of the estate must be feued to defray the expenses of a daughter's marriage, and once feued, the rents became nominal and unalterable. Then, a father's funeral ceremonies could not be duly performed until two or three hundred acres had been sold altogether. And thus it happened that, by the time Kristo Baboo became head of the family, scarcely anything was left to support his lofty pretensions. The old Rajah of Ghatghar, whose greed for land was only less than his lust for gold, had bought up lot after lot, until little remained to Kristo but the village and a few farms round about it. One year when there was a drought over all Bengal, the rice was burned up in the blade: there were no crops, the ryots had fallen into arrears with their rent, and Kristo was unable to pay the Government assessment, which was several years in arrears. The collector saw no prospect of recovering the dues, and after several warnings proceeded to distrain a considerable portion of Kristo's estate. This was bought in by the Government and presented as a reward to a Pathan officer who had been of signal service to the English during the Mutiny. Kristo Baboo had never got over this disgrace. He hated Shamsuddeen Khan as the author of his calamity, although the Pathan had only accepted what the Government offered him; and when the latter built a new mansion on the land which had once been Kristo's, the Baboo had gone solemnly down on his knees before the gods and prayed that the new possessor might never have enjoyment of his land until the soil of it covered him.

In course of time, as Kristo Baboo's circumstances grew worse, his richer kinsmen drew away from him, and refused to pay him the respect which they owed to him as head of the family; and there only remained his daughter and a host of poor cousins, who, having no better means of subsistence, adhered faithfully to his falling fortunes. But chief among all his troubles was the condition of his daughter. Radha had now been marriageable several years, but as yet the Baboo had been unable to find a suitable match for her among his acquaintance. He clung eagerly to the pride of his high caste, which was indeed nearly all that was now left him; but his means were so slender that he shrank from encouraging the advances of any wealthy suitor, who would expect to be treated to an expensive marriage ceremony and a heavy dowry. There would have been no lack of lovers, for Radha was beautiful as a queen, and the *ghataks* had trumpeted her praises all over the district.

Among the few that had ever been privileged to catch a glimpse of the maiden was Krishna, the priest's son. The young man had come unexpectedly upon Radha as she had finished bathing, and was standing by the edge of the tank wringing the water out of her dark tresses, and looking in her scanty drapery lithe and graceful as a nut-brown naiad. The girl fled, but not before she had marked that Krishna was rapt in admiration of her person: and Radha was too vain of her own charms not to triumph at the conquest she had made. From that hour Krishna was always to be found sauntering about the Lahories' tank, or prying so curiously at the Baboo's zenana windows, that it was a wonder how he escaped the staves of Kristo's servants. Sometimes a window would be thrown open as if by accident, and before it could be closed he would discern Radha's retreating figure as she fled backwards into the obscurity of the room. Once or twice a flower fell from the window, which he stealthily snatched up and concealed; and these were carefully preserved as his greatest treasures. But such courtship makes slow progress, and three years found Krishna and Radha still utter strangers to each other. But Krishna's love was not the less constant; and when his wife Chakwi was brought home, it was still Radha's image that was uppermost in his heart, and he could not help loathing his gentle partner, because of the bright vision that had crossed his path so long ago at the tank of Lahory.

Kristo Baboo was standing upon the steps, in close conversation with one of his guests, who was preparing to mount an active little pony that a *syce* (groom) held close by them. The Baboo was a middle-aged Hindoo, of a stout, almost obese figure, but with a high square forehead and fair features, indicating the purity of his Aryan descent. He wore only a waist-cloth of white cotton, with a snowy muslin *chadda* thrown loosely over his shoulder, and nothing to distinguish him from the others but the massive silver hookha that he held in his hand. His companion was a man of a very different stamp. His skin was almost as black as a negro's, and his round face, narrow brow, and irregular features contrasted strongly with the aristocratic countenance of the master of the house. He was dressed in a long *chapkan* or coat, cut in a fashion half oriental half European, which is much affected by the Anglicised natives: he wore a pair of white duck trousers, with patent-leather English boots; a heavy gold chain attached to his watch was wound in two or three folds about his neck; and a little gold-laced cap was perched jauntily upon his crisp black curls. In short, his whole appearance was such as may any day be seen loitering about the Presidency College gate, or Wellesley Square, or any of the other haunts of " Young

Bengal" in Calcutta. Though only the son of Ram Lall, the village oilman, Preonath had become a man of greater consequence than many a person of much higher birth: for he was a Bachelor of Arts of the Calcutta University, and Deputy Magistrate of the subdivision. The "Dipty Baboo," as he was called, was one of the most earnest suitors for Radha's hand. Many thought that it would be no great condescension in Kristo to give his daughter to so promising a young officer; but the Baboo had never been able to bring himself to sanction an alliance with a Sudra who did not even belong to the nine tribes of tradesmen with whom a Brahmin might drink water. Kristo was, however, litigious and oppressive, and lawsuits with his neighbours and tenants were of frequent occurrence, so he prudently kept friends with the Dipty, before whom such cases would generally come in the first instance; and though he never pledged his word to Preonath, he never gave him to understand that there were irremovable obstacles in the way of a marriage. On his part, the Dipty spared no pains to win Kristo's favour. He took up his quarters at the house of Lahory every time he visited Dhupnagar, although he knew that his old father, Ram Lall, had the little house in the bazaar swept and garnished for the reception of his great son. His origin and his father's status were sore trials to Preonath's pride. Were it not that the old man and the little shop in Dhupnagar were constantly before their eyes, folk would, he fancied, soon forget that Baboo Preonath Doss, B.A., and Deputy Magistrate, was the son of an oil-seller. But old Ram Lall would not resign the shop for all his son's entreaties and promises of support; and every time Preonath entered Dhupnagar, he was haunted by the dread of a meeting with his father.

"And you must then go to-day, Baboo?" said Kristo. "Well, we cannot detain the pillar of justice with us always. When may we next look for you in Dhupnagar?"

"It will not be long," replied Preonath: "the subdivision has been giving a good deal of trouble lately, and the Magistrate Sahib insists that I must be accountable for the discovery of all these robberies that have of late taken place. *Sri Krishnaji!* as if I could arrest a band of Sonthal highlandmen, armed with axe and spear, with the aid of my court clerks and half-a-dozen policemen. A likely thing indeed!"

"Very likely," rejoined Kristo. "But what better know these Englishmen? The Magistrate Sahib should come himself if he wants to rid the district of *dakaits* (robbers). He will find that there are Bengalees as well as hillmen among the thieves."

"How?" said Preonath, pausing sharply as he put his foot in the stirrup. "Whom do you mean? No one in Dhupnagar?"

"Umph! well, no, I don't know of any one in particular," said Kristo, stammering and reddening; "but that old scoundrel Shamsuddeen Khan who stole my land, is quite capable of stealing anything else, and his ne'er-do-well of a son has come back again from the army. Mind I don't say that any of them are mixed up in the robberies, but I should not be at all surprised if they were."

"It would never do to say such a thing to the Magistrate Sahib," said Preonath, reflectively. "The Pathan is a favourite with the English, and he has eaten—yes, actually eaten, with the Magistrate Sahib, and at the very same table; so it is impossible that he could have anything to do with the robberies. And now, am I at liberty to take my departure?"

"Go, my son, and may Vishnu be your preserver!" said the Brahmin; "and forget not to countenance me in my plea with Gunga Sahai, the dog of a money-lender from Gapshapganj—would that an evil eye might light upon him!"

"Fear not, my father, I shall do all that I can," returned Preonath in a whisper; "but Rakhaldass Sen has appealed to the Magistrate Sahib from my last decision in your favour, and if his honour should call for the record, I know not what may happen to me. Think of this, Kristo Baboo, and let it make you favourably disposed towards me in my suit for Radha."

"I do think of it, I will think of it," cried Kristo, hastily waving an adieu to the Dipty, and entering the house to conclude a conversation which had taken an awkward turn. Preonath looked doubtfully after him for a moment, and then applying the switch to his pony trotted off, followed by half-a-dozen ragged hangers-on of his court, who, by obsequious attendance on the Dipty, hoped some day to raise themselves from "expectants" to the position of salaried officials.

CHAPTER III.

RADHA'S THREE LOVERS.

WHERE the highroad leading from Calcutta and the other towns in the Hooghly basin crosses the low ridge that forms the eastern watershed of the Gungaputra, it passes through a green mango tope, beneath which a shrine had once been reared to some of the Hindoo deities. The little temple had long ago been deserted, unless when a passing traveller took shelter from the heat beneath its white dome, or a band of belated pilgrims to the Linga of Dhupnagar passed the night there. The tope had a bad name among the country people. The priest had never prospered while the shrine was still in existence. His children had been carried off by disease; his cows had been stolen; people refused to give anything to so ill-omened a temple, which, they said, must have been built over human bones; and the priest had in course removed his idol to some more auspicious locality. The people of Dhupnagar would hurry on that they might pass the Pagoda Tope before night fell; and if they were alone they preferred to seek hospitality at some of the wayside cottages rather than place themselves within the power of the evil spirits that infested the ruins.

At noon-tide on the day after the Dewali Puja the temple had a single occupant, who had evidently ventured to pass the night in the haunted locality; for the strip of matting which had served him for a couch was still spread out upon the floor, and by it was a small bundle of clothes which he had used as a pillow. He was a young man of eighteen or nineteen, whose fair face and open regular features, no less than his sacred cord, bespoke him a high-caste Brahmin. He had just finished bathing in the ruined tank, which was half choked up with the broad green leaves of the water-lily, and the white pith-like stems of the *sola* bushes. As he stood in the temple door adjusting his simple toilet, his eye followed the road as it wound down the valley—past hamlet and homestead —now lost in a patch of jungle, now skirting the green fields of some ryot's farm. Beneath him, at a distance of two or three miles, lay Dhupnagar, its white houses standing garishly forth in the blazing sunshine; and down in the bottom of the valley the Gungaputra was flowing swiftly along—an unbroken current of liquid silver—from the white minarets of Bhutpore on the north, until hidden behind the lofty terraces of the Ghatghar Palace at the other extremity. Beyond, the view was bounded by the low range of hills called, from its five peaks, "Panch Pahar," the skirts of which were clothed with a dense robe of jungle, while on its ridges and summits gigantic old *sal* trees waved like the plumes upon a warrior's basnet. There are few fairer scenes in Lower Bengal than that which greets the traveller's eye as he gazes from the Pagoda Tope into the valley of the Gungaputra. The wearisome flatness of the Gangetic plains has been exchanged for undulating slopes and rich meadows: a red earthy soil resting on a rocky bed, which here and there throws up a craggy peak above the surface, has taken the place of white sandy clays: the vegetation, if less luxuriant, has a hardier appearance: and the population are of a stronger and manlier cast than the lithe, slim Bengalees of the Hooghly valley.

"I must face my fate, whatever be the consequences," said the young man, as he looked nervously in the direction of Dhupnagar, "for I can delay here no longer. It would be all the same if I waited for a lifetime, for I should never be able to nerve myself more for the task. I might just as well have gone on last night; but I felt as if I would be carrying discord and trouble into a scene of happiness and gaiety, and I could not enter Dhupnagar upon a festival night: and then when the lamps were kindled, and the village shone out in one blaze of light, and sounds of music and revelry came floating up from the valley, I felt that I was indeed an outcast. The old temple sprang up all at once into a building of flame, and a dark figure passed athwart the light, which I am sure was my father's. My poor father! I wonder how he will bear it! He has such an easy, selfish nature, and is so worldly, that it will fall a heavy blow upon him. Perhaps he may curse me and throw me out of doors. Well, let him : I shall then, I know, be firm in the truth. It is not persecution, but silent reproach, affectionate entreaties, and tender pleadings, that can shake my resolution."

He had now completed his toilet and taken up his little bundle, but he still lingered by the temple door as if his heart failed him and his limbs were refusing to bear him on the road.

"I saw, too, where she was last night," he soliloquised, sadly. "When they placed these coloured lamps upon the terrace of Kristo Baboo's verandah a slim form stood out for an instant in front of the light, and then glided away towards the zenana. It *was* her, for no maiden in Dhupnagar—no, nor in all Bengal—has the same sylph-like form, or moves with so much grace. But why should I think of her now, when she would turn from me as from a pariah dog? I could never have won her as I was before—far less now. Then there is my wife, Chakwi. My wife! What wife can she be to me, or what husband I to her? God's curse upon Hindooism and its customs, for it has blighted my life, and the lives of every one connected with me. But I, for one, have broken with it, never to be reconciled. Would that I could as easily cast off its taints as I can fling from me the last of its emblems!"

As he spoke he again opened the bosom of his coat, and tearing off the *poita* or sacred cord, which marked his position as a Brahmin, he held it for an instant in his hands: "It was my father who blessed it and put it on me," he said, bitterly; "little did he think that the day would come when I should thus dishonour it. But the Christian Teacher rightly says, 'He who loveth father and mother more than me, is not worthy of me;' and how can I expect the eternal Brahma to lead me to truth and everlasting bliss, if I allow my mind to be warped by the fleeting affections of earth? God is my father and mankind is my brother, and thus perish everything that would tend to narrow the holy relationship;" and the young enthusiast broke the sacred thread into fragments, and flung them contemptuously upon the highway, trampling them under feet as he did so.

He had now wrought himself up to a pitch of strong mental excitement, and he set out with firm step along the road, and began to walk at a rapid pace down-hill in the direction of Dhupnagar. The road followed an easy declivity, and for some distance from the Pagoda Tope it was sheltered by clumps of tall bamboo planted by the wayside. But Krishna Chandra Gossain—for it was the priest of Dhupnagar's son, as the reader has doubtless already conjectured—recked little of shade or sunshine, but strode resolutely on with knit brows and clenched fists. Sometimes he would pause abruptly, muttering to himself, and wildly gesticulating. Sometimes he would halt with a look of uncertainty upon his face, as he half thought of turning back, and then again he would start with redoubled speed and a more determined resolution than before. It was no wonder though Krishna shrank from the journey, for he was going to face death; ay, death— the death of a lifetime—the terrible civil death that overtakes the Hindoo whose foot strays from the strait ordinances of the Brahmins. We have our martyrs in plenty—men who have devoted themselves for their faith to the most terrible deaths; but our Western imaginations fail us when we attempt to realise the lifelong persecutions, trouble, isolation, and scorn which beset the young Hindoo who dares to put himself in opposition to the errors of his countrymen.

As Krishna came out upon the open road, his eye fell upon a rider coming up the hill, followed by five or six half-clad attendants. At a glance he recognised Preonath, the Deputy Magistrate, the man whom, of all others, he was most anxious to shun. He knew Preonath to be a pretender to the hand of Radha, and he could not help entertaining feelings of dislike and jealousy towards him. There had, moreover, been an old rivalry between the two at the Presidency College, where Preonath, as the senior student, would have taken the wall of young Krishna, an assumption which the high-caste Brahmin refused to tolerate upon the part of an oil-seller's son. It was true that when Krishna's liberal instincts were aroused, and when he began to see how empty a boast was the pride of caste, he had sought to repair his error by treating Preonath with the utmost courtesy and even respect; but though they outwardly remained good friends, Preonath never could forgive his fellow-student for being a better-born man than he was, far less for having vaunted himself to be so. In their studies, too, each had endeavoured to surpass the other, but their intellects were very differently constituted, and rivalry between them was almost impossible. Krishna excelled in literature and ethical philosophy—could pen a Sanscrit *sloka* like Kalidasa, as his pundit boasted, or turn out a very creditable essay in English. It was in mathematics and law that Preonath had distinguished himself. His acute but superficial intellect lacked the guidance of taste in his literary studies, and his mind was too selfish to seek philosophical culture simply for culture's sake. Krishna had sought his friends among the little group of theistical students who adhere to either of the two sects of Brahmists; while cautious Preonath kept the most orthodox company in college, and never ceased to extol the blessings of caste, although he himself had none that was worth mentioning. The end of all this was, that Preonath, through the influence of his Hindoo patrons, soon procured a deputy magistracy, and was now on the highroad to official promotion; while Krishna, a disgraced and a broken man, was on his way to his father's house, which he would in all likelihood find to be no longer a home for him.

Had it been at all possible to avoid Preonath, Krishna would have gladly done so; but the Dipty was close upon him, and there was not a single bush or a tree by the wayside that would have screened him from observation. He must face his old rival; and with this resolution the thought of his altered circumstances came bitterly into Krishna's mind. He had just thrown away the last relic of his caste: what grounds had he now for claiming to be the superior of Preonath? Could he have gathered up and mended that cord which he had dishonoured at the Pagoda Tope a few minutes before, he would have been strongly tempted to do so. But now the deed was done, and he must abide by the consequences, whatever they might be.

"What! Krishna Chandra here?" cried the Dipty in amazement, as he perceived him. "How is this? We had not expected to see you before March." And Preonath got off his pony and greeted his old fellow-student with a great show of cordiality.

"Well, Preonath Baboo, I am glad to meet you," said Krishna, somewhat coldly. "You seem to have grown quite a great man in the district; I suppose I ought hardly to address my old class-fellow without 'your honouring' and 'my lording' him, now that he has become a great official."

"Not so great yet that he can receive adulation from his old friend and the son of Ramanath Gossain. But tell me, Krishna, how comes it that you are away from college just now? Is all well with you? I know your friends in Dhupnagar are in health, for I saw your father last night before the festival."

"Yes, yes—all is right; I have come home upon some private business," responded Krishna, hurriedly; "and as my time may be short, you will excuse me, Preonath, if I do not delay longer with you. I am very anxious to see my father."

"Of course, of course," said Preonath; "but you will come and see me before you return to Calcutta. I am very lonely at Gapshapganj among stupid old Bengalees, who are as ignorant as their own bullocks, and positive as pigs. Will you not come and spend a few days with me at my house? You are not one who troubles himself about his caste, or I should not have dared to ask you to be the guest of a poor Kyasth;" and as the Dipty said this he darted a keen glance towards Krishna, as if he would read in his looks what he wanted to learn.

"No, certainly not; nothing would give me more pleasure," said Krishna, speaking with incoherent utterance. "If I can so arrange it, I shall pay you a visit before I go back to college—that is, if I do go back, for really my mind is at present very unsettled."

"Just so," said Preonath, drily, as he looked doubtfully at the other. "Well, at all events your future does not depend upon your taking a degree, as mine did. Pious Hindoos will not tie the corners of their *cummerbunds* (waist-cloths, purses) any tighter because the priest of Dhupnagar is not a B.A. of the University."

"If a man escape the shafts of Yama, the god of death, he will not die," answered Krishna, shaking his head sadly. "You will never see me priest of Dhupnagar, Preonath, while sun and moon endure; at least not the priest of Siva's Linga. And now, farewell;" and with a wave of the hand to the Dipty, he walked rapidly down the hill to avoid further questioning.

"What in the thousand names of Vishnu is the matter now?" said the Dipty to himself as he remounted his pony. "What on earth *can* he be doing here when the college examinations are just beginning? He can't have been expelled from the Presidency College for misconduct. No, it's not that; he was always too shy and quiet—annoyingly quiet—for that. It is something about religion that is at the bottom of it. I should not wonder, now, if he had got up another beefsteak party as they did in the wild old days, for when I left college he was always sneering and scoffing at Hindooism. He can't have become a Christian. No, that would be too good to be real."

Thus the Dipty continued to muse as he rode along the road. He knew that there was something wrong with Krishna, and he was already plotting how he might turn the accident, whatever it might be, to his own advantage. He was perfectly well aware of Krishna's passion for Kristo Baboo's daughter, for he had often seen the wild impassioned verses in which the young student was wont to celebrate the beauties of Radha, and which were looked upon by their class-fellows as masterpieces of Bengalee poetry. And if, as he did not doubt was the case, Krishna had done something to compromise himself with the orthodox party, he would then at least have one dangerous rival removed from the field. " I would give a *lota* (cup) of silver to the temple of Tarakeshwar, that this young fool had turned Christian," he said, as he looked piously up towards the sky.

Hardly had he breathed his vow when his eye fell upon the shreds of Krishna's cord as they lay scattered upon the road before him. " What is that ? " the Dipty asked, as he pointed with his riding-switch towards the fragments. Four of the attendants rushed forward, knocking their heads against each other in their eagerness to pick them up. " Let me look at them," he continued, holding out his hand. The first glance confirmed his suspicion. " *Sri-Narayan-ji*," he muttered ; " the prayer of the pious hath its answer. It is —yes, it is a Brahmin's *poita*, and it is Krishna Chandra that has offered this insult to the sacred symbol. The temple of Tarakeshwar shall have its *lota*, if I should never earn another rupee in the world. What an ass, and father of an ass, is he, thus to throw away his high privileges ! "

" I shall keep this," said the Dipty to himself, as he carefully rolled up the broken cord ; " it is right that the Brahmins of the district should know how religion is dishonoured, and by a priest's son too. Jaddoo," he continued, turning to one of his followers, " stand apart here and hearken. They say that you have brains, Jaddoo, and if you will use them now in my service it may well be to your advantage. You saw young Krishna Baboo pass us on the road ? Well, I am told upon good authority that he has become an unbeliever, and an eater of beef and other abominations; and it is right that the good folks of Dhupnagar should be cautioned against so dangerous a character, lest they should suffer pollution in his society. Now, Jaddoo, you will go into the bazaar, and when they ask you for news, you will say that you have heard such things of the young Krishna Baboo, but that you do not think them true. You will tell them that you have heard of his eating and drinking with English and other unclean races ; that he despises the gods, and follows a new religion ; and that he has come back to Dhupnagar to destroy the caste and creed of everybody in it. You will tell them all this, and anything similar that may occur to you—but only as hearsay, mind; and do not let my name pass your lips, as you value my favour. You understand, do you not? Very well, you may return now, and if you manage this business properly, I shall soon require an extra *chaprassi* about the court. And stay, Jaddoo—do not go the way of Kristo Baboo's with your gossip; they will hear of it without you."

"It will be better that the Baboo should not see that I have any interest in running down Krishna," said he to himself; "but I shall take care to let them hear of it through another channel."

The Dipty's meditations were here interrupted by a violent collision, which sent both him and his little pony spinning to the wayside, where they fell in a heap, the one rolling over the other, until they settled down into the ditch, the Dipty being undermost. His ragged staff set up a howl of affected concern, and rushed to extricate him; while the cause of the accident, a young man in a semi-military attire, mounted upon a bony Waler mare, reined up his charger and began to anathematise the sufferer.

"May the Prophet confound thee, thou son of a burnt father!" cried the new-comer, speaking loudly in Hindustani, with a north-country accent, "that ridest along the highway like a bag propped upon the back of a mule. Say, thou brother of a wanton sister, what wouldst thou have done had my mare injured her knees against thee and thy wretched *tat* there? By the tomb of Shah Safi, I had rather thy neck had been broken!"

The speaker, a smart young Mussulman of twenty-two or twenty-three years of age, handled his riding-whip as if little would induce him to lay it across the Dipty's shoulders. He was dressed in a dust-coloured tunic, ornamented with gold embroidery about the sleeves and collar, and he wore yellow leather gaiters and long steel spurs. Round his close-fitting velvet cap were wound two or three folds of a *pagri*, or scarf

of green silk—the favourite colour of the Prophet—
which, ending in embroidered fringes, hung gracefully
over his shoulders. He rode with the lightness and
ease of a Sikh or Mahratta horseman, and managed
his charger with the dexterity and grace of a trooper of
the Irregular Cavalry.

By this time the Dipty had scrambled to his feet
with the assistance of his orderlies, and he stood with
lowering brows, rubbing his aching sides, but taking
care to keep his attendants well between him and the
horseman.

"I do not know who you are, sir, and it strikes me
you do not know very well who I am, else you had not
ventured upon this insult," said Preonath, slowly.
"I am Deputy Magistrate and Deputy Collector of the
subdivision; and the Bengal Regulations, as contained
in Sutherland's edition, lay down respecting the causing
of hurt or obstruction to wayfarers——"

"May Shaitan choke thee, O son of the one-eyed
and doomed to perdition! what have I to do with thy
Bengal Regulations? Where is it written that a magistrate shall ride along the highway with his head hanging down upon his breast, and his body swaying to and
fro like the head of the leading camel of a *kafila*
(caravan) for the Faithful to peril themselves upon?
Why didst thou not take to the roadside when thou
sawest me ride up?"

"Who are you that I should give place to you?"
demanded the Dipty, though in a less confident tone,

for he was conscious that his own inattention was in some measure to blame for the accident. " I have yet to learn that a Deputy Magistrate riding upon duty through his own district, must give place to any rude blusterer that sets himself to create a disturbance upon the highroad. You shall answer for this, sir."

"By the sword of the Prophet, and that I shall, in this very spot too!" ejaculated the imperious Mussulman as he made his horse curvet towards the Dipty, while he raised his whip high above his head to strike the terrified official. But the Dipty was too true a Bengalee to wait the descent of the blow, and he took to his heels, with all his followers before him. A low wall of ruined masonry that had once marked the *pomarium* of the deserted pagoda, stood close by, and towards this the Dipty retreated. When he had succeeded in scrambling up to the top, his courage revived a little, and he again addressed the Muhammadan who sat upon horseback in the middle of the road watching with a scornful smile the retreat of the Bengalees.

"It is not here that you can account for this conduct, sir," cried the Dipty, in desperation. "There is justice in the Englishman's court for the poor Hindoo as well as for the Muhammadan; and if you are Shamsuddeen Khan's, the Subadar's, son, my officials will know where to bring you a summons. There is not only the original ground of offence, the injuries caused to my person and to my horse, but there is now superadded language and gestures calculated to provoke a breach of the peace, the punishment for which, made and provided for in the Indian Penal Code, Currie's edition——"

"I should not like to hear the language calculated to provoke a Bengalee to break the peace," said the stranger, with a derisive laugh; "for it must be indeed more awful than the words engraven upon the seal of Suleiman, the son of Daoud, the mention of which makes all the powers of evil to quake. But hearken, Baboo; thou hast thyself disproved the accusation, for instead of provoking thee to a breach of the peace, my language provoked thee to run away. What says the Penal Code of that? and what will the English Magistrate Sahib say to the courage of his Bengalee Deputy, when thy charge comes up before him?"

Preonath bit his lip and was silent, for he knew how well founded was the Mussulman's taunt. Mr Eversley, the Collector of the district, was a civilian of the old Anglo-Indian school, who rated his native subordinates very cheaply, and who was never ill pleased when anything occurred to expose them to ridicule. The stranger marked the impression that he had made, and continued :—

"Go home, oh thou! and thank thy abominable gods —which may the Prophet speedily exterminate—that thy bones are whole; for if Pearl's knees had been as much as grazed by thy carelessness, it would have been many a day before thou hadst been able to take thy seat in *cutcherry* again. And now again begone, lest I give you some real cause to sue for damages. Take my advice and walk on foot in future, as every Bengalee should do, for horses were made for men and for your masters. Again be off, O infidel! and may the Prophet convert thee to the true faith, if he should think a dog like thee worth his pains."

With this parting benediction the haughty youth rode off, turning now and then to cast a threatening glance backwards at his Hindoo opponents. As the waving green turban of the Mussulman began to disappear down the slopes, the Dipty's courage revived, and he cursed the stranger by as many of his three millions of gods as he could readily remember in his agitation. When his pony had been caught, and the Dipty assisted to the saddle, he proceeded to quote whole pages from the Penal Code and High Court Circulars, illustrative of the injuries that had been sustained by his person and feelings: he conjured his attendants to treasure up the minutest particulars of the encounter; he made a formal minute of the occurrence in his pocket-book; and then he rode angrily homewards, racking his brains for a convenient means of revenging himself upon his enemy. Little cared Afzul Khan for the Dipty's threats as he descended the slope towards Dhupnagar at a hand-gallop. He soon passed Jaddoo, who had started off to fulfil his master's orders in the village, as soon as he saw that the altercation was not unlikely to end in blows, and who was now trotting quickly along the road, his mind filled with visions of his future greatness, when once he should become a belted messenger in the Dipty's court. As Afzul slackened his rein at the end of the village, he passed a weary-looking wayfarer who stood half concealed by the shade of a banian-tree, as if doubtful whether he should venture into Dhupnagar. It was Krishna who was bracing up his nerves for the trial that awaited him.

CHAPTER IV.

FATHER AND SON.

OLD Ramanath Gossain had again seated himself by the shady door of his temple, and beside him still sat Three Shells, the money-lender. The priest had returned from breakfast before the end of the mahajan's protracted devotions, and the two resumed their gossip. Ramanath dearly loved to discuss the affairs of his neighbours. It was almost his whole occupation to sit by the temple door, hot weather and cold, and give and receive the news of the village. There was not a soul in Dhupnagar with whose family affairs Ramanath was not intimately acquainted. He could tell the exact number of wives in each man's family, could call all the children by their proper names, and could calculate to a rupee the annual income and expenditure of every one around him. But with all his love for tattle Ramanath was no slanderer. It was rather because in his easy, good-natured way he took a fatherly interest in the villagers' wellbeing that he loved to discuss their domestic concerns. Nothing pleased him so much, not even a donation to the shrine, as when a neighbour came to ask his advice; and though his experience of the world was very limited, his natural shrewdness made him a safe and cautious counsellor. But there was one subject that Ramanath carefully excluded from conversation, and that was the domestic relations of his son and daughter. He was well aware that Krishna's aversion for his wife was the talk of Dhupnagar, and that many orthodox Hindoos were disposed to blame himself for not stretching his paternal authority to hasten on the consummation of the marriage. But it was all for the best that Ramanath had acted, for he well knew that nothing would be so likely to confirm Krishna's aversion for his bride as any show of paternal coercion. And so, although he received with great complacency all the praises that Three Shells could lavish upon his son's learning and high character, he promptly repressed any remarks that would tend to turn the conversation towards Krishna and Chakwi's ill-assorted union.

But there was no lack of free topics. There was the young Rajah of Ghatghar, who, while yet a ward of Government on an allowance of five hundred rupees a-month, had spent five thousand, and had now got to the end of his father's savings before he had been full five years in possession. His father—peace be with him— who was such a miser that he would have eaten the mangoes and sold the stones, never thought that his money would come to an end in this fashion. The Rajah kept horses to run races with the Englishmen; and madams came from Calcutta and the up-country towns who would soon help him to eat up the Ghatghar property. His Dewan (agent), too, was making a pretty penny off his master's improvidence; people said that he had already acquired estates of his own in the Backergunge district. "And the ill wind from Ghatghar may blow good to somebody else, eh, Three Shells?" and Three Shells meekly owned that he had had the great honour of ministering to the Ghatghar Rajah's present necessities. Then the Subadar's wild young son, Afzul Khan, was come back again to the village. Folks said that he had shown himself to be bold as a tiger while the English were fighting in Bhootan with the square-faced Budhists, but that he would not behave himself in cantonments when the war was over, nor be submissive to the Sahibs. It was a pity for his father, who was a respectable man—that is, for a Muhammadan and a kine-killer. It was not likely that the young fellow would be long in the village before he played some mischief. Had he not attempted to carry off Belputtee the ryot of Milkiganj's daughter before he went away to the army; and when the ryot's servants had driven him off with clubs, had not the wanton slipped away next night of her own accord and abode in the Mussulman's zenana. It was a great scandal; and though the Subadar had given the ryot two hundred rupees to take back his daughter, silver will not lacquer disgrace. Might the gods defend all virtuous women who had not a husband's protection, against him and the like of him. Here Ramanath shifted uneasily as conscious that Three Shells' petition was directed more at his family than to the gods. Then these night robberies were getting more and more common. What an awakening that was for poor Peary Lall, the landholder of Kadimkote on the other side of the Gungaputra, to be roused by the blaze of his own roofs, and to find half-a-score of armed *dakaits* ransacking his house and untying his cattle! Resistance! How could Bengalees resist hill-men armed with sword and spear and the terrible Sonthal axe? The policemen came next day, but they were afraid to venture beyond the passes of Panch Pahar; and the Superintendent Sahib had said that the thieves did not belong to his district, and that all he could do was to report them to Government. But it would be long before the Government thought of compensating poor Peary Lall for his eight cows and his wives' jewels worth five hundred rupees.

"Take care, friend Three Shells," remarked Ramanath, drily, "that they do not call in some night to help you to sum up your accounts. A wealthy mahajan like you would be better worth fleecing than a poor zemindar who has nothing but what he can scrape off the soil."

Three Shells smirked and said that he rested in safety under the protection of the gods and the Linga of Dhupnagar; what little money he had was all in the hands of clients; and though they searched his house from top to bottom, the *dakaits* would not find as much silver as would make a nose-ring for a three-year-old child.

While the two sat in the shade of the temple conversing in this fashion, they were startled by a loud exclamation from the porter, who threw down his hookha in astonishment, and sprang to his feet to greet his young master as Krishna entered the court-yard. Ramanath sat in speechless amazement at the unexpected sight, and rubbed his eyes to convince himself that he was not dreaming. Krishna's haggard aspect and jaded appearance at once informed him that something was seriously wrong. His first impulse was to get rid of his companion, for he noticed that Three Shells' little red eyes were like to start out of their sockets with curiosity, and that he was looking from the one to the other for an explanation. But after the first shock of surprise was over, Ramanath's countenance told no tale, and he welcomed his son with dignified and affectionate gravity. Raising his clasped hands to his brow, and bending his head almost to the ground, Krishna stood before his father waiting for his blessing.

"You have come somewhat before you were expected, but not sooner than you are welcome, my son," said the priest, placing his hand fondly upon the young man's head. "You are tired with your journey and the heat; speak not a word until you have come into the house and rested yourself. Peace be with you, good Three Shells," and taking his son by the arm to conceal his own trembling gait, Ramanath descended the steps of the temple and moved off in the direction of his dwelling.

But Three Shells was not to be thrown off thus easily. "Let me welcome you again to Dhupnagar, Krishna Baboo," he said, following them closely with hands respectfully clasped and head bent eagerly forward, fawning upon the young man like a cringing spaniel. "May I hope that your learning and virtues will shed light upon the village for some length of time? Your propitious name has made Dhupnagar famous among Calcutta pundits. I pray that all may be well when you come among us thus suddenly."

"Enough, Three Shells," cried the priest, impatiently; "my son is tired, and cannot stand chattering here with you. Go in peace. Hai Modhoo! attend this worthy mahajan, Tin Cowry Baboo, to the gate;" and away went the priest with his son, leaving Three Shells to pocket the rebuff under a profusion of low bows and salaams.

"Commend me to such courtesy," muttered the money-lender angrily; "a man may learn good manners that has never been to Delhi. But go thy ways, Ramanath Gossain; sorrow has set his foot on your threshold this morning, else may I never draw a pice of interest again. It is not for good that that young fellow comes here to-day in this fashion. Modhoo, my good friend, Modhoo."

"Baboo," answered Modhoo, sententiously, as he came slowly up to the speaker, for he did not like the mahajan, who was stingy in his largesses to the temple attendants.

"That gate of yours was very brilliantly lighted last night, Modhoo," said Three Shells, affably; "it was quite an ornament to the village. You are a good man, Modhoo, and you will get a great reward some day for your services to the shrine."

"Umph! some day," said Modhoo, drily, as if he would have preferred a less indefinite time of settlement. "One would need a reward, for it is poor work, if *all respectable* Baboos did not give me a rupee apiece when they come to the temple."

"Very true, my good Modhoo, and that reminds me of my duty," said the mahajan, blandly, taking a rupee from his bag and putting it into the man's outstretched palm. "How glad I am to see your young master again! He has come home quite unexpectedly, has he not?"

"We did not look for him just quite so soon," said Modhoo, with an appearance of reserve.

"Not quite so soon," re-echoed the mahajan; "but he was expected, then, about this time? It is strange that Ramanath Baboo did not mention it. It will be private business that has brought young Krishna home, then?"

"Very private," said Modhoo, with a mysterious shake of the head.

"Very private, you say. It occurs to me just now, Modhoo, that I forgot to notice you last time I was at the temple. However, it is not too late yet, and here is another rupee for you. And does this private business that you speak of relate to your young mistress?"

"I have not heard that it relates to my young mistress," said Modhoo, pointedly, as if there were some great secret in his possession, which was only to be wormed out of him piecemeal.

"What in the name of Siva can it be then?" said the mahajan to himself. "Good Modhoo," he added aloud, "I have been blind not to have noticed your obliging manners before this time. Here is another rupee to you; we must be friends after this. And now, Modhoo, tell me truly what is the cause of Krishna Baboo's coming home?"

"I know no more about it than you do," answered Modhoo, curtly.

"No more about it than I do," re-echoed Three Shells, angrily; "why then, you rascal, did you tell me that it was very private business?"

"Just because I did not know anything about it," said Modhoo, sturdily; "if it had not been very private I should have been able to tell you what it was."

Muttering a curse upon his grinning interlocutor, the mahajan shuffled away impatiently from the temple, determined to find some explanation of the mystery in the bazaar. "Three rupees thrown into the water," he growled. "I might have known that if there was any secret it would not have been intrusted to that churlish slave. But it will be strange if I do not get an inkling of it from somewhere before long."

Not a word passed between Ramanath and his son as they crossed the temple courtyard and entered the little wicket that admitted them into the compound of the priest's house. Ramanath's dwelling was a large brick building, in the usual quadrangular form of Hindoo houses. The Gossain family had been much more numerous at the time of its erection than Ramanath's modest household, which now occupied only a small corner of the house. The *zenana*, or female apartments, took up a whole wing of the upper floor, and the only other habitable apartments were the *boita khana*, or sitting-room, where the priest received visitors of distinction, and the rooms which had been set apart as the study and bedchamber of the priest's son. The latter were furnished in a semi-European style, with some pretensions to taste and neatness, and they contained a fair collection of popular English works, which Krishna had picked up among the book-stalls of China Bazaar. These rooms were generally shut up during the young man's absence; for, except an occasional glance at an odd number of the 'Shome Prokash,' which his son would send him from Calcutta, the priest never read anything but Puranic books of devotion; and the ladies of the household did not know even their letters.

Before Krishna had conceived a fixed aversion to his wife, he had dreamed of teaching her all that he himself knew, and of making her a marvel of learning among her countrywomen. But though Chakwi would have been delighted by such a mark of her husband's regard, and would have exerted her utmost to please him, Krishna had never taken the pains to teach her anything. Nevertheless, the poor girl kept good watch over her husband's treasures. No servant was allowed to enter Krishna's room except when she herself was present. She saw that each book was carefully wiped and replaced in its proper order; that they were put forth into the sun in the damp, rainy season, when white mould gathered about the precious volumes; and that fresh leaves of the *nim* tree were scattered over the bookcase to repel the white ants, the Indian bibliopole's greatest enemies. It was out of pure devotion to her husband that Chakwi undertook this task, for she herself bore no goodwill to the volumes which she had come to connect with Krishna's heretical leanings and neglect of herself. Sometimes as Chakwi lifted a book, she would shudder to think that it might perhaps contain some blasphemous writings against the gods; might, indeed, be one of those wicked books that the Padre Sahibs wrote to beguile men into the religion of the white Christ. There were books, too, with pictures of English ladies, at which Chakwi would look with curiosity not unmingled with awe; for it seemed to her a terrible thing that women should not only dress themselves in such a monstrous costume, but should be represented as unblushingly walking arm-in-arm with their husbands before the eyes of all the public. Chakwi had grave doubts about the moral tendency of books that were illustrated in such a fashion. But whatever they might be they were her husband's, and that was enough for Chakwi.

It was to these rooms that the priest now led Krishna. Not a word passed between them until they had entered, and the priest sat down faintly upon a couch. Krishna threw himself upon his knees before him, and would have embraced his feet, but Ramanath took both his son's hands in his own, and held them tightly in his nervous grasp. The young man buried his head in his father's lap and sobbed aloud, and the priest sat with ashy face and quivering lips, his eyelids closed tightly, as if he would fain shut out the scene before him. It was a moment of bitter suspense, and each shrank from being the first to begin the dread explanation.

At last Ramanath broke the silence. "Krishna, my son," he said, gently passing his hand over the young man's thick black curls, "tell me what evil has befallen you, for I can see plainly that something serious has happened. Let me know the worst, for I think I can bear it now, whatever it is."

A stifled sob was Krishna's only rejoinder. "Courage, my son," said the priest; "in whom can you confide, if not in your father? You are all my happiness in this world—my hope of salvation in the next; say what it is, and we will bear the sorrow together."

"It is that thought which maddens me," cried Krishna, wildly. "I can bear my lot without a murmur; but what have you done, dearest father, that grief should thus be brought to your door? My father, did I say? You are my father no longer, nor am I your son. I have discarded my faith and my caste, and with them all my future prospects in life, all my present position in society. I have now nothing but the possession of that truth which I have sacrificed so much to obtain, and the hope of that eternal reward which the one God will give to him who denies himself for His service."

The priest heaved a deep sigh, it might be of relief, or it might be of anguish at the announcement. "Have you turned Christian?" he asked, with a groan.

"No," said Krishna, "I am of the congregation of God. We hold that the one God is our Father, and that the human race is one vast family of brothers and sisters. We protest against the degradation of the Eternal by idolatry, and the usurpation of sacred attributes by erring creatures. The whole system of caste is one great pernicious lie, feigned to give the Brahmins sovereignty over their fellows, and no one may follow the God of truth while he lends himself to the maintenance of such a falsehood. So I have renounced my caste; would, father, that you could view my conduct in a true light! Would that your eyes were opened to a sight of the truth!"

But to this appeal the priest made no response. "Do you follow Debendronath Baboo?" he asked, in a calmer tone.

"I do not," said Krishna; "the Adi Somaj seeks to temporise with darkness, to free the mental faculties while they fetter man's social relations with all the old chains of Hindooism, and to substitute for Nature's simple ritual the affected liturgy of the Vedas. I have cast in my lot with the Progressive Brahmists."

"Do the Calcutta Brahmins know of your perversion?" was the father's next question.

"I myself proclaimed it to them," said Krishna, rising to his feet with an air of pride. "I threw down my gage to the foremost pundits of the Sanscrit College, and challenged them to prove the inspiration of the Hindoo Shastras, offering to make a public recantation of my opinions if they could convince me by their arguments. But none of them came forward, and the Brahmins ordered all the caste students in the college to expel me from their society. Then it was that I publicly freed myself from the trammels of Hindooism, and joined the little band of reformers that are so nobly devoting themselves to the regeneration of our country. My guardian, Poorno Baboo, turned me out of his house, and I had no choice left but to come and tell you what I had done, and to shape my future career by your decision. O father," added he, again throwing himself upon his knees before the old man, "I cannot say forgive me, for my conscience tells me that I have chosen the right part; but think kindly of what I have done. You know how I love you, my father, and consider what a price I shall pay for my principles if I forfeit your affection."

"Krishna," said the old man, solemnly, "it would have been lighter for me to have stood by your funeral pyre on the banks of the Gungaputra, and to have committed your ashes to the bosom of the sacred stream, than to hear from your own lips that you have forsaken the faith of your fathers. O gods! that my son should be the first to cast dishonour upon the Gossains of Dhupnagar."

"I have done no dishonour to our name," cried Krishna, starting up indignantly: "I have taken a step of which the purest Brahmins in Bengal might well be proud. Who says that it is a dishonourable thing to forsake all for the service of God? But forgive me, my father," he added; "I am indeed forgetting myself. I who have to bear the world's reproaches, need not chafe at the words of a parent."

"You have forfeited all your hereditary advantages," said the priest; "you have renounced your caste, and your position among the honoured of your countrymen; you have disqualified yourself for following the profession of your fathers, for inheriting the family possessions; you have thrown away rank, and affluence, and the prospect of future wealth: tell me now, son Krishna, what have you got in return for these sacrifices?"

"The approbation of my own conscience, and a knowledge of the truth," said Krishna, boldly; "compared with which, all the riches of Calcutta are but as so much dirty dross."

"Conscience!" echoed the priest, testily; "will conscience fill your belly when I am dead and the temple gone to strangers, and you are reduced to shift for a living? Knowledge of the truth! ay, feed upon that. The truth of to-day will be the truth of to-morrow— that is, if your nerves and senses remain unchanged— won't it? A little addition to the nervous current, a slight disturbance of the brain's equilibrium, and what becomes of the truth then? The truth is now falsehood, and something else is truth, and will continue so just as long as your stomach keeps its present tone. Have not you yourself told me so? Is it not thus that a plain Hindoo like me reads the lessons of your English masters? Truly it is a superlative thing this truth of yours, that you should make yourself a beggar, and plunge your family into mourning because of it."

Krishna made no answer, for he knew enough of his father's disposition to be aware that the priest's feelings were most easily relieved by sarcasm. Like many good-natured men, Ramanath was irritable enough at trifles; but when a blow of any magnitude fell upon him, he braced himself up manfully to bear his troubles. His mind had already grasped the worst possible consequences of Krishna's imprudence, and he was now seeking for some means of obviating them. There still remained a gleam of hope. In the solitude of Dhupnagar, away from all the heretical influences of the Calcutta Brahmists, who could say what changes might not come over his son? Hindooism had, too, among its resources, pleasures of which the young man knew nothing; and the best Brahmins in all ages had not scrupled to employ voluptuous allurements to restrain the wavering in the ways of religion. Though pure in life himself, and ashamed of the excesses of his countrymen, Ramanath felt at that moment as if he would willingly sacrifice his son's morals to save him from apostasy. Then there was another expedient that might be tried, and the priest almost started from his seat as the idea flashed across his mind. Krishna was still madly in love with Kristo Baboo's daughter, and as against his passion for her, his new opinions would, the priest thought, count for little. Yes, that was a certain remedy. Much as he disliked polygamy, he would willingly promote a marriage with Radha as the price of his son's recantation. There was, to be sure, poor Chakwi: it would be a heavy grief to the girl to see another come between her and the coveted affection of her husband. But hundreds of thousands of Hindoo wives had patiently to put up with the same; and Ramanath, much as he loved his daughter-in-law, unhesitatingly resolved that the peace of the family would be cheaply purchased at the expense of Chakwi's happiness.

"You have acted in this matter with the hot-headedness of youth," said the priest at last, "and time and reflection may bring you to a better way of thinking. Surely it is not the son that I have begotten that would doom my old age to misery. Consider, Krishna, how much my future weal depends upon my having a son to perform my funeral rites. You will think of this, and think deeply, before you designedly put your father's salvation in peril."

"O father," cried Krishna, "would that you could see how vain are the rites you mention, and how contemptible such oblations must be in the eyes of the Eternal! There is a purer and more spiritual life among the poor Theists than any that you have ever experienced in this idol-tainted town."

"Krishna," said the priest, sternly, "you must not speak thus to me, the bond-servant of the dread Siva. I have ever allowed you too much licence in religious matters, and this is the sad result of my laxity. We will talk no more of this at present. Avoid making any parade of your new faith, lest sooner than you can anticipate, the time may come when you would wish your acts undone and your words unsaid."

"Nay," said Krishna, "I must go out into the world and proclaim to my benighted countrymen their deliverance from idolatry and the tyranny of caste. Accursed be the man that would lie idle while such a glorious work is waiting to be achieved."

"You quit not this house," said Ramanath, firmly,

"if my paternal authority is to have any weight with you. What call have you to unsettle men's beliefs, when you have nothing certain to offer them instead? Is it for the sake of establishing a single abstract doctrine, the individuality of the Supreme, which lies at the very root of our own religion, though time and men's fancies may have clothed it with various disguises? It seems to me that you wish to roll back the religious progress of two thousand years, and to reduce us to the simple worship of our Aryan ancestors, who could only discern in the elements and the agencies of Nature the ministries of an unknown deity. Remain here, and seek a surer faith for yourself before you assail other people's."

"How can I remain here?" said Krishna, as he bent his head sadly: "you forget, my father, that I am an outcast, and may not stay here without defiling the household. I have done you harm enough already, without making your home a scandal among your caste-fellows."

"Krishna," said the old man, sadly, "though you came to me with your hands red from the blood of a Brahmin, you would still be my son, and my roof would shelter you so long as I was beneath it. Here you may abide in comfort and quietness. These rooms are yours, and Bechoo, who has no caste to break, will gladly cook for you and be your attendant: with your advanced views you will not scruple to take food from his hands; and here you will remain, my son, until you again awake to a proper sense of your privileges as a member of our holy thrice-born order. O Krishna! your father will have a heavy heart until that happy day arrives."

The concluding words quite unmanned Krishna, whose enthusiasm was as easily quenched by kindness as it was kindled by opposition. He sank down upon the couch as the old priest rose from it, and burying his face among the cushions, lay there for a long time in an agony of tears and prayer. Ramanath carefully shut the doors of his son's apartments, and went slowly across the courtyard in the direction of the temple. There, in his favourite seat under the porch, the priest could best meditate upon what was to be done. The afternoon was well advanced, and the sun was fast declining towards the woody peaks of Panch Pahar. Calling to Modhoo to close the temple gate for the day, Ramanath sat himself down and tried to draw consolation and counsel from his hookha. The hookha was emptied and filled and emptied again that afternoon. The sun went down behind Panch Pahar: the ruddy crimson skies in the west changed first to a pale red and then to a dusky umber, dark as the giant outline of the trees that stood out in colossal relief upon the crest of the hills. Darkness set in, except where here and there a death-pyre lit up the waters of the Gungaputra, or the myriads of fire-flies illumined the forest. A cool breeze came sweeping up the valley, stirring the *peepul* leaves above the priest's head to a ghostly fitful shiver. The jackals began to peep from their covers; the pariah dogs came boldly into the compound snuffing for garbage; the night settled down, but still Ramanath sat and smoked by the temple door. It was the bitterest pipe that ever he had smoked.

CHAPTER V.

THE COUNCIL OF FIVE.

JADDOO, the Dipty's "expectant," did his work well. Coming into the village in a careless saunter, he lounged about from shop to shop, and from house to house, giving and receiving the news of the day, casually mentioning always that he had met Krishna, the priest's son, on the highway, and had heard a current report that the young man had turned a Christian, and a beef-eater. This astounding intelligence speedily took wing and flew over the town; and long before Jaddoo reached the further end of the bazaar, he was gratified by meeting his own story so exaggerated and coloured, that he, the author, might have been pardoned for disowning it. Shama Churn, the grain-seller, confidently asserted that Krishna had not only eaten beef, and drunk spirits in the company of English Sahibs, but that he was in the habit of frequenting European *nátches* (balls), and of dancing like a wanton or an infamous play-actor. Nitye, the village Kobiraj or quack doctor, who had not forgiven Krishna for administering quinine to the fever-stricken peasants, two years ago come the rains, had an inkling of the business which brought the young man to Dhupnagar:—it was nothing more or less than a conspiracy to exterminate caste among the townsmen by means of European medicines, into which the dust of human bones and other abominations had been covertly introduced; and if any one was so irreligious as to accept anything from Krishna's hands after this warning, his blood was on his own head and not on his, Nitye, the Kobiraj's. Dwarkanath, the schoolmaster, had heard from one who ought to know, that the temple of the Linga was about to be turned into a Christian church, and he could even lay his thumb upon the exact spot where the butching-house—without which, as they were all well aware, no Christian church could exist—was straightway to be erected. And Three Shells, the moneylender, who on entering the bazaar had greedily caught up the news, soon had his little mite of gossip to contribute. He had heard a report that Krishna's wife was forthwith to be divorced, and an offer of marriage made to Kristo Baboo's daughter; and that failing the maiden and her father consenting to a Christian marriage, as was very likely, the young man was to bring home a fine European madam from Wellesley Street, or the Bow Bazaar. He, Three Shells, had heard, but could not believe, such a calumny: it was too profligate, too atrocious a deed to be done in a godly town like Dhupnagar; but a score of voices instantly protested upon their personal knowledge that Krishna was capable of even worse wickedness than that.

By sunset the whole village was in an uproar. Folks gathered in knots about the bazaar, or squatted upon the door-steps, discussing the scandal with their neighbours over the way. Nothing was to be heard but abuse of Krishna, and of his father who had exposed the young man to the contaminations of Calcutta. Everybody agreed that nothing of such importance had occurred in the district since the Chota Lord Sahib (Lieutenant-Governor) had camped a night in the village on his way to the Sonthal Pergunnahs, the year of the rotten mangoes. Many put on their best *chaddars*, and went with an offering to the temple in hopes of hearing further intelligence; but the gate was shut, and Modhoo, who sat before it imperturbably smoking his hookha, gave all comers stiffly to understand that he had no orders to admit them. All attempts to elicit information from the surly porter failed; and in the evening numerous little groups had assembled upon the village green, to talk over the awful calamity that had befallen Dhupnagar, and to peer through the gaps in the bamboo hedge to see if they could glean anything of what was going on in the temple; but nothing was to be seen but the old priest sitting smoking under the porch.

In a separate corner of the green, under the shade of

the *babul* trees (acacias), which a former magistrate of the Gungaputra had planted for the benefit of the town, the high-caste Brahmins held a solemn conclave. There were old Gangooly, the village headman; Dwarkanath, the schoolmaster; Prosunno, the *mookhtyear* or lawyer; Shama Churn, the grain-dealer; and Protap, the accountant and letter-writer. Three Shells had properly no vote in the matter, as his own caste was, to say the least, involved in doubt; but the Brahmins were his bondsmen, and could not well exclude him from their counsels. The mahajan went to work in his own wily fashion; he professed to lament the calamity that had befallen his friend Ramanath, and while he enlarged upon the judgments which would surely overtake the village if Krishna's impiety were altogether condoned, he entreated the Brahmins to deal leniently with the young man for his father's sake. The Brahmins did not very well know what to do. If the offender had been a poor man, with only a cow and a *bigah* of land, they would have made short work with him; but Ramanath was one of the heads of the village, of a family that had been honoured in the place for many generations, and he was more wealthy than even Three Shells himself. But most of the Brahmins were more or less at Three Shells' mercy, and rather than displease him, they were prepared to proceed to the utmost extremities against their castefellows.

"In the Council of Five is the voice of God," said

old Gangooly, the village headman; "my friends, let us not proceed rashly in this matter. We must summon the Brahmins and deliberate what is to be done. The gods forbid that we should needlessly lend our ears to evil rumours of a brother. The words of a backbiter are like the stream of the Gungaputra, they gather as they go."

"Who talks of evil rumours and backbiters?" cried Prosunno, the lawyer, who was the money-lender's factotum, and felt bound to display his zeal when his master's testimony was assailed; "you surely do not say that worthy Three Shells would come to us with words of falsehood in his mouth. No one is so blind as he who wilfully shuts his eyes. Did not half-a-score of respectable in-dwellers see the young man as he slunk through the back lanes of the village towards his father's house? And has not this trustworthy follower of the Dipty Baboo" (here Jaddoo made a low salaam to the company) "brought news from Calcutta, which completely confirms the evil tidings? Why then talk of rumours unless you wish to shirk your duty, Mr Headman?"

"The gods forbid," said the perplexed Gangooly. "I have been forty years headman of Dhupnagar, and my father and grandfather were headmen before me, but such a scandal never came before me or them. As I said before, I am willing to call a 'Panchayat' upon the business."

"It is my opinion," said Dwarkanath, the schoolmaster, sententiously, " that something should be done to stop the godless teaching of the English. If Krishna Baboo had been educated at my school, I warrant that he had never thought of turning Christian. But what can we expect when lads are sent to a college where they are told that the earth is a round ball, and that it is continually moving round about the sun ?—ha! ha! What fools they must be to have eyes in their heads and yet believe such stuff! If we were to mind what the English teachers tell us, we should soon be all Christians and kine-killers."

"This is, indeed, the Black Age," snuffled Three Shells, turning up his eyes,—" but what can we do? The evil is already committed, and punishment will not mend matters. Let me entreat you to take no notice of this affair, for my heart is sore for Ramanath Gossain. It were much better that we should try to propitiate the gods, that their wrath may not fall upon Dhupnagar because of this impiety. As for myself," continued Three Shells, with an affected shudder, " I think I shall gather together my little property and return to my own country, that my eyes may not be grieved by the sight of godlessness."

At this, Protap, and Prosunno, and Shama Churn, and Dwarkanath burst forth into a howl of grief, for they knew that if Three Shells left the village he would gather in all his debts, which meant utter ruin to themselves.

" What! the worthy Three Shells leave the town, and

for such a cause! Never should it be said that the Brahmins of Dhupnagar gave offence to so excellent, so religious a man by their laxity. They would do anything he might choose to direct. They would hold a Panchayat, and put Krishna out of caste that very night. They would make such an example of the priest's family that the name of heresy should never again be breathed in Dhupnagar. But Three Shells must never speak of leaving. It would be a less calamity were the sun to desert the firmament, than that Three Shells, who had been a father to the village, should turn his back upon his children."

Even old Gangooly, who had less cause to fear the mahajan than any of the others, joined in their entreaties, and expressed his willingness to call a council of the Brahmins. To this the faction of Three Shells gladly assented, and messengers were despatched throughout the district to summon the few Brahmins who had a right to be present, and to invite Kristo Baboo and the Rajah of Ghatghar, to sit upon the Panchayat which was to take place next afternoon at the house of Gangooly, the village headman. It was also necessary that a summons should be served upon Krishna and his father, for the Panchayat could not venture to decide against persons of their standing without first hearing what they had to say in their defence. None of the Brahmins were willing to undertake the errand to Ramanath. Respectable men like Gangooly felt for the priest in his trouble, and were unwilling to be the means of adding to his affliction by further ill news; and the others did not wish to bring down upon themselves the wrath of so influential a man. When at last it was apparent that no one would volunteer his services, Gangooly made choice of Prosunno, the lawyer, ostensibly because he was the best business man among them, but really because he and all his townsmen hated Prosunno as a sneaking, officious mischief-maker, the cause of more than half the discord in the village, and a spy and tale-bearer to the money-lender. Prosunno would fain have declined the mission, but the other Brahmins, each of whom was glad to escape the unpleasant task, unanimously confirmed the choice; and the dread of exciting Three Shells' anger deterred the lawyer from returning a flat refusal.

The announcement of this resolution served to quiet the public curiosity, and the people began to move away in the direction of their houses. It was little marvel though they talked, for a case of heresy in Dhupnagar was more than a nine days' wonder. All the Rajah of Ghatghar's wickednesses, all the excesses of young Afzul Khan, the Subadar's son, even the raids of the Sonthal *dakaits* were as nothing compared to the perversion of the priest's son. Violation of caste was a scandal hardly known in Dhupnagar. Sometimes a Brahmin would so far forget himself as to indulge in a *liaison*, or even to marry, with a woman of low caste or no caste at all. And instances had been seen of a twice-born Hindoo emerging from the shop of Rutton Pal, the *kulwar* or spirit-seller, with an unsteady gait and idiotic demeanour which too clearly indicated that the restraints of caste had been temporarily forgotten. But prompt submission, a fine or so, and a feast to the Brahmins, had caused such slips to be glossed over, and the regulations of caste had been maintained without the necessity of a public example. But this was a different case. When the matter went before a Panchayat it could no longer be hushed up, and the people amused themselves by conjecturing how Ramanath and his son would ward off the terrible doom of excommunication. It would cost them the bulk of half a lakh of rupees, Ram Lall, the oilman, was ready to warrant; but what mattered it, since they were well able to afford the money? It was fortunate for Krishna that Ram Lall's caste did not entitle him to a seat on the Panchayat, for the old man heartily shared the hatred of his son the Dipty. Nitye, the quack doctor, was doubtful whether the high-caste Brahmins would, after all, fall out among themselves. If the offender had been a poor man there would have been little doubt of his being punished; but had they not winked at old Hem Chunder when he married the rich leather-seller's daughter, of whom he begot Prosunno, the lawyer? Bah! what Brahmin ever saw a speck of dirt upon another Brahmin's *dhoti* (waist-cloth)?

At sunrise next morning, Three Shells and Prosunno met together before the gate of the temple. Although the hour of morning worship had arrived, the door was still locked, and Modhoo did not seem to be in any hurry to respond to their loud knocks. The money-lender carried a garland of brilliant flowers, in which the bright blossoms of the *champak* mingled gaily with the white flowers of the *kundoo* and the blue petals of the water-lily, as an offering to the Linga. Confident that he had a good excuse in this offering for seeking admission, Three Shells knocked loudly at the gate, and reviled the memory of the ancestors of Modhoo, the porter, who lay in bed like a lazy fellow while the sun was mounting to mid-heaven, and whose sloth prevented devout worshippers from paying their morning devotions. Modhoo having recounoitred his visitors through a slit in the gate, leisurely set about his toilet, which consisted chiefly in stretching and shaking himself and in binding his long red turban round his head. The porter suspected that the early visit of these two worthies betokened no good to his master, and so he admitted them with curt civility, scarcely deigning them a stiff salaam as they walked past him towards the temple. Early as it was, Ramanath was before them engaged in the ceremony of morning worship; and the money-lender and Prosunno did not venture to intrude themselves upon his devotions. Whether the trouble that had befallen him had rendered Ramanath more pious than ordinary, or whether he had observed his visitors and conjectured their motive, it is certain that his prayers occupied him a good hour longer than usual; and Three Shells and Prosunno were left to stand sweltering in the sun, for they could not venture to come under the shelter of the temple porch until the priest had invited them. Meanwhile Modhoo, who had seated himself at his ease in the shade to enjoy his morning smoke, scarcely concealed his exultation at their embarrassment, and the position of the confederates was not rendered any more comfortable by the porter's broad grins. At length Ramanath's prayers and the envoys' patience were alike exhausted. Slowly the priest rose to his feet and placed an offering of rice and ripe plantains before the idol, accompanying each act with a *mantra* (prayer) which Three Shells thought might well have been dispensed with; and it was not until he had deliberately gone through the minutest injunctions of the ritual, that the priest came to the temple door and acknowledged the presence of his visitors by an affable salaam and an invitation to enter. After the usual greetings had been interchanged, Three Shells slipped into the temple with his offering, leaving Prosunno a fair field for delivering his message. But though he prostrated himself before the Linga in the attitude of prayer, the usurer kept his ears open to catch every word that passed between Prosunno and the priest.

"These are evil times," said Prosunno, with a sanctimonious sniff, as he accepted the priest's invitation to sit down. "The judgment of the gods must be near at hand when mankind disowns their power and impurity is openly committed in the sight of heaven."

"Umph!" said the priest, who knew what was coming, and was determined to do battle with Prosunno; "I don't know that the world is any worse than it used to be. Your father, Hem Chunder—may his memory be preserved—was, in my way of thinking, just as good a man as you are, Prosunno."

"Hem!" said Prosunno, drily; "there is an evil spirit abroad upon the land. The English teachers are covertly sowing the seeds of irreligion, and who knows what the crop may be like? I say foul befall the Brahmin who countenances those that would sap the foundations of our most holy faith; and three-fold woe to those who expose the young of their families to the contagious influence of Christians and kine-killers."

"Indeed!" said Ramanath, calmly, as he smoked away at his hookha without ever offering a whiff to his visitor, a sure affectation of superiority which did not fail to increase Prosunno's discomfort. "You did not think so, friend Prosunno, when you went to learn law from the English Sahibs at Hooghly. I have heard, too, that after you came home you boasted of being the only lawyer in the Gungaputra district that had learned the Sahibs' law from the Sahibs themselves. Did the Christians and kine-killers do you much harm that time?"

"I spoke not of law teachers," said Prosunno, somewhat discomposed, "but of those who teach systems of philosophy and religion contrary to the Shastras; and many of your friends in Dhupnagar think that you have erred with respect to your son Krishna Baboo."

"Oh, they think that I have erred, do they?" said the priest, sarcastically. "And have they sent you to tell me so, Prosunno? It is surely a propitious day for my family when the good folks of Dhupnagar have sent their sharpest lawyer to aid me in managing my domestic affairs. This kindness is all the greater that it is entirely unsought on my part. I hope my wife and daughter-in-law are included in your commission?"

Prosunno's wrath was kindled by this taunt, for it was not long before that the Brahmins of Dhupnagar had been obliged to restrict his marital powers of inflicting chastisement upon the ladies of his zenana. "Jesting may do for the Hoolie festival, maharajah, but to-day is a day of earnest words," he said, testily. "I have come to summon you to answer before a Panchayat of your townsmen for the character of your family."

"*You* have come to summon *me!*" cried Ramanath, losing all self-control; "you, the grandson of a vile leather-seller, summon Ramanath Gossain whose Brahmin's blood runs as pure in his veins as it did in those of his forefathers when they first came to Bengal forty-five score years ago. Hound! it would only be the meet desert of your insolence if I were to have you driven from the temple with clubs. What can I or my family be to Sudras like you?"

"I crave your pardon," said Prosunno, cowering before the priest's anger; "I crave your honour's pardon if I have offended you. Remember, if you please, that I am only delivering a message from my fellow-townsmen; and I pray you also that you will recollect how the Brahmins, yourself among the rest, have condoned the blot in my pedigree and confirmed me in all the privileges of my father's caste."

"But they couldn't put a Brahmin's heart in a Sudra's body," said the priest, turning away haughtily; "they could not make you anything but the half-bred sneak that you are. Begone, sir! and tell those who sent you that I will be at their Panchayat, and that some of them will wish that they had sat down upon red-hot iron before they seated themselves to try the caste of Ramanath Gossain and his son. Modhoo! attend this Baboo to the gate."

"You will repent this violence, Baboo," cried Prosunno, whose rage was now fairly kindled, but who nevertheless took the precaution of moving away half-a-dozen paces before he ventured upon a retort; "your language, sir, is actionable, and I shall make you pay for it. The Penal Code, Chapter XV. clause 5, see Mayne of Madras's edition, expressly says, "Whoever with the deliberate intention of wounding the religious feelings of any person utters any word, or makes any sound in the hearing of that person, or places——"

"By the three heads of Siva!" cried the priest, interrupting him, "if you stand there giving me back answers, you shall have something to sue for. Here, Modhoo, Bechoo, Ram Singh, quick with your *lattees* (quarter-staves) and drive this fellow outside the bounds of the temple."

Modhoo caught up his club with alacrity, but the lawyer did not wait to add an assault and battery to his proposed action against the priest. He took to his heels with such goodwill, that although first one and then another of his loose native shoes fell from his feet as he ran, he never stopped to take them up, nor paused in his flight until he had reached the village green, where several of the townsmen were already assembled waiting for his return.

"Fling his shoes over the hedge after him, Modhoo," said the priest, "and never allow that spawn of a Sudra to pass my temple doors again."

Modhoo picked up the shoes with much affectation of disgust, and flung them over the hedge with so just a regard to the laws of projectiles that one fell with a thud upon Prosunno's sconce, and the other plumped into the ample stomach of Protap, the accountant, with such force as caused the fat Baboo to double himself up in a contortion of pain. This signal of defiance, coupled with the exaggerated accounts which Prosunno gave of the priest's insolence, excited the popular anger in a tenfold degree against Ramanath; and even old Gangooly vowed that the Panchayat would make him bitterly repent his effrontery. But Three Shells had yet to come out, and so the Brahmins hung about the green, waiting to hear what further news the money-lender would bring them. But Three Shells was apparently in no hurry. The Brahmins were much discomcerted at the sober countenance which they had received in the prosecution. The needy Rajah of Ghatghar had long been scheming to obtain a loan from the wealthy priest, and would not damage his chances of accommodation by taking part in a hostile meeting, but he civilly excused his attendance upon the plea of ill health. Kristo Baboo, whose voice would have gone a great way in determining the decision of the village council, was less polite. Mindful, perhaps, that his own domestic arrangements were open to censure, and perhaps grateful for old kindnesses done to him by Ramanath, he returned for answer that the villagers were ever too ready to meddle with the affairs of their betters, and that there was none among them of good enough caste to try Ramanath Gossain. Kristo's reply disconcerted the Brahmins more than they cared to admit, for they had made themselves sure of the co-operation of a man who prided himself so much upon his orthodoxy. Gangooly would fain have seized the opportunity to urge that the matter should be dropped or postponed, but Prosunno threatened him with the vengeance of all the Brahmins in Bengal, and the possible loss of his office, until the pacific Gangooly was obliged to proceed with the business. Then a controversy sprang up as to whether Three Shells might not be permitted to sit upon the Panchayat. Although the moneylender was generally very reticent about his caste, he laid some pretensions to Brahminical dignity; and the village Brahmins when they had once borrowed his money could not well refuse to meet him upon an equal footing. Prosunno the lawyer, and Protap the accountant, were ready to vouch for him being a good Brahmin. Shama Churn, the grain-dealer, who was to some extent in Three Shells' power, but was still a conscientious man, held his peace. Dwarkanath, the schoolmaster, who was just about to redeem the mortgage upon his house and garden, openly demurred, unless Three Shells could establish his caste upon better evidence than verbal assertion. And old Gangooly, the village headman, settled the discussion by flatly declaring that no one should join the Panchayat who was a stranger to the place, and of more than doubtful antecedents. A wordy warfare sprang up, in which the lawyer and accountant fought a stout battle on behalf of their patron, and argued the point so keenly that the minority were beginning to yield. But what was detaining the money-lender himself all this time in the temple?

CHAPTER VI.

THE PRIEST SCOTCHES A SNAKE.

AFTER the priest had routed his first opponent he again sat down quietly to his hookha. Three Shells, still prostrate before the idol, was now praying in a loud, whining tone, repeating the names and attributes of Siva, and pleading for preservation from all sorts of danger, both likely and unlikely. The money-lender had marked Prosunno's discomfiture, and fearing lest the angry priest might be disposed to treat him as an accomplice, he had some difficulty in summoning up courage to face Ramanath. At last, when he could in decency pray no longer, and when he had spent an unconscionable time in arranging his offering of flowers, Three Shells came forth, concealing his apprehensions under his usual fawning demeanour. With a low salaam and a fervently-ejaculated prayer for the continuance of the priest's life and prosperity, Three Shells would have gone on his way, but the priest beckoned him to stay.

"Three Shells, my friend," said Ramanath, affably, "sit ye down; I have a few words to say to you."

Three Shells took his seat on the other side of the temple door in considerable surprise. "Aha," thought he, "Ramanath Baboo, like a wise man, is going to solicit my assistance in this matter, but he shall pay for it, I promise him;" and, pleased with his new importance, Three Shells made a ridiculous attempt to inflate his skeleton of a body into consequential and dignified dimensions.

"Speak on, Ramanath Baboo," said he, with an air of lordly condescension; "anything that I can do for you will be gladly performed. There is, of course, my duty to society and to religion, which a holy man like you will not expect one to transgress."

"Certainly not, Three Shells—certainly not," cheerily responded Ramanath; "your duty to society and religion—it is quite proper that you should regard both; I am only going to tell you a little story."

"Indeed?" said the mahajan, looking straight before him with half-closed eyes and his face puckered up into a contemptuous smile; "and what may it relate to? Say on, Father Ramanath."

"Two years ago come the next Jagannath Puja," the priest began, "there came three Hindustani pilgrims to the temple door, telling me that one of their company was lying sick unto death at the Pagoda Tope. He was a poor Brahmin who had been at Puri, had spent all his money, and had caught jungle-fever by the way, and he was now lying in that ruined temple without a friend to comfort his last moments—without a hand to close his dying eyes. Well, taking Modhoo with me, I set out for the Pagoda Tope, and, sure enough, there was the man lying upon a strip of tattered matting in the vestibule of the old temple, perishing of thirst and hunger. Modhoo broke a coco-nut and poured the milk down his throat, and the poor wretch revived a little. We tended him all that day, and as the heat declined the fever left him; so we called three or four kindly ryots, and placing him on a *charpai* (four-legged wicker bedstead), bore him to my house. But Yama, the god of death, had laid his hand heavily upon him. The luckless creature raved the whole night, and died a little after sunrise next morning."

"Peace be with him! You did well, very well, Father Ramanath, to show compassion to a helpless stranger," said Three Shells, with an air of patronising benignity. "Verily the gods will reward you manifold. But as touching this matter of your son Krishna which you doubtless wished to speak to me about———"

"He raved, as I said, the whole night," interrupted Ramanath; "ah! it is an awful thing, Three Shells, when the gods deprive the guilty of their reason. This man had been a terrible sinner. There was hardly a crime in the power of man to commit which this poor wretch did not lay to his own charge. He spoke of drugging lonely travellers with the deadly *dhatura*;

of despatching with his knife the wayfarer that had taken shelter beneath his roof; of robbing the widow of her ornaments and the maiden of her honour; worse than all, he talked of a priest butchered at the altar, and the shrine of the gods plundered of its wealth. This man was a Brahmin of Lootua, a village on the higher waters of the Soane, a place you may perhaps have heard of.—But what ails you, Three Shells? You look as if you were going to faint. The sun is too strong for you, eh? Sit a little farther back into the shade, man."

A terrible change had come over Three Shells' aspect. His face had turned of an ashy-grey paleness, his eyes were distended until they seemed to have started from their sockets, his lower jaw had fallen as if paralysed, and a gurgling inarticulate sound in his throat failed to find expression in words.

"Sickness had brought the poor wretch to repentance," continued the priest, turning away his head carelessly in the other direction, "and he set out on a pilgrimage to Jagannath to seek rest for his conscience; but he might have gone to the world's end before a soul like his could have found any peace but what the gods in their goodness had provided for him at Dhupnagar—the peace of death. An hour or two before he died, his senses returned to him, and he told me his sad history. He had led a terrible life, had that Brahmin; but he told me of an accomplice who was even more steeped in crime than he was. This person was

—dog, and son of a dog!" exclaimed Ramanath, starting to his legs, as Three Shells with a howl of despair prostrated himself before him and attempted to kiss his feet, "pollute not with your unhallowed lips the feet of a pure Brahmin. Back, wretch, lest I blast thee with a look!"

"Mercy, mercy!" groaned the usurer, as he raised his hands in supplication. "Protector of the poor! upon thee, upon thee! Your slave is your protected! O Asylum of the Universe! defile not your sacred foot by crushing a mean worm. Have mercy upon me, holiest of priests! have mercy upon me!"

"Aha, Three Shells! you have heard my little story before," said the priest, looking down with a glance of scornful loathing at the wretch who lay writhing before him. "I will spare you the repetition of it then, and come to the *hasil* (moral), which you will find to be as pithy a one as is in all the fables of Pilpay. It is this —mind your own business and let your neighbours' alone. And now begone, and never set your foot within this temple again, if you would rather have whole bones than broken ones. I need hardly tell you that if this Panchayat takes place to-day, I shall have matters to lay before the members that they little anticipate. They will scarcely be prepared to learn that you have not left them an undefiled Brahmin in the village, but Kristo Baboo, to hold a Panchayat upon Ramanath the priest. Moreover, I shall have a messenger going express to the English Magistrate Sahib at Bhutpore, as soon as the Panchayat is over. Can he execute any little commission for you, friend Three Shells, in that quarter?" added Ramanath, tauntingly.

"There will be no Panchayat, maharajah," said Three Shells, humbly; "no indignity shall befall your honoured family that I can prevent. Am I not your bond-slave? Do you not give me life? O maharajah, overlook my error towards you!"

"Begone then," said the priest, sternly, "and take care how you again intrude yourself into my presence. Yet, stay a moment, Three Shells," he continued, as the mahajan was sneaking away humbly from the temple: "it may prevent mistakes if I tell you that I have written down this little story we talked of, and given a sealed copy to a trusty friend, who will place it in the hands of the Magistrate Sahib if anything unusual were to happen to me—that is, if I were to be suddenly found dead, or the like. You understand me, Three Shells? Ah, I see you do. Peace be with you, Three Shells." And the priest bestowed a derisive salaam upon the retreating money-lender.

Three Shells slunk quietly out of the temple gate and passed along the back of the thorny bamboo hedge, beyond which he could see the elders impatiently waiting his arrival on the village green. He paused for an instant, but his mind misgave him, and he hurried off by a back lane in the direction of his house, and was seen no more of the villagers for several days.

The threatened Panchayat never was held for the trial of Ramanath and his son Krishna. While the Brahmins loitered about the village green waiting for the appearance of Three Shells, Modhoo came forth and summoned the village headman to wait upon his master. When alone with old Gangooly, Ramanath was able to show the headman excellent reasons why his family should not be made the subject of public interference. His son was no Christian: of that the priest would assure them; and his house was his own, and his son was welcome to remain there as long as he pleased. But let the villagers beware how they meddled with Ramanath Gossain's domestic matters. The temple was his own, the Linga was his own, and what prevented him from doing with them as he thought fit? The folks of Gapshapganj would only be too glad if he would transfer his shrine to their town; and Ramanath himself owned lands in Bhutpore where he could build a temple. This threat was sufficient for the headman. Dhupnagar owed all its prosperity to the popularity of the Linga, and to the crowds of pilgrims that resorted to it. If, as Gangooly afterwards told his fellow-townsmen, they drove away the priest in disgust, they might as well yoke the donkey's plough* and sow salt upon the site of Dhupnagar, for the ruin of the village would be certain. The priest did not dis-

---

* *Gudhe ka hal* (the donkey's plough) was driven over the site of a captured town as the emblem of degradation and ruin, and salt was sown in the furrows.

miss Gangooly until he had convinced him of the folly of trusting to popular rumour, and made the headman thoroughly ashamed of the ingratitude of himself and his fellow-townsmen towards a family to whom the village stood so much indebted.

Dwarkanath the schoolmaster, and Shama Churn the grain-seller, readily seconded Gangooly's proposal that the matter should be quashed in spite of the outcries of Three Shells' dependants, who called all the gods to witness that the Brahmins of Dhupnagar were compounding sacrilege against their holy order. Prosunno, the lawyer, who had his own private insults to avenge, was especially vehement, until reminded by old Gangooly how slender was his own claim to caste consideration, and that those who had made him a Brahmin would have little difficulty in unmaking him. The village elders speedily agreed that they had acted upon insufficient information, that the priest's son had not become a Christian and a kine-killer, that no breach of caste had taken place, and that those who had raised such reports were liars and *dullals* (brokers, a common term of abuse). Jaddoo, the Dipty's expectant, who still loitered about the village in the hope of being able to carry his master the news of Krishna's condemnation, was observed by old Gangooly sneaking about the village green, endeavouring to pick up scraps of the elders' conversation; and the old headman, not sorry perhaps to find a convenient scapegoat, gave orders that he should be driven from the town as a liar and a mischief-monger. A magistrate's hanger-on is as unpopular a character in a Bengalee village, as a sheriff's officer, or process-server, is in an Irish hamlet. And the townsfolk willingly seized clubs and slippers to fulfil the headman's behest. Jaddoo protested his innocence, and menaced them with his master's wrath, but all to no purpose. His voice was drowned by the thud-thud of slippers upon his sconce, his bones were nearly broken by the whacks of cudgels, his clothes were torn off his back, he was thrown into the gutter, and rolled over the gravelly road; and finally, he made his escape from the village, more dead than alive, never pausing to examine his injuries until he reached the crest of the ridge and the shelter of the Pagoda Tope.

But the villagers, ever ready to grumble at the doings of their betters, were far from satisfied with the decision of the Brahmins. They had looked upon Krishna's excommunication as certain, and now they felt as if they had been unjustly balked of a sensation. If Krishna had been a poor man, they argued, instead of the son of a rich priest, his caste-fellows would not have scrupled to throw him off; but what wonder was it though men forsook the gods and the customs of their country when twice-born Brahmins durst not say to such that they were doing wrong. The lower castes, jealous of the Brahmin's position and privileges, are sharp critics of the latter's shortcomings, and though they would gladly welcome any relaxation of the Brahminical restrictions that would admit themselves to a closer intimacy with the favoured class, they are ever the first to taunt the Brahmins with tolerating laxity in any other form.

Ram Lall, the oilman, who hated Krishna on his son the Dipty's account, and would have gladly seen the young man degraded, was one of the mouthpieces of popular discontent. When the Dipty's expectant was driven from the village, the old man had retired to sulk in his shop, and to pray that no signal judgment might fall upon Dhupnagar because of the impiety of its inhabitants. Moreover, Ram Lall that same evening, although notorious as *parcus deorum cultor et infrequens*, made an offering of a two-pound measure of flour and half-a-dozen ounces of clarified butter, together with a huge basket of flowers, which cost only the trouble of gathering, to the clumsy pillar-stone at the east end of the village, which stood for the *gram deota*, or *genius loci*, of Dhupnagar. By this unwonted manifestation of piety the oilman meant to show, not so much his reverence for the *gram deota*, as his contempt for Ramanath and the Linga of Dhupnagar. But Ram Lall's ostentatious devoutness only caused a hearty laugh to the Brahmins, who were well acquainted with the old man's penuriousness, and who jestingly said that surely the gods would be good to Dhupnagar since Ram Lall had spent eight annas in their worship. But Ram Lall, as well as the rest of his townsmen, was quite aware that the prosperity of the village depended upon the temple, and that if they drove Ramanath and his idol away by their scandal-mongering, their craft was in danger to be set at nought; for no pilgrims would then repair to Dhupnagar—there would be no yearly *mela* or market at which the tradesfolk might reap a golden, or at least a silver, harvest—and rich devotees, with their trains of attendants, would no longer frequent the village at festal tides. No doubt religion was a matter of great importance—so, also, was the preservation of caste; but it was more especially the Brahmins' business to attend to these things; and the good folks of Dhupnagar had no intention of breaking with their livelihood in their zeal for orthodoxy.

CHAPTER VII.

SHAMSUDDEEN KHAN, THE SUBADAR.

A FEW hundred yards out of the village, by the side of the road leading down to the fords of the Gungaputra, stood a large house, of a style not often seen in the Lower Provinces. The walls were compactly built of brick and lime, but without verandahs, with narrow stanchioned windows, and with small turrets surmounting each angle of the building. The aim of the architect had apparently been to combine the semblance of an up-country chieftain's *muhil*, or citadel, with the conveniences of a peaceful dwelling-house. Another novel feature was the tastefully laid out gardens that flanked the mansion upon either side, and filled up the background as far as the commencement of the jungle. Shamsuddeen Khan, the proprietor, had seen the imperial gardens of Delhi and Agra, and in spite of his rough profession he had always cherished a passion for flowers; and now that he was an old man, and no longer able to sit firmly in the saddle, he was well content to turn his sabre into a pruning-knife, to spend his days among his roses and passion-flowers, and to smoke and dream of old times under the tulip-loaded boughs of the *dhag* tree by the side of the little marble fountain that dropped a tiny jet of water into the basin at his feet.

Shamsuddeen Khan had well earned his repose and the reward which the British Government had bestowed upon him for his services. When the Pindarry bands of Kurreem Khan were routed near Gungraur in Malwa, a little boy was found among the prisoners, with whom no one would acknowledge relationship until a kind British officer took the waif into his own household. The young Shamsuddeen was brought up in his benefactor's regiment, and became a trooper almost as soon as his legs could straddle across a saddle. His patron, Captain Walesby, attended to his military education, and made him the best swordsman and "tent-pegger" in a crack corps of irregular cavalry; while old Ahmed Khan, Captain Walesby's butler, superintended the lad's religious instruction, and brought him up as a stanch Muhammadan of the Shiyia persuasion. The young Shamsuddeen rapidly became a favourite in the regiment, both with his English officers and native comrades. The latter made him the spokesman of all their little grievances, and the former were always glad to oblige so active and respectful a soldier. If a man wanted furlough, it was Shamsuddeen who was deputed to beg it from the colonel; if the colonel wanted a batch of lusty recruits, it was Shamsuddeen who was sent to beat up for them. In war Shamsuddeen Khan's reputation was no less favourable than in peace. In the Afghan campaign, where, as everybody who reads Sir John Kaye's delightful history will remember, Walesby's Horse did such distinguished service, Shamsuddeen won a commission by his determined bearing in every engagement; and his promotion was accompanied by an eulogium in General Orders upon his long service and good conduct. At the same time Shamsuddeen had an opportunity of clearing off his debt of gratitude to his commandant. In the night attack upon Sale's brigade in the Khurd Cabul valley, Colonel Walesby was recognised as he rode from the Political Agent's tents to join his regiment, wounded, and carried off a prisoner by the traitorous Afghans who had obtained admission into the camp; and there is little doubt that he would have been reserved for cold-blooded butchery, had not Shamsuddeen, without orders, and heedless of Sale's "assembly" bugles, followed up the retreating Ghilzyes with a score of troopers, until they were compelled to abandon Walesby in their flight. All through Walesby's illness, in the miserable Afghan winter, Shamsuddeen tended his patron with the carefulness of a son and the tenderness of a woman; until the colonel declared that he had been repaid tenfold for his early kindness to the Pindarry orphan.

In course of time Shamsuddeen remained alone in

the regiment. Of the early comrades of his youth the bones of some lay bleaching in the Afghan passes; others had found a grave in the sandy plains of the Sutlej, and those who had survived the wars had long since retired to spend their pensions in their native villages. Though General Walesby was dead and buried in Cheltenham churchyard, Walesby's Horse was still Walesby's Horse, and Shamsuddeen Khan was now Subadar-major of the regiment, with many streaks of silver in his black hair and beard. Then came the Mutiny; and when the troopers of Walesby's began to growl about greased cartridges and interference with their faith, and to listen to the lying agents of the Badshah of Delhi and the Nana of Cawnpore, Shamsuddeen Khan remained faithful to the salt, and did his best to strengthen the wavering allegiance of his comrades. And when Walesby's troopers held a midnight muster upon the Pultunpore parade-ground for the purpose of shooting their officers, and declaring for the Moghal, Shamsuddeen Khan had dashed into their midst, pistoled Reissaldar Ahmad Buksh, the ringleader, at the risk of his own life, and made such an eloquent appeal to the loyalty of the men that eighty of the best soldiers in the regiment came to his side and assisted him in escorting their officers safe to headquarters. For his fidelity Shamsuddeen was made a Khan Bahadoor in the Order of British India, and the Government further rewarded him with a small estate rent free in the vicinity of Dhupnagar, which had come into the hands of the District Collector from the distraint of Kristo Baboo's property.

In quitting the regiment in which his life had been spent, Shamsuddeen Khan felt like a man who has broken off all the associations that bound him to earth. His heart was still in his old corps, and it was still his pride to know every officer and every trooper in Walesby's. Regularly as the Durga Puja came round, Shamsuddeen paid a visit to Walesby's Horse, no matter how far off they were stationed; and his coming was welcomed with all the honours that would have been paid to the general commanding the division. It was good to see the old soldier receiving the salutations of the beardless recruits with whose fathers he had ridden side by side in the Afghan and the Punjab wars, and to hear the words of encouragement and counsel which he addressed to them. The troopers felt that Shamsuddeen Khan was an honour to their regiment, and would proudly boast that the commander-in-chief, Sir George Blitzen Sahib, who would hardly look at an Englishman under the rank of a field-officer, was wont to shake their old Subadar cordially by the hand whenever his Excellency met him.

There was no house in all the Lower Provinces where an old soldier was made so welcome as at Walesbyganj, for so Shamsuddeen had named his house, in memory of his benefactor and the old corps. Troopers of Walesby's going and coming between Calcutta and Upper India would make a long detour to pass a night under Shamsuddeen's roof, and to hear his stories of the storming of Ghizni, and the charge at Sobraon. Retired Rajpoot officers of other corps taking a trip for their sins to the shrine of Jagannath at Puri, or the Linga of Dhupnagar, never failed to pay their respects to the old man as they passed through the valley. Zealous Mussulman as he was, the "Service" overrode all sectarian feelings in Shamsuddeen's mind, and the Hindoo was as cordially welcomed at Walesbyganj as the Muhammadan, provided he was a soldier. The Subadar did not, however, carry his tolerance beyond the limits of the army, and treated the civilians, his Hindoo neighbours, with the utmost *hauteur* and contempt. There was no other Mussulman near Dhupnagar except the broken-down landholder who dubbed himself the Nawab of Panch Pahar, in virtue of some post which his ancestor held about the Nazimat Court of Murshedabad, and who affected to look down upon the Subadar as an upstart and a parasite upon the British. On his part, the Subadar was nowise anxious for the intimacy of so disreputable an old spendthrift, who had spent all his belongings, down to the bare walls of his paternal mansion and the few *bigahs* of land that surrounded it, upon brandy and dice and loose company, in a way that could not but bring the holy faith of Islam to discredit among the surrounding infidel. Bhutpore, at the head of the valley, had once been a populous Muhammadan town in the days of the Moghals; but, as the number of ruined mosques testified, the Faithful had fallen upon evil times, and, except one or two grey-bearded Moulavis, the Mussulmans had all sunk into a menial condition. Consequently Shamsuddeen was almost wholly cut off from the society of his co-religionists.

When the Subadar quitted Walesby's Horse he took with him his orderly, Agha Khan, an Afghan from the Khyber, who had been in his service since the army of retribution had returned from the burning of Cabul. The Subadar's fondness for Agha was one of those attachments that no one could explain. The Khyberee was a loutish, unshapely soldier, whose insubordinate temper was perpetually bringing him into quarrels with his comrades. From the hour of his enlistment Agha had never been out of trouble; and his *duffadar* (corporal) used jestingly to calculate that all the entries against him in the defaulters' book would alone fill an ordinary-sized volume. The adjutant had pronounced him incurable, and Colonel Walesby had threatened to have him drummed out of the regiment the next time that Agha was brought before him. But the Gwalior war soon broke out, when discipline was less strictly enforced, and those officers who had been hardest upon Agha's shortcomings, could not but admire the daring recklessness with which he had broken his ranks and galloped up to the mouth of the Sindhia's guns at Maharajpore. The Subadar took him for his servant immediately after the action, and quite melted the rough Khyberee by his kindness. Shamsuddeen was eating in his tent when the trooper came to him, and when he had commended his bravery and told him of the promotion in store for him—the first words of kindness and sympathy that Agha had heard since he quitted his native hills—the man dashed his hand rudely in Shamsuddeen's salt-dish, swallowed a mouthful, made a low salaam, turned on his heel and strode out of the tent without a word of thanks. Shamsuddeen perfectly understood the significance of this act; and well did Agha fulfil his profession of fidelity. He had received a great slash across the shoulder from a Sikh sabre as he was dragging his master from the bloody mud of the Sutlej in the grand charge which Walesby's Horse made at Aliwal, and he had received in his own thigh a thrust from a bayonet which a sepoy had meant for his master when the troops at Pultunpore mutinied in the 'Fifty-seven. These injuries had improved neither the symmetry of Agha's appearance, nor the equanimity of his temper; and it was rarely that he ever opened his mouth to say anything civil even to his master. Strange to say, the Subadar, who had the reputation of a martinet as far as every other person was concerned, never allowed himself to be disconcerted by Agha's insubordinate language. The wags of Walesby's had a joke that the Subadar was afraid of Agha, and that the Khyberee was thus the real commandant of the regiment, for the Subadar ruled the colonel, and Agha the Subadar. Facetious young subalterns took a delight in dubbing the old curmudgeon "commandant sahib," until the Khyberee was like to handle his dagger for very passion.

There was one, however, with whom Agha never lost his temper, and whose caprices he was never tired of humouring. Shamsuddeen had married a Pathani wife when Walesby's Horse were serving under Sir Harry Fane in the Army of the Indus, and in due time a little boy made his appearance in the Subadar's tent. Agha had been the little Afzul's nurse almost from his birth, and the ungainly trooper would stalk about the bazaar with the infant in his arms quite composedly, in spite of the jeers of his comrades at his awkwardness as an ayah. The trooper would walk from one end of the cantonment to the other to humour the child's slightest whim, and would cheerfully stint his own expenditure that he might buy toys and sweetmeats for him in the bazaar. The boy grew up to know his power, and lorded it over Agha right despotically; and the poor man would hardly have dared to call his life his own if Afzul had thought fit to require it. While a child Afzul was trained to arms, and before he had entered his teens he was as fearless a rider as any trooper in the regiment. Agha taught him to ride and to "tent peg," to hurl the quoit like the Sikh Alkali, and to wield the lance like a Mahratta horseman. But there were some of Agha's instructions of a less edifying character. Though with his comrades he had maintained a taciturn reserve, and had never let out any of his antecedents previous to joining the regiment, he opened his whole heart to the boy, and never tired of telling him of the wild life which men lived beyond the frontier,—where there was no red-coated infidel to keep the sons of Islam in bondage; where each man righted his own wrongs by the sword; where men were not fettered by laws written on paper; and where a stout heart and a strong arm were of more avail than miles of land or lakhs of rupees. He had stories, too, to tell of the terrible blood feud handed down through half-a-dozen generations, each of which had vainly shed its quota of blood to appease the family quarrel; of the plunder of villages and the abduction of virgins; of conspiracies, intrigues, and the other lawless and romantic phases in the wild life of the trans-Indus tribes. The effect of such a training upon an impulsive young lad may easily be conceived. Afzul grew up to hate the restraints of law and discipline, to revile English rule, and to long for some field where more licence was allowed to strength and passion. He had more than once proposed to Agha that they should run away to join the Afghan tribes; but a sense of duty to the Subadar steeled the trooper against the temptation, and for once in his life he had warned the father of his son's intentions.

It was Shamsuddeen's greatest ambition to see his son take the place in Walesby's Horse which he himself had filled so long; and so, when he quitted the service, Afzul was left behind him in the ranks of the regiment. Agha would fain have stayed with his young master, but the Subadar would not hear of such a thing. A private trooper had no use for a servant: he himself had never had one until he became an officer; and his son must learn to wait upon himself until he won his commission. But when his father had left the regiment the lad's conduct became less guarded. He associated with the wildest and most dissolute men in the corps, and gave himself no trouble to conciliate the good opinion of his superior officers. Much would have been, and much was, pardoned to his father's son, but the discipline of the service could not be infringed with impunity, and the young man had been more than once before a regimental court-martial for wildness and insubordination. When the regiment was sent to Bhutan, during the brief campaign against the insurgent chiefs of that country, a remarkable change came over Afzul. So long as the regiment was in the field, it did not contain a more zealous and orderly soldier than the Subadar's son, and none so eager to undertake any duty that involved fatigue or danger. The officers were delighted with Afzul's alacrity and bravery, and his speedy promotion was looked upon as a certainty. Old comrades of his father, who had hitherto held their peace or shaken their heads gravely when Afzul Khan's name was mentioned, never ceased now to sound his praises; and the Subadar's retirement was cheered by glowing descriptions of his son's good qualities from his former friends and officers. But when the times of "piping peace" returned, and the regiment was sent back to the plains, Afzul speedily effaced these good impressions, and was reported to the commandant as more insubordinate and ungovernable than before. The colonel, an old officer who had served with Shamsuddeen, and respected his bravery and probity, was unwilling that his son should be made an example of in the corps; and so he sent for Afzul and told him plainly that he must either reform or quit the regiment. Afzul haughtily took him at his word, applied at once for his discharge, and threw old Agha into a cold sweat by appearing before him one morning dusty and wayworn at the gate of Walesbyganj. Agha concealed and fed the young prodigal until the Subadar was prepared for the bad news, and a pardon obtained for Afzul's misconduct. Shamsuddeen was almost heart-broken at the failure of his hopes, but he never as much as said to his son that he had done wrong. Not so Agha, who did nothing from morning to night but harp upon Afzul's profligacy, although the young man gave little heed to his rebukes. Although he was rich enough to make his son independent of any profession, Shamsuddeen was bitterly disappointed that he should have left in disgrace a service where he himself had obtained both honour and rewards. He considered the army the only honourable career for a Muhammadan gentleman, and the favour of the British Government the highest distinction which any native could obtain. He had fondly hoped that Afzul would revive the good reputation which he himself had left in the army, and that his loyalty and bravery would increase the patrimony which he would inherit at his own death. Now that all these prospects were blasted, the old man thought it mattered little what Afzul did.

Afzul Khan was no stranger in Dhupnagar when he came there after leaving the army. During two furloughs he had already succeeded in scandalising the quiet inhabitants. He had carried off Bel-puttee, the ryot of Milkiganj's daughter, and beaten the girl's brother within an inch of his life. He had almost ridden over old Gangooly, the village headman, in the middle of the bazaar in broad daylight, thus offering a wanton insult to the representative of public authority. He had borrowed money from Three Shells at seventy-five per cent, and had treated the mahajan to a sound bambooing when he came to claim his interest. He was perpetually getting into some trouble or other with the villagers, and the Subadar was constantly annoyed by complaints of his son's riotous conduct. Shamsuddeen took these matters, however, very coolly. If a man behaved himself inside the lines, he must be allowed some licence among the civil population. After all, the offended parties were only Hindoos, and it was doubtful whether to torment them was not a meritorious act for a true Muhammadan. As for the carrying off of the girl, young men would be young men, and he had seen many a wench taken away from her friends across the crupper in his old campaigning days. He paid Three Shells' claim, and threatened the usurer with personal chastisement from his own hands if ever he lent his son another anna. But when Afzul one day announced to his father that he was bent upon having Kristo Baboo's daughter to wife, the old man saw that this was a more serious caprice than any that the lad had yet taken into his head. Kristo was a Hindoo of high caste and consideration, and his family could not be dishonoured with the same impunity as the poor ryot of Milkiganj's. Then the difference of creed prevented all prospect of securing an alliance by fair means. Shamsuddeen did his best to drive the passion out of the lad's head ; but Afzul was obstinate, and swore by the tombs of Hassan and Hussein at Kerbela that he would not live another twelve months without the girl though he were to be made Lord Sahib of Bengal. The Subadar knew the young man's headstrong nature too well to hope that advice would influence his conduct, and so he contented himself with ordering Agha to keep the child out of mischief. But Agha was the worst possible mentor that a fiery young man could be put under. Advancing years and wounds had not yet tamed the native lawlessness of the Khyberee, and he was ever more ready to abet than to check the irregular conduct of his young charge.

On the same morning as Prosunno and Three Shells had paid their visit to the priest, Shamsuddeen Khan was seated in his little arbour, breakfasting upon a simple repast of sliced *hilsa* fish and custard apples. Behind him stood Agha, who still deigned to wait upon his master's meals, although he would not have done a similar service to a Lieutenant-Governor. Both master and man still retained some traces of their old calling. Though his uniform had been laid aside for a loose coat of striped silk, the Subadar still clung to the gaiters and the flowing turban of the Irregular trooper, and from sheer force of habit he carried his long cavalry sword with him wherever he went. Shamsuddeen Khan was still erect as an arrow, and his grey hairs and long flowing white beard gave him an appearance of great dignity. The naturally unshapely figure of Agha had been still more contorted by his wounds; and his broad shoulders were so bent as almost to give him the appearance of being hump-backed. He wore his coarse black hair long, in the Afghan fashion; his surly features were disfigured by the loss of an eye, which had been knocked out in a bazaar brawl; and a cynical sneer had for many years been stereotyped upon his large mouth. Agha was always dressed in a cast-off suit of the Subadar's regimentals, in the tarnished embroidery of which he took no little pride. At his girdle he wore a long straight dagger, with an antiquely-shaped silver hilt, in which was concealed a lock of hair belonging to Sayyid Saffia Shah, a celebrated saint of Agha's own tribe. In the potency of this relic, whether for defence or attack, Agha placed implicit confidence; and whether or not the holy Sayyid nerved Agha's arm in the hour of need, it was certain that he never had occasion to strike twice.

"These roses," said the Subadar, looking up from his plate, "are the richest that we have yet had at Walesbyganj. I never saw finer in the Shalimar. You remember the roses of the Shalimar, Agha?"

"Am I a *mallee* (gardener)?" was Agha's tart reply. "I remember Madam Dilnawaz's house behind the Shalimar well enough, but I never saw any roses except on the cheeks of her and her damsels."

"A soldier has no business to know anything of such wares," said the Subadar, shaking his head; "but you were ever prone to mischief, Agha. Is the child at home?"—among themselves the two old soldiers always spoke of Afzul as "the child." "At what hour did he return from Panch Pahar last night?"

"He did not return from Panch Pahar last night," answered Agha, curtly.

"Is he at home now?" demanded the master.

Agha nodded.

"It was this morning, then, before he came," said Shamsuddeen, with a sigh. "When I was at his time of life, if I had stayed outside the lines after the last post I would have tasted of the guard-house, as sure as my name was Shamsuddeen."

"And a good thing it was for you too," said Agha, sneeringly.

"But I shall keep better discipline with you all after this; I am determined on that," said the Subadar, somewhat nettled by his follower's remark. "I shall muster the house every night at ten and lock the gate with my own hand, and if any one is outside after that, he may remain there till daybreak."

"You have said so a hundred times before, but you never did it yet," was Agha's comment.

"You grow impudent, O thou!" cried the Subadar, in a rage. "I shall have to send you back to your hills again;" and seeing Agha inclined to grin at this terrible threat, which he had heard uttered half-a-dozen times a-day for the last six years, he bawled out, "'Tenshun! Silence in the ranks!" At the word of command Agha clapped his hands to his thighs, drew himself stiffly up behind his master's chair, and stood still as a mute, waiting to hear what the Subadar had to say farther.

"I do not approve of the child's going so much to Panch Pahar," said Shamsuddeen; "he will learn no good from that bankrupt old scoundrel who calls himself a Nawab. If the falcon is shot among a flock of kites, who can blame the archer? If a horse run away with a herd of wild asses he will soon try to bray like them. They drink abominations which the Prophet, upon whom be peace, has interdicted, and the Nawab's house is the resort of gamblers and dancing courtesans. It is no place for a young soldier. I would rather my son had been thrust through with a Bhutia's spear in the last war, than that he should live to become a low, cheating debauchee like the Panch Pahar man."

The Subadar turned half round to Agha, as if expecting him to make some remark; but the trooper still stood at "attention," with his lips firmly pressed together.

"And now he has got some vagary in his head about the daughter of this Hindoo Lahory," continued the master, "and there is sure to some mischief come of it. Was there no maiden of Islam fair enough for him that he must seek to mate with this she-infidel? I do not approve of young soldiers marrying, for a man who wishes to do his duty will have no time to trifle away with women; but now that he has left the service, I should have no objection to his marrying three or four decent girls of his own faith. But nothing less will serve his highness than a high-caste Brahmini, who will be almost as easily won by a Mussulman as a Peri from Paradise. He is making my old age miserable, Agha. Why don't you answer me, sirrah?"

"Answer you what?" returned Agha, imperturbably.

"What am I to do with the child? He is getting wilder and wilder every week, and each new fancy that he takes into his head is more extravagant than the one that went before. His bickerings and excuses are wearying my life out as well as my substance. What would you do, Agha, if you had such a son?"

"Slay him," said Agha, in a snappish tone of decision.

"Ah, Agha! it is easy for you to say that," said the Subadar, in a lachrymose tone, at which the trooper made a ludicrous grimace; "you know nothing of the feelings of a father. Whatever may be his faults,

Afzul is my only son, and who would lay my grey head in the grave if he were gone? Allah is my witness that there is no reasonable licence which I would withhold from him. You know I never said a harsh word to him about the Milkiganj girl. But what's to be done about this daughter of Kristo Baboo's? I do not see any prospect of the child's obtaining her."

"I would burn down the house and carry her off by the strong hand," said Agha, after a short pause, during which he seemed to be absorbed in deep reflection upon the case.

"Ay, and be thrown into Bhutpore jail next day for it," said the Subadar, impatiently. "Tush, Agha! speak sense. Why will you always forget which side of the frontier you are standing on? If we were in Afghanistan, now, it might be a just and honourable way of settling the difficulty; but it does not become persons who are so much indebted to the English Sircar (Government) as me and my son to do anything against their laws. Not that I consider there is anything morally wrong in a true believer carrying off a Hindoo damsel; it might even be the means of bringing an infidel to the faith of Islam. But it's no use speaking of such a thing in the Lower Provinces here."

"Let us go to Afghanistan then," said Agha, in a more serious tone than he had hitherto used. "There is little good in staying here in subjection to Nazarenes. Once beyond the border and Afzul may have any woman that he is strong enough to take."

"Don't speak nonsense, man," said the Subadar, impatiently; "we should be just as likely to get all our throats cut. I have lived sixty years under English rule, and never found any restrictions upon liberty but what was for the good of the public. Just think, if you had a daughter, how you would like Kristo Baboo to come and take her away from you."

"I have no daughter, and if Kristo Baboo took her away I would bury my dagger in his fat paunch," retorted Agha, with slight regard for logic, but with an emphasis which showed that he had little belief in the application of the moral law to the intercourse of Muhammadans with the infidel.

"You will get yourself into trouble yet with your bullying, swaggering manners," said the Subadar; "if the men of Dhupnagar had the spirits of pariah dogs they would give both you and Afzul skinsful of broken bones some dark night. But tell me, Agha, what has the child been saying to you about the Hindoo girl?"

"Nothing; what, in the name of Eblis, have I to do with him and his wantons?"

"'Tenshun! speak respectfully, fellow," cried the Subadar; and Agha, thus admonished, fell once more into a stiff military attitude. "Well, I want you to find out what schemes the child has in view about Kristo's daughter. He tells you everything, and you must tell me, so that between us we may keep him from harm's way. After all, we must pardon something to youth, and not allow the child to come to grief for lack of good advice. Where is he now?"

"In bed: where else would he be? You know he won't rise for these good two hours," replied the trooper.

"More is the shame, Agha,—more is the shame. I must really do something to bring you all back to discipline. You will order the garrison—the household, I mean—that after this they must turn out every morning at sunrise. Late hours are an unsoldierly habit, and an ungodly habit; for have not set times of prayer been appointed by the Prophet, upon whom be peace?"

"So I may tell them," said Agha, with a contemptuous sniff; "and if you had a *duffadar* with a heavy bamboo to beat sleep out of them you would likely be obeyed; but it is folly to expect people to get up at sunrise who only go to bed at the false dawn."

"Don't bandy *bat-chit* with me, slave, but go and do as you are bid," cried the Subadar, losing his patience; "and mind that you report to me at breakfast-time to-morrow what the child is saying about the Hindoo girl. 'Tenshun! 'Bout face! Mar-ach!"

Agha never ventured to gainsay an order delivered in military fashion, and he stumped away with the eye-side of his head turned up towards the sky in a queer expression of cynical amusement. The trooper knew his master's weakness and his own power, and did not give himself much trouble about the Subadar's rebukes. Though in the regiment Shamsuddeen had shown himself an admirable disciplinarian, he was perfectly unable to govern a private household. All the duties of his previous life had been regulated by military formulas, which were in a manner self-enforcing, and which, at any rate, could be applied without much mental exertion. The Subadar had always regarded the life of a civilian as one that could have but few cares and anxieties; and when he had settled down at Walesbyganj, it was with the determination that worldly troubles were to give him no more annoyance. A household of a dozen servants and a score of tenants would, as he thought, need no supervision; and so he contented himself with laying down stringent rules for their guidance, never doubting that they would dare to disobey his instructions. But the servants soon began to get lazy and slight their work, except in the stables, which were under Agha's special supervision; and the tenants began to be backward with their rents, and to pester their landlord with their quarrels among each other. It was then that Shamsuddeen saw how powerless he was to enforce his orders, and that he could no longer support his authority by the guard-room and a court-martial. Discipline was once broken through, and the Subadar felt that he had not the energy to put it in force; and so he contented himself with forming resolutions to keep better order, which were never by any chance put into execution. The household would have gone to rack and ruin but for Agha's ill-temper. Both servants and ryots had a wholesome fear of the trooper, who had indeed a rough-and-ready way of putting things to rights which kept the timid Bengalees in a constant dread of offending him. When two of the Subadar's tenants came bawling for mutual justice, Agha would hear both their cases with the gravity of a Radamanthus; and if both were wrong, as was almost always the case, he would order plaintiff and defendant to be seized and bambooed until the soles of their feet were as soft as a jelly. In spite of Agha's churlish habits he was invaluable to the Subadar, and without his presence the affairs of the Walesbyganj household must very soon have come to a dead-lock.

CHAPTER VIII.

THREE SHELLS' CONVERSION.

WHEN the meeting of the village elders broke up after they had come to a resolution that the matter against the Gossains was to be set aside, Prosunno, the lawyer, left the green in disgust at the apathy of his castefellows, and went strutting angrily through the bazaar in the direction of his own house. He for one had made up his mind that the prosecution against Krishna should not be dropped. Provided they got a market for their wares, these grovelling traders cared nothing for the purity of religion; but Prosunno's practice lay in the Gapshapganj court, and it was nothing to him though the village should go to wreck and ruin. His own influence in Dhupnagar would not avail him much against a person of the priest's standing; but with Three Shells' assistance he might still hope to compass his revenge. The mahajan could at least excite a popular commotion by means of his many debtors, and when the attention of the other Brahmins throughout the district had once been attracted to Krishna's perversion, Prosunno had little doubt that the excommunication of the priest's family would speedily follow. There were Lingas, moreover, at Bhutpore and Gapshapganj, whose priests would give their ears to get a handle against Ramanath; and Prosunno mentally resolved that before many hours passed he would lay the matter before them.

As the lawyer walked along, engrossed in his vindictive reflections, Gopi, the usurer's clerk, plucked him by the *chaddar*, and summoned him to his master's house, where the worthy Baboo Three Shells was anxiously awaiting him. Prosunno turned and retraced his steps to the money-lender's dwelling, wondering how Three Shells could have slipped out of the temple unobserved, and what had been the issue of his interview with the priest. The mahajan's residence was a compact little house of *cutcha* masonry—that is, it was built of brick and mud instead of brick and lime. The walls were of great thickness, the few windows opening to the outside were narrow and barred with iron, and the door was made of heavy planks of teakwood, strengthened with bolts and plates of metal. Three Shells did not keep many servants, and the villagers could glean but little information regarding what went on in the interior. The money-lender's food was brought to him at stated hours, and he ate it in his little open sitting-room facing the doorway. Gopi, his clerk, and Prosunno, the lawyer, were the only persons who had the *entrée* to the house, and neither of these had much opportunity of prying into the mahajan's private affairs. Three Shells invariably received them in a little office off his sitting-room, and he had given them sharply to understand that when they did not find him there, it was *darwaza bund*.* Strange stories were told in the village of the interior of Three Shells' dwelling. Some would have it that he sat all day surrounded by coffers of pearls and rubies; others were sure that his zenana contained beauties of surpassing loveliness from Persia and Kashmere; while a third party was not less confident that scenes were enacted there which would make the blood curdle and the hair turn white to witness. Lights might be seen streaming through the narrow windows night after night until the morning watches; and what else could Three Shells be doing sitting up so late, but endeavouring to bring back by magic exorcisms and the aid of demons the *paras patthar*, or philosopher's stone, which a holy Brahmin had, ages before, thrown into a bottomless pool of the Gungaputra? But whatever shapes the popular conjecture might assume, the villagers took good care not to obtrude them upon the mahajan's ears.

On this occasion, much to Prosunno's surprise, Three Shells was not to be found in the sitting-room or office. "Go straight before you and ascend the stair," the

---

* *Darwaza bund*—literally, the door is shut; the native equivalent to "not at home."

clerk said, in a nervous whisper, "and take care what you say, for the Baboo's liver is boiling."

"Oh ho!" said Prosunno to himself, while he groped his way along a narrow dark passage, "Three Shells must have heard that the Panchayat has broken down; I do not wonder that he is in a passion. But so much the better; I shall have the less difficulty in persuading him to extreme measures. He is the only man in Dhupnagar who can lay the pride of these cursed Gossains."

Prosunno cautiously stepped up a rickety stair, every step of which creaked beneath his tread. He peered cautiously through the darkness as he went, for some sign of the splendour with which rumour had fitted up the money-lender's apartments; but the staircase might have been of ivory and sandal-wood for all that Prosunno could see. He felt his way to the landing and stood there, undecided as to where he should turn himself. If he were to advance another step he might find himself in a forbidden apartment, and then the angry mahajan would very likely turn his passion upon him. After a few minutes' deliberation, Prosunno ventured to announce himself by a forced cough; but still no answer was returned, nor could he see any indication of the mahajan's presence.

Presently he heard a low wail issue from the adjoining apartment—a wail such as the hungry cheetah utters when forcibly torn off his prey. Remembering the stories he had heard of Three Shells' habitation, Prosunno's hair began to stand on end; but his curiosity almost mastered his fears, and though he was trembling like an aspen, he eagerly inclined his ear in the direction of the sound.

"Would to the gods that I were either dead or avenged upon him!" Prosunno heard uttered in tones of heartfelt agony. "Fool that I was, ever to have come to Dhupnagar! And yet who could have thought that Prem Singh would come here to die, when I had sent him thousands of miles away into the Deccan? It is the gods' doing : it is their doing, undoubtedly. What is it that always tempts me, wretch that I am, to put forth my hands against their servants? O blessed Kali, my mother and protectress! keep my head in safety and from shame, and a Brahmin shall henceforth be to me as sacred as my father. But no, I *will* be revenged upon that priest; I must, for while he lives my life is not my own. O Vishnu Vaikuntha, the destroyer of sorrow! must I then dye my hands once more in holy blood? O gods! my wealth is yours, all yours, down to the uttermost cowrie—not one pice shall my nearest and dearest deprive you of; only, *only* let me live my allotted days and die in peace at last."

Prosunno could hear the wretch beating his bosom with his hands, and dashing his forehead against the floor or the wall. The lawyer would fain have listened to further revelations, but these fragmentary confessions had not tended to increase Prosunno's confidence in his patron. So he again coughed loud enough to attract the money-lender's attention. But Three Shells was too much immersed in his own guilty reverie to heed the interruption. The lawyer heard him again burst forth into a torrent of passionate exclamations, but they were uttered so rapidly in a strange Hindustani *patois*, that Prosunno could make nothing of them. He was still listening eagerly, and was so much absorbed in thinking of what he had just heard, that he did not mark the money-lender's movements, until Three Shells sprang out from the room and caught him by the throat. Prosunno made an effort to free himself, and the two rolled over on the floor, each locked in the other's embrace. The struggle lasted but an instant, for the puffy and effete Bengalee was no match for the spare, sinewy, up-country man; and Three Shells soon had his long lean fingers buried in the flesh of Prosunno's fat neck, while the other feebly attempted to gasp out a supplication for mercy.

"Wretch! I would strangle you where you lie, if it were not that I would be doing you a kindness," hissed Three Shells in the lawyer's ear; "but live—live to be my slave, my tool, my fetch-and-carry cur, and I shall give you crumbs or kicks as you deserve them. But mark me, seek not to pry into my secrets, or your curiosity will meet with a more terrible reward than you think of."

So saying, Three Shells dragged the lawyer to his feet, and thrust him head-foremost into an adjoining room. Prosunno reeled forward like a drunk man, gasping for breath, and with his eyes rolling sightlessly in his head. His progress was arrested by a pile of cushions, over which he stumbled and fell headlong on the floor; and there he lay, stunned with the fall and his fright. When he ventured at last to open his eyes, he saw Three Shells sitting cross-legged on a couch, and smoking furiously at a huge silver hookha. A window had been thrown open, and the light now streamed full upon the mahajan's countenance. An expression of forced composure was stamped upon Three Shells' features; his eyelids drooped, but now and then his small bloodshot eyes flashed forth with a quick, angry glare, his thin hard lips quivered impatiently, and he ground his teeth savagely, as he struggled to keep back the torrent of rage and despair that was rending his bosom in search of an outlet. Prosunno felt himself in the position of one who, without knife, or rifle, or prospect of succour, has brought a tiger to bay. He continued to lie speechless on the floor, only holding up his clasped hands before the mahajan in abject entreaty for mercy.

"Sit up," said Three Shells, curtly, as he pointed to a low seat before him. Prosunno scrambled up hurriedly enough, and took a seat among the cushions. "Compose yourself," was the money-lender's next order. This command was not so easily obeyed, but, nevertheless, Prosunno did his best to assume a confident bearing. He sat upright, and endeavoured to look the mahajan fixedly in the face, but he cowered and quailed as often as Three Shells bent one of his keen angry glances in his direction; and his hands seemed to be unaccountably in his way, his legs refused to bend easily beneath him, and his neck appeared to have grown too weak to support the weight of his head. Two large horse-pistols lying on the couch, with which Three Shells' hands kept nervously playing, did not assist Prosunno in regaining his assurance. "Compose yourself," again said Three Shells, spitefully, as he marked and gloated over the terrors he was exciting; and he fingered the butt of a pistol, while Prosunno again raised his clasped hands in mute entreaty for mercy. And thus the two continued to sit, the mahajan still smoking, and keeping his eyes steadily fixed upon the lawyer, whose increasing uneasiness seemed to have the effect of allaying his own fury; while Prosunno squatted with downcast eyes and parched mouth, his frame motionless, except when a convulsive shiver showed the apprehensions under which he was labouring.

"Speak!" cried the mahajan, at length, contemptuously puffing a mouthful of smoke in the direction of Prosunno; and seeing that the latter did not stir, he said again, sternly, "Speak, slave."

Prosunno shifted himself uneasily upon the cushions, made a mouth as if he would speak, and lost heart again as he saw the money-lender's hand still grasping the pistol: at last he stammered out—

"Sir, believe me, sir, I could not help it. All that

I could do was done, to stir up the Brahmins against Ramanath and his son. How can I answer for their obstinacy? And am I not here, your slave, ready to obey each and all of your commands? What does it please you that I should do? Shall I go forth and stir up the people to take staves against these unclean dogs of Gossains?"

The mahajan's answer was to hurl first one pistol and then another in rapid succession at the lawyer's head. Prosunno was, however, on the alert; and the first missile was avoided by an adroit duck of the head, but the second grazed his poll, inflicting a slight wound upon the scalp. Prosunno threw himself forward with a howl, and lay extended at full length before the mahajan.

"Prosunno," said the money-lender, in slow and emphatic tones, "if you venture to raise as much as a finger against my most excellent and honoured friend Ramanath Gossain, or any of his family, I shall murder you myself, and throw your body to be devoured by the jackals of Panch Pahar."

The lawyer started up at this unexpected intimation, and scanned the mahajan's face anxiously, to see whether he was speaking in jest or in earnest. But Three Shells' countenance wore a look of grim determination, which showed that he was not to be trifled with, and so the lawyer could only bow his head silently in token of assent.

"And hark ye, Prosunno," continued the money-lender, "you will go out into the bazaar and take steps to stifle all gossip about this affair of Krishna Chandra Gossain. When you hear a trader speak an evil word of the lad or his father, you will ask them if they are desirous that I should reclaim my money, principal and interest, at a day's warning. You will give everybody to understand, moreover, that the priest and I are greater friends than ever, and that if they offend him they offend me beyond forgiveness. You will take heed to do all this, Prosunno, and what is more, you will contrive that the priest shall learn all that I am doing in his behalf."

Prosunno acquiesced by a gesture, and the money-lender went on:—

"For the insult you offered him to-day at the temple you will apologise upon your knees, and render, besides, any other atonement that the priest may desire. Shall I have to order twice?" he added, as Prosunno showed his unwillingness by an impatient gesture; but the lawyer hurriedly raised his hands to his forehead in token of submission. "It is well; and now attend to your other instructions. I wish to know in whose hands Ramanath Gossain has placed a sealed packet of great importance. You will make private inquiries until you have found out this, Prosunno, and when you have discovered it you will instantly let me know. Go now, and return to-morrow at sunrise and report the news of the bazaar."

The lawyer rose, and after salaaming almost to the

ground, was slouching out of the house when the money-lender's voice recalled him.

"Stay, Prosunno," said Three Shells: "I believe I could have you transported for life to the Andamans if I pleased. Forgery aggravated by perjury is punished by the Magistrate Sahib in that way, isn't it? Ah! I thought so: but it is not enough—I must be able to hang you, Prosunno—d'ye hear, to hang you? Not that I would do it, for you are much too useful to me for that; but I must have you in my power. However, we can devise some means for arranging that afterwards. Go now, Prosunno—go in peace."

Prosunno staggered forth from the money-lender's house with these terrible words ringing in his ears. He was faint and sick at heart, and would have been hardly able to walk the length of his own house had not his bosom friend Protap, the accountant, been passing that way and lent him assistance. Prosunno gave out that he had been suddenly taken ill on his way home from the temple, and said nothing of his having been at the money-lender's. He was indeed ill, but it was in mind, and not in body: and he kept his house for the remainder of the day, soothing his feelings by beating his wife Dossee on the pretence of the rice at breakfast-time having been over-seasoned with *chillies*, and racking his brains as to the real purport of his late conversation with the usurer.

Three Shells still sat where Prosunno had left him, agitated by a torrent of contending passions. The temporary relief which he had experienced in the lawyer's humiliation soon died away, and the remembrance of his interview with the priest, of Ramanath's threats, and of the dangerous position in which he had placed himself, came back with all its terrors. At the very height of his prosperity, at the time when he fancied himself most secure from recognition, the Nemesis of his past life had swooped down upon him, and borne him off to the dizzy verge of ruin. Well might Three Shells recoil from looking over into the dark abyss of the calamitous future, for pale ghosts hungry for vengeance were hovering under, ready to seize him, and the weight of former crimes hung heavily about him to accelerate his fall. He burrowed his head among the cushions of the couch as if he would hide himself from memory, but his restless spirit gave him no peace. At last, as if struck by a sudden idea, he sprang to his feet, and tearing open an *almira* (cupboard) he took from it another hookha and filled it from a parcel of dried-hemp leaves; and sitting down again, began to smoke furiously. As the fumes of the *ganja* mounted to his head, the pale agony of the money-lender's features changed to an expression of settled savage ferocity, and he clenched his fists and struck angrily at the side of the couch as if he were assailing an enemy. He was rapidly becoming intoxicated, and as his spirits rose the sense of danger lessened, and he became more able to lay plans for saving himself. Ramanath was the only man in

Dhupnagar who possessed the power of harming him, and if he could be removed, and the sealed packet of which he had spoken secured, Three Shells might face the Magistrate Sahib as calmly as any man in Dhupnagar. But how was this to be accomplished? There were difficulties in the way of no ordinary magnitude, and the money-lender felt that he must go cautiously to work.

"And this is the justice and providence of the gods!" said Three Shells to himself, angrily. "I do not believe that there was a more religious man in Dhupnagar, or a more respectable, than I was until this morning. I gave more money to the Linga than any one in the village, and I never sent a Brahmin from the door without a bellyful. And this is my reward. I am compelled to become as bad as ever, or my life is not worth a four-anna bit. The gods never give a man a chance in this world, and what's the use of spending money on their worship? Why, it is not longer than two days ago that I gorged a Kanouje Brahmin with curds and sweetmeats until the rogue was not able to crawl out of the courtyard from sheer surfeit four-and-twenty hours after, and this is my reward! But I'll none of that trusting in them longer. I'll save myself by killing that cursed priest; and then, when once I am safe, may dogs devour me if ever I spend as much as another cowrie upon temple or priest! But softly, Three Shells; keep well with the gods until you are in sure ground: it will be time enough to turn your

back upon them when you are out of this scrape. I
must be more pious than ever, and more liberal to the
Linga to conceal my intentions towards the priest. I
wonder if Kalee would aid me against Ramanath if I
prayed her assistance, and gave a costly present to her
temple at Bhutpore. I shouldn't wonder, for the goddess could not be very friendly at heart to so popular
a shrine as the Linga and to its priest. But that will
take more money. I shall be beggared by this devotion. And there are these lazy blackguards eating
up all my substance, and doing nothing for it. But
I must make them work. It is easy for them to idle
so long as they get me to fill their bellies. *Qui hye?*
(who's there?)

"Salaam!" responded a deep voice from a remote
apartment; and in a few minutes a tall muscular
Hindustani, with a swarthy face and small lowering
forehead, entered the room and saluted the money-
lender.

"Well, Mohun," said the mahajan, making an
attempt at affability, "and how is the time passing
with you? You must be dull, Mohun, in these hard
times when so little is doing; it is about time Panchoo
and you were thinking of another job."

"Yes, Baboo," replied Mohun; "but we were thinking
that we had just done enough in this place. Since the
affair at Peary Lall's, over the water, the police are keeping such a sharp watch upon the country-side, that we
may as well walk into the *zilla* (county) jail at once

as show our faces outside after nightfall. Panchoo and I have been thinking of going home to our own country."

"What!" cried Three Shells, starting up in wrath; "going home to your own country without settling the debt of five hundred rupees which you have owed me since you came first to the valley, and the interest, which makes it one thousand two hundred! Slaves! shall I have to give the hint to the Dipty Baboo who are the Sonthalis that are plundering in his subdivision?"

"Nay, Baboo," said Mohun, composedly, "you will not do that for your own sake. Remember that it was you who suggested the robberies and received the *loot* (booty); the English Sahibs would be as hard upon you as upon Panchoo and me."

"Fool! don't you know that I could purchase my own pardon by informing upon you?" said the mahajan, maliciously; "but don't be afraid, Mohun; I would never try such a trick—that is, so long as you made yourselves obedient and useful to me. But never speak of going away. I shall have such work for you as you little dream of before long, and then you may go back to your country with your waistbands stuffed with gold mohurs. And to show you how friendly I am, I will put you up to a trick. The ryot of Gaogong comes today for two hundred rupees which he has borrowed from me. The man is a coward, and his house is hidden in the jungle, and Panchoo and you will have no difficulty in breaking in and carrying off the bag. And as a proof of my liking for you both, I shall only ask the half for my share. There—you won't find such a generous master in every place."

Mohun salaamed his thanks, but still he seemed dissatisfied. "But one might as well be in prison as shut up here," he grumbled; "we never get out of doors night or day unless to do mischief. I had rather be with Bhugvan Dass and his men in the jungle than cribbed up here."

"Tuts, Mohun!" said the mahajan; "keep up your spirits. Bethink you how much better you are under shelter of a good roof, with as much food as you can eat, than shifting for yourselves among the jungles of Panch Pahar, without a full meal once in a week's time. Wait until after nightfall and we shall send along to Rutton Pal's for a gallon of arrack, and that will make the time pass more merrily; and now go and prepare Panchoo for his evening's work."

The man left the room, and Three Shells again resumed his pipe of *ganja*. He was now more than half intoxicated, and his spirits were as extravagantly high as they had been depressed before. "Who need be afraid when he has such fellows as these in hand," he chuckled, "and can manage them as I can? That fellow, Mohun, will do anything, if he is only properly worked. He shall kill Ramanath, for I dare not do it myself. No, I could never carry another priest on my conscience; and then I'll poison Mohun—I don't mind that; there can be no sin in putting such a scoundrel out of the world. Sin! the gods should reward me for it. And then when all that is settled, I, Three Shells, shall be king of Dhupnagar. I shall foreclose upon the Ghatghar property, and turn that young blackguard of a rajah out neck and heels. I shall build a female school, and make a *pukka* (macadamised) road between the village and the ferry of the Gungaputra, and get the thanks of Government and the Kumpshiner Sahib (Commissioner) as a model landlord, and perhaps be made a Rae Bahadoor—who knows? Then where would Kristo find such a match for his daughter as Baboo Tincowry Dass Rae Bahadoor, the zemindar of Ghatghar? Oh ho! I trow they will lick their lips at me then; and Ramanath will salaam to the ground, and come to meet me at the gate whenever I go near his temple. But stay, Ramanath will not be there; where will he be? Ah, let me see: he will be killed. And I will build a temple—such a temple! the Linga's temple would not be a kitchen to my temple. What's that? Is that the Linga standing there in the middle of the floor? I'll just say my prayers before it and go home. Can't think what is become of Ramanath this afternoon. Oh, I know now; he is killed—killed—ay, killed by the Sonthal *dakaits*. Well, I must just say my prayers without him. Obeisance, O obeisance to the glorious, the everlasting Siva, whose alms-dish is a skull! But stay, there's a priest: O gods! it's the priest of Lootna, and his breast is all bloody. Gopi! Mohun! Panchoo! save me! save me from him!"

The mahajan fell forward upon the floor in an agony of drunken sickness, and Mohun and Panchoo, alarmed by his outcries, entered the room and laid him to sleep upon the couch. These worthies improved the occasion by searching for some key to the place where the money-lender kept his treasures; but Three Shells was too experienced a person not to have taken due precautions against any such accidents. They rummaged the mahajan's room from top to bottom, and found nothing worth pillaging except a small bottle of French brandy, which at once approved itself to their palates, and with which they retired to their own room to drink and play cards until sunset.

CHAPTER IX.

THE PRIEST'S ZENANA.

THAT eventful day passed very quietly away in Ramanath's household. Krishna kept his room in obedience to his father's orders, and no one saw him save old Bechoo, his attendant, who had long been a servant of the house, and who gave himself little trouble about religion or caste. The priest had as yet made no remarks to the ladies about his son's return, but it was impossible that Krishna could remain long in the house without their knowledge. The Thakoorani was too apathetic to trouble herself about the matter, further than to inquire whether her stepson had brought his usual present of *Belatce mithai* (European sweetmeats) from Calcutta, a delicate attention which Krishna had this time unfortunately overlooked in his perplexity. But Chakwi naturally took a deeper interest in the matter. When the poor girl heard of her husband's return, she put on her finest clothes, and her most costly ornaments, perfumed herself with attar of roses and sandal-wood powder, and sat down in the zenana to wait for a summons to her husband's presence. But Chakwi waited in vain. Day broke upon her as she sat shivering in the cool morning breezes within an embrasure of the zenana window, her pale cheeks and eyes red with weeping, contrasting sadly with the gay flowers in her hair and the flash of jewels about her dusky neck. She had looked across the court to her husband's windows the livelong night, feeding her eyes upon even his shadow, as he chanced to come between her and the lamp, and listening breathlessly to every footstep that fell upon her ear.

"He is busy with his books and his learning, and forgets how the time passes," Chakwi kept saying to herself; "but he will come yet for all that—he will come." But when the light was put out in Krishna's room, the light of hope was also extinguished in Chakwi's heart. "I had better have been a widow in reality," sobbed Chakwi, flinging herself upon a couch in a torrent of tears, "than to be thus tortured with false hopes. It were better I had never loved at all, than to have my love thus put to scorn."

Still Chakwi hoped against hope, and sat through the long dark watches praying the gods that her husband's love might be inclined towards her. Surely he could not be so heartless as to desert her altogether. Was she not his wife, and as such lawfully entitled to claim his love? Why, the very Brahmins would take her part if she were to complain to them; but it was love freely tendered from the heart, and not a forced show of affection, that Chakwi pined for. Had Krishna become enamoured of some Calcutta damsel, that he thus continued to slight his wife? Surely she herself was not so ugly that he need loathe her; and if a warm heart could make any husband happy, Krishna need not seek after strange women. Hark! that was a step coming in this direction. Such a firm elastic tread could only belong to Krishna; and Chakwi began to tremble, and put her hand upon her side to help her to breathe! Poor fool! it was only Ramanath going to bed—slow-footed and heavy-hearted enough, doubtless. Surely that was Krishna's door that creaked. A long breathless pause,—until a repetition of the noise shows that it came only from a loose venetian on the opposite verandah. She counts the howls of the jackals prowling about the compound, hoping that he would come before she counted fifty—a hundred—two hundred—a thousand. At last, at last, he comes! She would have known his step among the tread of an army, said Chakwi to herself, as she sprang up and stood with clasped hands in the middle of the room shivering with anxiety. Alas! it is only poor old Doorgee, the *dhye* (waiting-woman), whose rheumatism keeps her from rest at night, hobbling along the passage. But still Chakwi hoped on, and waited on, until the flush of the false dawn lightened the court for a few minutes, and she knew that morning was at hand. "I wish I were dead," said Chakwi; "I wish he were dead, and I would make myself *sati* for him, though all the Sahibs in Bengal tried to keep me from the pile, and then he could not help loving me in heaven. Oh me! but my heart is sore;" and the poor weary watcher laid her head against the cold damp wall, and in a few minutes had forgotten her sorrows in sleep.

But her slumbers did not last long. Already the sun was up and shining fiercely into the window, and Chakwi, mindful of her household duties, sprang to her feet. She pushed back the thick black tresses which hung in dishevelled locks about her face and neck; she took the white rosebuds, now, alas! faded and shrivelled like her own hopes, from her hair, and put them into a little vase of water, that they might perchance revive a little; and she stealthily divested herself of her rich dress and jewellery, and slipped on the simple white muslin raiment which she ordinarily wore. It was less easy to remove those tell-tale traces of tears which clung to her cheeks and eyelids, defying alike water and towel. But Ramanath was in no mood that morning to notice Chakwi's appearance, and when he had saluted her in his usual affectionate way, he took up the offerings and went away to the temple. It was with a heavy heart that Chakwi set about the ordering of the house and the preparation of the morning meal; but labour lightens sorrow, and she tried so zealously to engross herself in the work, that the servants wondered at her unusual sharpness and activity, and imputed her briskness to joy at her husband's return.

After breakfast Chakwi went to her own room and sent for old Doorgee, her nurse, to whom alone the girl could freely open her heart. But Doorgee could tell her nothing about what she most wished to know, although the old woman shook her head and said that all could not be right, for Krishna Baboo was strictly confined to his own rooms and saw nobody but Bechoo, his attendant. Was there any other news in town? the girl had asked, half dreading to hear that Krishna had come home to marry Kristo Baboo's beautiful daughter, for she knew the village gossips had talked of such a match. Doorgee, however, could tell her nothing, though she thought there was something unusual going on by the stir about the village green; but she was just going into the bazaar to buy rice, and would give her young mistress all the news on her return.

While Doorgee trotted away upon her errand, Chakwi again attempted to forget her cares in bustling about the house. She had seen that the breakfast that morning had contained a large supply of those dishes which she knew to be her husband's favourites, and had made Bechoo take him a quantity large enough to satisfy two men of moderate appetites. She went herself to the tank and drew a pitcher of cool water from the shady side upon which the sun's rays had not yet fallen, and wrapping a wet napkin round the jar, had set it forth in the sun to cool for her husband's refreshment. She might even have carried her complaisance so far as to pour it into the big silver jug called a filter which Krishna had brought home among other newfangled contrivances, although Chakwi had serious misgivings about the orthodoxy of water prepared in such a fashion; but then the jug stood in her husband's rooms, and there she might not enter unbidden. She would have liked to muster courage enough to question the priest about Krishna, but Ramanath was still at the temple; and so she fidgeted about until Doorgee's return, hiding a heavy heart under an active, cheerful demeanour. She had occasion frequently that morning to pass the windows of her husband's room, and actually saw Krishna standing in an abstracted reverie looking out into the courtyard; but the young man's thoughts had little connection with the poor girl to whom an untoward fate had linked him. Poor Chakwi! your misfortunes are but too common. What cares little Rama for Sita when they are made to take up house together? They were but infants when the bonds of marriage were fastened upon them, and the key of the padlock given to death to keep. Sita is a nice playfellow, but then there is this disadvantage, that she does not go away when Rama gets tired of her. Let them live as turtle-doves or as game-cocks: it is all one under this happy dispensation. Love indeed! a *fico* for love if it were not a nice thing to read about in a song or a story; but in real life—— Is there any word of love in the work of Manu, king of men, who came down from heaven to give laws to mortals, and to set society on its legs? I trow not. It is only in the pages of crack-brained poetasters like Vyasa and Kalidass that we read of such an absurdity. The Hindoos are a practical people, let them thank the gods for it, and manage their marriages much better than we silly Englishmen, who leave green heads to settle a matter that would be so much more wisely arranged by grey ones.

"How shocking is all this!" says Mrs Mayfair, who has done me the honour to skip thus far over these humble pages; and who, having married her eldest daughter to Sir Invoyse St Leger, the eminent banker, in spite of Miss Frances's passion for her penniless cousin, Jack Churchmouse the curate, can speak with authority upon the subject. "How I pity these wretched Hindoos and their unhappy marriages! nothing done to consult the poor things' feelings, nothing left to the heart—no place given to sentiment or affection. It is really so distressing, that I must remember to give a ten-pound note to the India Mission next May meetings. I must go to Exeter Hall at any rate, to see that Clara is sufficiently civil to Mr Smelters, the rich ironmaster, who has become quite serious of late, and to keep that young pauper Linesley of the Temple from dangling at her heels. I'm sure the minx must give him some encouragement, or he would never persist so. Ah, well! these poor Hindoos and their unhappy unions —my heart quite bleeds for them."

Go now, dear Mrs Mayfair, and drop in your shekel with a clatter upon the plate, that everybody may know *you* don't give a mite when there is good to be done; or, better far, put your name in a conspicuous place upon the subscription-list, that men may see your good works, &c. Your offering will be blessed—I know it will.

There is a river in Monmouth and a river in Macedon. Bengal and Belgravia both begin with a B; and marriage is an institution in both. But to resume: When Chakwi saw Doorgee coming back from the village as fast as her old legs could bear her, she knew by the nurse's tremulous gait and dejected looks that there was bad news to be told. "It is as I thought," said Chakwi to herself; "he has come to marry Radha Lahory. Well, it is all one to me whom he marries, for he will never lay his love upon me. And why should I wish him to be miserable as well as myself? It is enough that one should bear the sorrow. But if he would spare me only a little portion of his love, for I will not need it long—I feel that;" and stifling her sobs, Chakwi sat down upon a couch and prepared herself to hear the tidings that Doorgee had to tell her.

Doorgee unburdened herself of the gossip of the bazaar with very little reserve, told Chakwi that her husband had become both a Christian and a kine-killer, and assured her that a Panchayat was about to excommunicate him for ever from the Brahmin caste. This news was so startling, and so different from what Chakwi had expected, that she hardly knew how to receive it; but there was one faint gleam of light issuing from the dark cloud, to which the girl eagerly turned her eyes. If Krishna had become a Christian he could never marry Radha Lahory; and what prevented her from changing her faith as well as her husband? She would be put out of caste likewise; but what was caste to Chakwi, compared with the love and society of her husband? She might be punished in another life, but she was certain that she would be happy in this one. Chakwi was almost horrified to find how easily she could stifle the scruples of religion by the promptings of love, and she began to fear that some evil spirit must be putting such ideas in her head.

It was late in the evening when Ramanath came home from the temple, for he had avoided the house all day on purpose that he might not be troubled by his wife and daughter-in-law with awkward questions regarding Krishna's return. The victory over Three Shells and Prosunno had raised the priest's spirits, but he knew that a still more difficult task had to be achieved before he could reclaim his son from heresy. His hopes of success rested chiefly upon the young man's passion for Radha Lahory, and he was now willing to make any sacrifice to bring about the match. The Lahories were of excellent caste, and of as long standing in Dhupnagar as the Gossains themselves: and though they were poor, Krishna had no need to seek for a wealthy wife. He himself would clear off Kristo Baboo's debts, and quietly lend him a hand with the marriage expenses; and there was little doubt that

Kristo would be glad to get clear of his daughter in so honourable and convenient a fashion. But then there was Chakwi—and the priest's heart sank at the thought that his plans could not be carried out without causing sorrow to his daughter-in-law, for, next to Krishna, Ramanath loved Chakwi better than any one on earth. But what was a woman's tears against the honour of the Gossains, and the prosperity of the Linga of Dhupnagar? It was, as Ramanath tried to assure himself, a matter of the highest religious importance, in which family affections could not be taken into account; for if Krishna persisted in his perversion, there was a serious danger that the service of the Linga might be interrupted at his own death. True, he might adopt a son, or might even appoint an orthodox Hindoo trustee for the temple worship; but Ramanath chose rather to ignore these simple remedies, and to assure himself that the course upon which he had set his mind, was also the one that would be most agreeable to the gods. Besides, many a wife had to put up with the same, and why not Chakwi? It might even come to pass that Krishna would love her better after his second marriage than ever he had done before. Beauty was only skin-deep; and when his son was disenchanted of Radha Lahory's charms, the patient gentleness and pure loving heart of Chakwi could not fail to make an impression upon him. It was right, however, that Chakwi should be protected against the new wife; and he, Ramanath, would take care that his favourite's interest came to no harm in the marriage contract. He even made up his mind that the ample dower which Chakwi had brought with her should be placed at her own absolute disposal, and that would enable the poor girl to hold her own in the family against the penniless beauty. Many in his position would think such an arrangement to be foolishly liberal, but the Gossains of Dhupnagar were too high-hearted to be mercenary.

While Ramanath was endeavouring to persuade himself that he was doing everything for the best, and to silence any objections that conscience might suggest upon the score of Chakwi, the door of the room was softly pushed up and Chakwi stood before him. The priest opened his eyes at the change in her personal appearance. She was dressed in a plain white sheet of coarse cotton, her jewels were all laid aside, she had put away her rings and bracelets, she had strewed ashes upon her hair, and had adopted all the other signs of Hindoo widowhood. Her face was deadly pale, and she trembled in every limb as she stood before the priest. Ramanath knew what was coming, and strove to nerve himself for the scene.

"Chakwi, my daughter, what ails you that you have dressed yourself in these weeds?" said Ramanath, gently, as he drew the girl towards him. "Your friends are all alive and well; why then should you thus forebode calamity? Remember that they who sorrow before they need, sorrow always more than there is need."

"Oh, father! how can I be but sorrowful," cried the girl, burying her face in the priest's hands, "when I know not whether I am wife or widow at this moment? though a widow I have been, and a widow I shall be all the days of my married life. But tell me, father, what have they done to my husband? have they put him out of caste?"

"Why should my son be put out of caste?" asked the priest, evasively. "There are few Brahmins in Dhupnagar that can afford to make light of the caste of a Gossain, far less to refuse him *hookha-pani* (smoking and drinking)."

"But has not Krishna fallen away from the gods, and turned a white Christian?" asked Chakwi, looking up searchingly in the priest's face.

"The gods forbid," said Ramanath, fervently. "Krishna is no Christian, nor will he ever be one. In the course of a few weeks he will show the world that there is not a better Hindoo in Dhupnagar. Poor girl!" added the priest, as he recollected at whose expense Krishna's orthodoxy was to be demonstrated; "would that my boy only knew your worth half as well as I do!"

"How, then, did they dare to talk in the bazaar of my husband's perversion, and to speak of excommunicating him?" said Chakwi, indignantly. "What can have made them venture to take such a liberty with our family?"

"Evil hearts speak with evil tongues, my daughter;

but what has a good girl like you to do with the chatter of the old *randis** and cheating dealers that meet to make noise in the bazaar? It were as profitable an occupation to listen to the wrangling of two she-parrots. Persons of our caste and station must not heed what the envious rabble says about them."

"Alas! then," said Chakwi, "I had almost dared to hope that my husband had been excommunicated, for then I might have gone forth with him, as Sita did with Rama, to cheer and comfort him in his banishment. There is no poverty, no trial, no scorn, that I would not gladly endure for his sake; I would follow him through the world like his slave or his dog for only a dog's share of his master's regard. I might have compassed his love in adversity, but in his father's house what wants of his can I supply? Oh, father! tell me how I may win my husband."

"The gods help you, Chakwi, my child," said Ramanath, wiping his eyes with one hand while he embraced the girl's neck with the other. "It was an evil hour for you when I sought you from your dead father. But cheer up; all may turn out well yet, for I have a scheme which may melt this stubborn husband of yours, and secure you at least a share of his love. Ask not what it is," he added, as Chakwi looked up in his face with a glance of eager inquiry, "for I must keep

---

* *Randi* is a term of abuse applied to females. Query, Is it connected with the Scotch "randy," to which it exactly answers in meaning?

my own counsel in the matter; but trust me, my poor little lotus-bud, that I will do all for you a father can do."

The priest pressed a kiss upon Chakwi's brow, and gently put her out of the room, bolting the door behind her.

"What demon of mischief sent her here to unsettle all my plans just as my mind was fully made up?" said Ramanath, impatiently. "I believe, if that poor little thing came crying to me, I should break off the marriage with Radha even after I had tabled the money. I cannot think why I should be so foolishly soft-hearted. Now my dear father—peace be with him—would beat his wives until the zenana rang with wailing like a burning-ghat at burial-time; but I could never bear to see a woman cry all my life. The faintest whimper was always enough to turn my scolding into coaxing, and they can wheedle me out of anything directly they begin to snivel. It is a shame that a man should be so weak. I believe I should have done my duty as a husband better, had I made more use of the bamboo; and yet I never had anything to complain of. I would almost as soon give up my life as vex poor Chakwi; but what can I do? A marriage with Radha is my only resource for saving the boy; and if that fails me, I believe I shall have to turn him out of doors after all."

Ramanath rose, yawned, and paced up and down the

room two or three times with the air of a man who has quite made up his mind. "I had better go to bed now," he muttered. "The Thakoorani will be sleeping, that is one comfort, and I shall not be bothered with her queries. I used to grumble at her drowsiness, but it is an ill quality that is not serviceable sometimes."

CHAPTER X.

THE DIPTY CATCHES AN IDEA.

IN the centre of the town of Gapshapganj stands a large prison-looking building, distinguished by some pretensions to architecture from the *cutcha* houses and mud huts which surround it. The doorway is guarded by a Bengalee policeman, in red turban and faded blue jacket, who slopes his baton over his shoulder with an imposing air of authority. Other members of the force, in a *déshabille* approaching more or less nearly to perfect nudity, lounge or loll about the doorway. It is here where the deputy-magistrate for the subdivision of Gapshapganj and Dhupnagar holds his court; and the groups of people that we see pressing round about the door are lawyers with their clients, suitors or complainants, who have come in from the country with their pieces of stamped paper, to seek for justice at the feet of that Noushirwan of the nineteenth century, our old friend Baboo Preonath Dass, "the Dipty." The Dipty is the great man of Gapshapganj, and the *amla* or officials of his court are persons of scarcely less consideration. That fat consequential-looking native who elbows his way through the throng with so little ceremony is the *nazir* or sheriff, who receives as many salaams as might have sufficed for the Padshah of Delhi. Here stands the court interpreter, listening with half-closed eyes and vacant countenance to the pitiful tale of wrong and oppression which a poor ryot pours into his ear, in the hope of securing a friend in court when his complaint is taken up. *Chaprassis*, or belted messengers, are bustling in and out of the court-house, summoning now one and then another of the litigants. Smug-faced and sharp-eyed Bengalee lawyers are there in plenty, handling their bundles of papers, declaiming among themselves in loud tones, and now and then stopping to whisper into a client's ear. Notice among others our friend Prosunno, standing in eager converse with a wealthy landlord from the Dhupnagar valley. Prosunno is held in great estimation by the landlords of the district for his cleverness in rebutting their tenants' charges of rack-renting and oppression, and for the command which he always has of exculpatory evidence. Less successful pleaders did not hesitate to say that Prosunno gave more employment to the professional perjurers who skulked about in the vicinity of the court-house, than all the other lawyers in Gapshapganj put together. But all successful men have to put up with calumnies; and so long as his witnesses were unchallenged by the magistrate, Prosunno did not trouble himself about such aspersions.

Inside the court-house a more animated scene was going on. Upon the bench, a railed-in platform raised a few feet above the level of the ground, sat Preonath in all the dignity of a deputy-magistrate. Before him sat or stood half-a-dozen of court officials, clerks, or police inspectors, each endeavouring to make as much noise as he could under pretence of keeping silence in court. In one corner some half-dozen decree-holders were asssailing a clerk for documents; and the official on his part was enumerating all obstacles, possible and impossible, in the way of making out the papers, in the hope of extracting a fee from the pockets of the impatient litigants. Preonath's court was no exception in respect of venality to other tribunals of the same grade. Silver was the "open sesame" to every official's good graces, from the old registrar to the latest-appointed policeman; and if Preonath was above temptation, it was because he knew that honesty was the best policy for a man in his position, and not on account of any abstract scruples about the purity of public justice. Jaddoo, the late "expectant," stood with folded arms behind his master's chair, grave and dignified as became a paid orderly and a member of the uncovenanted Civil Service. A belt and badge had now repaid the bruises which the enraged villagers of Dhupnagar had inflicted upon him as a tale-bearer.

Jaddoo was now Preonath's head orderly, an office which was most conveniently filled by the man who had the least scruple about doing dirty work, and who could best forward any private objects that the magistrate might have in view for the time being. There were several circumstances which had recommended Jaddoo to the magistrate's notice. He was not only a poor relation—for there was some cousinship between Jaddoo's father and old Ram Lall, the oilman—but he was the stanchest and most ingenious liar in the whole of the subdivision. Jaddoo's brother, moreover, was a servant in the house of Kristo Baboo; and the Dipty, who took into account every circumstance that might advance his suit for Radha, had calculated upon Jaddoo's connection being convertible to his advantage.

To-day Preonath is engaged in police business. Here is old Gangooly, the headman of Dhupnagar, come to report another aggravated robbery within his jurisdiction. The tenant of Gaogong—a spare, hard-faced farmer, who, unused to the presence of justice, keeps well in the rear of the headman, and seldom ventures to speak louder than a whisper—was robbed last night of two hundred rupees; and his wife and daughter had lost all their jewellery. By the mouth of his spokesman, Gangooly, the ryot deponed that he and all his family had been sleeping, when two robbers burrowed a hole through the mud walls of his cottage, and one had seized him by the throat and held him down, while the other rifled the house, and stripped the terrified women of their ornaments. When the robbers had taken everything of value, they went away swearing that they would shoot any one who dared to lift a head before sunrise, and the ryot and his family had lain in bed expecting every minute to be murdered, until daylight came in, when the head of the house had gone to Gangooly and reported the robbery. Gangooly and the Dhupnagar policemen, two venerable watchmen of the Dogberry and Verges type, testified that they had gone to Gaogong, and examined the hole through which the thieves had entered; that they had found no other traces of them there or anywhere else; and that they had no hope of being able to discover the depredators but in his worship's wisdom, which was like that of Vrihaspatti, the teacher of the gods, and in his judgment, which was as a turner's lathe making all things even; adding thereto many flattering compliments to the magistrate's learning and sagacity. Then began the cross-examination. It was the magistrate's cue to bully the village authorities into some admission which would give his officers ground to work upon, and the village police in their turn did all they could to shift the responsibility from their own shoulders.

How could the complainant be sure that there were exactly two hundred rupees in the bag? was the first question put by the Court.

Sure! how could the complainant be otherwise than

sure? Had he not the very day before hypothecated his crop of betel and two oxen to the worthy Baboo Three Shells, the money-lender, that he might raise the expenses of his son's betrothal? Sree Krishnajee! why should he tell a falsehood? lying would not bring back his money.

"And you suspect nobody, Mr Headman? Come now, no trifling with me," said the Dipty, who never missed an opportunity of hectoring the archon of his native village. "Is there no one in Dhupnagar who was likely to have done this? Recollect your duty to the Government, and do not attempt to screen your townsmen."

Gangooly called the waters of the Ganges and the holy Linga of Dhupnagar to witness that he was not the man to conceal an offender or to trifle with the administration of justice. But who was there in Dhupnagar that would have done such a thing? The Huzoor (honour-magistrate), who well knew the people of his native town—and surely Dhupnagar was honoured in being the birthplace of so wise, so distinguished, so beneficent a ruler — knew also that there was no one there who would plunder a neighbour's house.

"And was there nothing about these robbers that could serve to identify them?" asked the Dipty, turning towards the complainant. "Can't you tell us something about their appearance or their voice that would lead to their detection?"

The farmer of Gaogong whispered into Gangooly's ear that he had been too frightened to look at them. Their faces were muffled up, as he thought, and the one who spoke did not speak like a Bengalee. His tongue was like that of an up-country man.

"An up-country man. I suppose you mean a Hindustani or a Mussulman," said Preonath, his face lighting up with a gleam of spiteful intelligence as he eagerly caught at the remark. "Think again, Headman; are there no Mussulmans about Dhupnagar who could have committed this robbery?"

Gangooly again called the gods to testify that there were no thieves in Dhupnagar. The only Mussulmans in the village were Shamsuddeen Khan the Subadar, and his family; and the gods forbid that the magistrate's slave should say a word against a man who stood so high in the favour of the English Sahibs, although he was a kine-killer. There were turbulent and evil-disposed Mussulmans in the retinue of the Nawab of Panch Pahar; but the ferryman on the Gungaputra swore that no one had crossed the river that night, so they could not have been the offenders. If Gangooly, the humblest of the magistrate's menials, might be permitted to make a representation, he would say that the robbery was doubtless committed by Sonthals from beyond the passes of Panch Pahar, who had so often molested the peaceable people of the valley.

But the Dipty had got hold of an idea and would

not willingly abandon it. "What sort of men are the Subadar's family? Are they all regular, well-disposed persons, or are there any *badmashes* (blackguards) about Walesbyganj who bear a troublesome, unruly character, and who would be likely to want money? Come now, headman, give me a straightforward answer."

Gangooly hummed and hawed, blushed up to his eyes, and then turned pale. He knew that it was running a great risk to tamper with the reputation of the Subadar and his son, and he knew also that there were many facts which circumstantial evidence could twist to the disadvantage of young Afzul Khan. But it was hard that a peaceable man like him should be thus innocently embroiled with a truculent young swash-buckler like the Subadar's son.

"A liar's face is black, but the man who speaketh truth shall prosper," said the proverbial Gangooly in desperation, when he saw that the Dipty was not to be put off with evasions ; "and the Muhammadan's son is an up-handed youth, who drives us Hindoos before him as if we were dogs or lepers. He is, moreover, a spendthrift and a waster, for he gambles with the Nawab of Panch Pahar, and frequents the company of naughty women. But how could it be otherwise? Man or beast will after kind, and the leopard will as soon cease to thirst for blood as the Mussulman to give over oppression. But remember, O Dipty Sahib, that I have not said anything against the youth in this matter of the robbery, for the man who secretly slanders his neighbour, sows brambles which will entangle him as he returns the same way."

"That is as much as to say that you are kept from speaking your mind through fear of this Afzul Khan. Now hear me, Mr Headman; these robberies are bringing the subdivision into disrepute, and the Magistrate Sahib has given a *hukhm* (order) that they must be put down. You have confessed that there is a disreputable young man in the village, and you hint also that you are afraid to say what you know of him because of bodily injury which might be done to you on that account by this Afzul Khan. Now no magistrate could tolerate such a state of things; and I warn you that, unless you give me some certain information regarding these thefts, another headman will have to be appointed to Dhupnagar."

"My fathers have been headmen of Dhupnagar since the English Sahibs obtained the stewardship of Bengal, Behar, and Orissa, but it must be as the gods will it," said Gangooly, beginning to whimper. "I have always tried to be a faithful servant to the Government and my townsfolk, and it is no shame to a man that he is not a seer. Question on them, your honour, and I will tell you everything I know against the lad."

In a short time all the evil reports that scandal had ever breathed of young Afzul Khan were wormed out of the timorous headman, who between the fear of the Subadar's vengeance and the threat of losing his office, was in a state of no ordinary perplexity. He saw clearly that the Dipty was anxious to get up a case against the young Muhammadan, and though he was quite certain that Afzul had no connection with the thefts, he knew also that his irregular habits and lawless bearing gave some colour of likelihood to suspicion against him. So he raked up the old stories about the ryot of Milkiganj's daughter, and other scandals of the same type, the beating of Three Shells, the orgies at Panch Pahar, Afzul's visits to the shop of Rutton Pal, the spirit-seller, and his riotous and unseemly carriage on foot and on horseback by street and by highway, and the offence which was thereby given to the decent and orderly lieges of Dhupnagar. Preonath knew all those stories before, for his father Ram Lall kept him well posted up in the gossip of his native town; but he shook his head with an air of sad gravity as the headman repeated each successive enormity, and made frequent entries in the note-book which lay open before him upon the desk.

"It is really a very serious and deplorable case," said the Dipty, shaking his head with an affectation of melancholy solemnity, "when a young man of respectable parentage and considerable substance embarrasses himself by extravagance and improper conduct, so that to maintain his pleasures he is obliged to resort to unlawful means of obtaining money. There is no crime so wicked, no deed so audacious, that such a person will not be tempted to commit. Nay, even the law itself, in the persons of its officers, they will contemptuously set at defiance," added the Dipty, indignantly, as he remembered how Afzul had ridden himself down at the Pagoda Tope. " I know nothing of this young man—it is probable that I may never have set my eyes upon him; but from what this worthy headman has deponed, I have no hesitation in saying that he is a most suspicious and dangerous character."

A murmur among the *amla* and the lawyers applauded the Dipty's eloquence and the justice of his remarks. A queer twinkle might have been observed in the eyes of Jaddoo as he stood behind the magistrate's chair, for the astute orderly had no difficulty in conjecturing why his master should be so anxious to get up a case against the Muhammadan. The Dipty had taken no further notice of his *rencontre* with Afzul at the Pagoda Tope, but he was not the man to dismiss an insult thus readily from his recollection.

" As yet I see no grounds for proceeding against the suspected party," continued the Dipty, " but it is a great matter to have got a clue. We must give this Muhammadan and his accomplices their swing for a while, Mr Headman, and keep a strict watch upon all his movements. When he goes out at night you or your policemen must keep him constantly in sight, and come to me next day with a report. If this be done we shall soon put a stop to these robberies, and have the thieves fast in Bhutpore jail."

But Gangooly had another protest to make. Did his honour the Dipty think that he and his policemen had wings, that they could keep sight of the swiftest horse and the fastest rider in all the country? The only horse among them was his own pony, which only went four miles an hour, except when Lutchmun was behind with a stick to belabour it, when it could manage five. Why, even Eversley Sahib Bahadoor could not ride so fast as the Muhammadan, and how could they be expected to keep him in sight? His honour the Dipty should bethink himself how such orders were to be executed; for as the law said, "He that devised impossible tasks for another devised only——"

"Now, headman, don't argue with me," interrupted Preonath, angrily; "it has been evident to me from the first that you are some way interested in screening this malefactor. But mark what I tell you: if you do not get me a conviction for these thefts before the month is out, there will be a change in the headmanship of Dhupnagar."

"The gods' will be done," said Gangooly, sulkily; "a man can do but his best. My fathers have been headmen of Dhupnagar since the British got the stewardship of Bengal, Behar, and Orissa, and they were never asked to run against a race-horse."

The Dipty struck his desk with his clenched fist, and was making an angry rejoinder, when a breathless messenger dashed into the court, covered with sweat and dust, without a rag of clothes upon him except his waist-cloth, and with his shoes slung over his shoulders, and hardly taking time to salaam to the Dipty announced that the Magistrate Sahib Bahadoor had taken horse, and was even then riding in the direction of Gopshopgunj. In an instant all was confusion. Policemen rushed off to don their turbans and waist-belts, clerks began to scribble as if for life and death; and Preonath, having hurriedly thrown a bundle of miscellaneous papers upon his desk, called an important revenue case, in which our friend Preonono made his appearance for the defendant; and by the time that Mr Eversley had arrived at the Gopshopgunj court-house the Dipty was sitting engrossed in the pleading, and so intent upon his work that he was for a few minutes oblivious of the magistrate's presence.

It should be remarked that the movements of a district magistrate are always a matter of the highest importance to his subordinates. The public business carried on by native officials is almost all eye-service, and it is essential to their comfort that they should know when they are under the observation of their English superiors. Like a wise official, Preonath took all necessary precautions in this respect. He tied the magistrate's confidential orderly he feed his *khan-samah*, and he secured the friendship of the chief officers of the Ellenpore court by frequent complimentary largesses; so that Mr Eversley could not put his foot in the stirrup to ride in the Gupshapganj direction without a friendly warning being conveyed to the Diputy to put his house in order.

The Bhurpore magistrate was a wiry little man of about forty years of age or upwards. His face, neck, and hands were burned as brown as a brick, and his long brown beard was bleached and grizzled by exposure to the weather. There was little appearance of official pomp about him as he dashed up to the door of the Gupshapganj court-house. He wore a yellow tussur silk jacket, which might have weighed an ounce and three quarters, a pair of white duck trousers tucked inside long riding-boots, and an enormously broad puthai, which gave him the appearance when walking of an animated mushroom; but he had eschewed all such vanities as gloves, waistcoat, collar, or necktie. As he came up, the Gupshapganj policemen drew up in line, with the sergeant at their head, executed an elaborate military salute, which the magistrate carelessly returned with the shaft of his hunting-whip; and handing his horse, a beautiful Waler mare, to the nearest orderly, who received the animal with hardly less respect than he had vouchsafed to its master, the magistrate walked into the court compound. The lawyers salaamed low, and the satries on the outside of the crowd set up a false cry of '*Inhasi Justice!*, Magistrate Sahib! *Kumpani ka dohai!*' (the justice of the Company!—which was promptly silenced by blows from the nearest policeman. Brijo, the perjurer "in largest practice," made off for the jungle as fast as he could; sweepers were sent off to clean and water the streets; and everybody in Gapshapganj could see by the bustle and hubbub about the court-house that the "Big Sahib" had come to the village.

CHAPTER XI.

EVERSLEY SAHIB.

MR EVERSLEY, the Collector of the Gungaputra district, was an official of a type that has almost passed away. He had been brought up in the strictest traditions of the Haileybury school, and had adhered through all his life to the conservative principles of " old civilianism." His deepest conviction was that the service was "going to the devil," and that every fresh change which was made in its constitution was merely an extra acceleration to its downward progress. When the " competition wallah " came in, Eversley foresaw certain ruin to the English interests in India; and to this day he firmly believes that the introduction of the new system was mysteriously connected with the Sepoy Mutiny, which followed after a short interval. "Competition wallahs!" he was wont to exclaim; "as well put the country under a commission of schoolmasters at once. But we'll lose the country with all this Greek and Latin; take my word for it, we'll soon lose the country." Mr Eversley was very sparsely imbued with these classical languages, and his contemporaries at Haileybury say that it was a marvel how the Court of Directors ever allowed him to come out to India at all. He had never been able to make a hexameter in the whole course of his life, and there is grave reason to doubt that he was ignorant of even the barest elements of the Greek accidence. But he had acquired a marvellous colloquial familiarity with the Eastern vernaculars, and he knew the habits and feelings of the Bengalees better than any other officer in the Lower Provinces. He could cross-examine a ryot in the *patois* of his own village, and repay with interest the slang of a bazaar shopkeeper. There was no chance of Eversley falling into such a blunder as that which was laid to the charge of Muffington Prig, the magistrate of the neighbouring district of Lallkor, who once, in taking the deposition of a witness in a criminal case, had expressed his displeasure that evidence of such importance should be given on the authority of a third person, and ordered the police to take care that "Fidwi" should be brought before him.* But for all that, Mr Muffington Prig was a rising man in the service, and had obtained as much promotion in twelve years' time as Eversley had in twenty. True,

* Mr Muffington Prig's little mistake is a well-known Indian joke. The witness in a respectful way gave his evidence in the third person, saying instead of "I saw," or "I heard," "*Fidwi* (your slave) saw or heard this or that."

he never could understand what a Bengalee said to him; he could no more sit a horse than he could have ridden upon a griffon; and his enemies even whispered—for the charge was too serious a one to be openly advanced—that he had once in a sporting mood gone out "pig-shooting," the enormity of which offence could only be paralleled by the butchery of a fox in an English hunting county. But then he wrote leaders in the 'Bengal Peon;' he was known to be the author of at least one article in the 'Chowringhee Review,' and he had edited an edition of the 'Mofussil Magistrate's Manual;' all of which eminent literary undertakings clearly marked him out for advancement. Eversley, on the contrary, had difficulty enough in making decent English of an official report, and pert young undersecretaries at the Bengal office took a delight in girding at his orthography and syntax. Mr Muffington Prig's judgments had been more than once spoken of with high encomiums by Mr Justice Tremor in the Appeal side of the High Court; but Mr Eversley's law never came before the Bench except to be reprobated. Lawyers complained that he did not know even the rudiments of the Codes; but there was no magistrate in the Lower Provinces whose decisions were received with more general satisfaction, or from whose judgments there were fewer appeals. The magistrate of the Gungaputra's rough and ready way of settling cases was better relished by the natives than the elaborate findings of the Lallkor archon, which were generally unintelligible to the suitors until they had fee'd their lawyers to tell them which side had gained. The people knew that Eversley would do what he saw to be right independent of Act or Code, and they had more confidence in his sense of justice than in the written law. But in spite of all these drawbacks Mr Eversley's name was well mentioned in high places, for the Government knew that he was a trustworthy and energetic officer, who could well be relied upon to meet an emergency.

It was clearly understood, however, that the magistrate of the Gungaputra was not a man who was likely to receive further promotion. So far was he from courting favour in Calcutta, that he had never hesitated to non-suit or decide against the Government itself when it came into his court with a weak or an illegal plea, notwithstanding a hint from the Board of Revenue that the magistracy of Colrapore would likely be soon vacant by death, as it was now nearly six weeks since the present incumbent had taken up his appointment. But neither Colrapore nor Saugor Island would deter Eversley from doing justice when on the Bench, and the Board was fain to leave him alone, for fear of a public outcry. But it was little wonder then though Mr Eversley's official reputation was thrown far into the shade by Mr Muffington Prig, for that excellent official had not only never decided against the Government in a single suit, but had always succeeded in showing that the law was clearly in its favour. It only remains to be added that Mr Eversley was a mighty hunter, a pillar of the Tent Club, and a patron of the turf, although he had never betted sixpence upon horse-flesh since he came to India. His exploits among the "wild pigs" were the favourite talk of the Bengal and the United Service Clubs; and he had shot as many tigers in his time as "Tiger Brown" of the Junglywallah Cavalry, or Bounceby of the Toshakana Office, whose feats, moreover, mainly rested upon their own personal assertions. He preserved the tigers in his district as strictly as a Norfolk squire guards his pheasants; and great was his indignation at the scandalous conduct of Muff. Prig of Lallkor, who determined to stamp out beasts of prey, and had offered a reward of five rupees for every tiger's head brought to his office. When it came out that the artistic natives of Lallkor had taken to the manufacture of tigers' heads, and that Mr Prig had paid away several hundred rupees for clever imitations, composed of glass eyes, bamboo splits, and tiger-skin, Eversley was as much delighted as if he had been promoted to a Commissionership. The news of a tiger was the signal for the instant adjournment of the Gungaputra court, no matter how important might be the business before it. Styles, the great wit of the Calcutta bar, used to tell how he had managed Eversley when pleading before him in a criminal case, which the magistrate refused to remand to give the prisoner's counsel more time to collect evidence. Styles had slipped out of court and given a countryman a rupee to tell the Magistrate Sahib that there was a tiger in the Panch Pahar jungles; and before ten minutes had passed, Eversley was on horseback and galloping down the valley at full speed with a dozen bearers behind him. But then Styles was not always remarkable for veracity when he himself was the hero of his own narrative.

Everybody salaamed down to the ground as the magistrate entered the Gapshapganj court-house, and the Dipty came down from the Bench and advanced with many bows to welcome his superior officer. Eversley gave him his hand, and threw himself unceremoniously into a chair, calling out as he sat down for a light to his cigar. Half-a-dozen fire-stands were obsequiously proffered, and the magistrate smoked away in silence until the Dipty had adjourned his court and cleared the room of officials. There only remained the Dipty's clerk and old Gangooly with his two watchmen, who had been hustled into a corner when the magistrate's arrival was announced, and who now stood as far away from the great man as possible, anxiously waiting for the Dipty's permission to depart. The Dipty, however, was too much engrossed in attending to Mr Eversley to be conscious of their presence. " Well, Baboo, and how is work going on?" the magistrate was saying; "as many cases upon your files as usual? This subdivision of yours is more litigious than all the rest of the district put together; and no wonder, for I am sure that I counted more than a dozen pleaders hanging about your *cutcherry*. I wish to heaven they would not let loose so many blackguards to prey upon the people! I would rather any day have ten *dakaits* (highwaymen) than one lawyer in my district."

"He, he! your honour is jesting surely," sniggered the Dipty; "but there are lawyers from Dhupnagar as well as Gapshapganj attending my court; one of them was pleading before me in an important rent case when your honour arrived."

"But talking of Dhupnagar," interrupted the magistrate, "what about these robberies? Something must be done, and that immediately; for these confounded papers in Calcutta are crying out about them, and urging the Government to send a special officer to the district. Special officer indeed! much good would a special officer do in my district. It is that confounded *soor* Muffington Prig who wrote that article in the 'Peon.' I know it was: no other fellow could have been so spiteful," added the magistrate *sotto voce*; and then aloud, "Have you got any clue to the depredators yet?"

"There was another robbery the night before last at Gaogong," said Preonath. The magistrate uttered an exclamation of annoyance, and began to smoke with short, fierce puffs.

"And has nothing been discovered yet? What is the use of your police? I'll suspend every man Jack of them if they don't get me a conviction within a week's time. You must stir them up, Baboo—you must stir them up, even if you should have to shut up your court, and go and stay upon the spot until some of these scoundrels are captured."

"I have received some information to-day," said Preonath, gravely, "which throws suspicion upon a new and altogether unsuspected quarter. The headman of Dhupnagar tells me that he suspects one Afzul Khan, a son of Shamsuddeen, the retired Subadar."

"If the humblest slave of the Huzoor—may his lordship live for a thousand years and his favour increase in the land!—might make a respectful representation, he would say that his honour the Dipty Baboo has mistaken his words," interposed old Gangooly, sidling forward into the magistrate's presence with profound salaams.

"What, fellow! how came you here?" cried Preonath, reddening at the interruption. "The headman, sir, is overawed by the young Mussulman, and it was with the greatest difficulty that I could get any information out of him. I would respectfully suggest, your honour, that a more efficient headman should be appointed to Dhupnagar."

"My fathers have been headmen of Dhupnagar since the English Sahibs got the stewardship of Bengal, Behar, and Orissa," said poor Gangooly; "but a man cannot see beyond eyeshot, nor hear where there is no sound. The gods know that I am neither diviner nor soothsayer. How, then, can I find out the robbers?"

"By keeping your eyes open and your wits about you, headman, as you will have to do a little better if you wish to remain in your present post," said the magistrate; "and now, Baboo, tell me what is this about Afzul Khan?"

"They will *have* it so then," said Gangooly to himself, with a sigh of resignation, "and the best thing will be to give them their own way, for there is little good comes of contending with one's masters. However, *I* wash *my* hands of false witnessing. And, after all, the lad is only a Muhammadan, so it does not matter quite so much whether he gets justice or not;" and consoling himself with this reflection, Gangooly held his peace, and allowed the Dipty to rehearse to Mr Eversley all the articles of impeachment against the character of Afzul Khan.

The magistrate listened gravely to the various charges. "But all these things," he said, "have no bearing upon the case in point, although they might help to strengthen a suspicion. Tell me, headman, what reason have you for thinking that Afzul Khan is mixed up with these robberies?"

"May it please your honour, I did not think that the Subadar's son was a robber," responded Gangooly, brightening up again. "I have always said, as the whole village says, that the robbers are Southals from above the passes; and what can I and my two watchmen do against half-a-score of men armed with axe and spear? It was his honour the Dipty Baboo who, in the depth of his great wisdom—of which we, his townsmen, may well be proud—discovered that the Muhammadan must be the robber."

"Indeed! and what grounds of suspicion have you against him?" inquired the magistrate, turning a searching glance upon the Dipty.

"Sir, your honour!" cried Preonath, eagerly, colouring up to the eyes in spite of himself, "I told you this man was under intimidation of the Muhammadans. It was with the utmost difficulty that I could draw any information out of him regarding this person's character. Besides, I had a hint from a most respectable Hindoo in Dhupnagar that the Subadar's family was connected with the robberies."

"And who may this most respectable Hindoo be, pray?" asked the magistrate, doubtfully, as he began to suspect that the Dipty had some personal interest in criminating Afzul. The aphorism "cui bono" was one of Eversley's few judicial maxims, and it was one that he never lost sight of when dealing with native cases.

"It was Baboo Kristo Doss Lahory," replied the Dipty, after some hesitation, for he was not sure that Kristo's words would warrant him in putting such a construction upon them. "He said to me that he should not be at all surprised if the Subadar and his son were at the bottom of these robberies the very last time I saw him."

"Now, Baboo, did you—who are a lawyer, and a

clever one too—actually give heed to what Kristo said of the Subadar's family? You know quite well that Kristo has never forgiven Shamsuddeen Khan for obtaining a part of his family estates, and that there is no ill turn which he would not do the Muhammadan if he could get off with it; and now, answer me plainly and truly, have you any personal quarrel with Afzul Khan?"

"What quarrel could I have with him, your honour?" said the Dipty, confidently. "So far as I know, I never saw the man in my life, and I have never heard anything of him except the information which has been lodged against him this morning. I trust you do not think, sir, that though I had any quarrel with him, I should allow it to influence my feelings as a deputy-magistrate? I am sorry that your honour should have formed so unfavourable an opinion of my character;" and Preonath put on an air of injured innocence as he looked Mr Eversley full in the face.

"Well, well, I hope not," said the magistrate, doubtfully, " but it is best to be careful. And after all," he muttered to himself, "it may be just the Dipty's officiousness and anxiety to fix the robberies upon some one of another faith." "And what do you propose to do?" he added aloud; "how do you intend to act upon this supposed information?"

"That will be for your honour to decide," replied the Dipty; "as you consider our suspicions unfounded, I suppose we had better take no further notice of them. I may, however, venture to remind your honour that the officers in the Sonthal Pergunnahs are positive that the robberies were not committed by men from their district. Shall I cancel this information against Afzul Khan?"

"No, certainly not," said the magistrate; "heaven forbid that I should allow my own prepossessions to interfere with the course of justice! and I would give heavy odds that the lad has no connection with these thefts. I have hunted with him in the Panch Pahar jungles, and I never saw any one that was a scoundrel ride so straight up to a boar." This comment was addressed rather by the magistrate to himself than for the Dipty's edification. "However, just keep a close watch upon him. If he is an honest man he will be none the worse for being under surveillance; and if he isn't, the sooner we send him to the Andamans the better. But who is to look after him? Do you mean to intrust the duty to these energetic officials?" looking towards Gangooly and his two ancient assistants.

"No, sir; I have an orderly who is a very clever detective, and I shall send him to Dhupnagar for this business. I suppose you think that we had better keep the matter secret until our suspicions are verified?"

"Certainly," returned the magistrate, "for the lad's father's sake, who, at all events, is a most excellent and loyal man. So take care of your tongues, my good fellows, when you go back to Dhupnagar, or if I hear of any gossiping about this business, there will be a vacancy in the village headmanship."

Gangooly swore by the thousand names of Siva, by the waters of the Gungaputra, and the thrice-holy Linga of Dhupnagar, that not a word should cross the lips of him and his watchmen; adding, also, that his fathers had been headmen of Dhupnagar since the English Sahibs had obtained——"

"Are there any tigers about Panch Pahar nowadays, headman?" interrupted the magistrate.

"By your honour's favour they are all exterminated," said Gangooly, with a low salaam: "the wild beasts of the jungle can no more face your lordship's presence than an antelope can look upon a hunting leopard. The mothers of Dhupnagar tell their children every day how the great Magistrate Sahib killed the big man-eating tigress at the Ghatghar ford, five years ago come the feast of Kalee. Do they not, Hurree? do they not, Lutchmun?"

Hurree and Lutchmun, the aged guardians of the peace of Dhupnagar, bowed almost to the ground, and whispered a chorus to their headman's eulogium on the magistrate's exploits. Mr Eversley sucked his cigar with a mollified air, for even district magistrates are mortal, and the Collector of the Gungaputra was not a little vain of his reputation as a sportsman.

"Well, headman, I am coming to Dhupnagar in a fortnight, and I shall want some sport upon the other side of the river. You will manage to provide a score or so of beaters for me, won't you?"

"Your lordship shall have the whole village, man and child, if you require them," said Gangooly, delighted with the commission; "and if any one dares to refuse, I will tie him by the great toes to the small end of a green bamboo, and let him hang there until he learn to reverence the Government."

"Nay, nay; 'ware the torture clause in the Penal Code," cried Mr Eversley, laughing; "eight annas a-head will be a more legitimate inducement. And do not forget to keep quiet about Afzul Khan, and to keep a good look about the village until you catch the real culprit."

Gangooly took his leave delighted with the magistrate's affability, and promising that his orders should be strictly obeyed; and the magistrate and the Dipty addressed themselves to the other business of the subdivision. It was not without a purpose that Eversley had conciliated the headman, for he had a sincere regard for Shamsuddeen, and would gladly have spared him any scandal regarding his son. The magistrate mentally resolved not to confide too much in the Dipty in the matter, but to take an early opportunity of investigating the robberies on the spot; for Eversley was one of those civilians who had little confidence in the integrity of natives, and who had incurred no small odium by steadily setting his face against their admission to offices of trust and authority. However, the public service lost little by Eversley's narrowness; for his distrust of his native subordinates only made him far more careful and energetic in the discharge of his own duties, and less ready to accept evidence at second hand than other officials who were more liberal in their sentiments.

"If a dog made a pilgrimage to Kasi (Benares), he is still but a dog when he comes back again," said old Gangooly to his two henchmen, as his pony jogged slowly up the road towards the Pagoda Tope. "Our Dipty, though he has got all the learning that the Calcutta Sahibs can put into him, is still no more of a gentleman than his old father Ram Lall, the oilman. You noticed, Hurree—you saw, Lutchmun—how politely the Huzoor Magistrate Sahib Bahadoor spoke to me. He is a great man, and of a good caste of Englishmen, and knows what proper manners are. But when had an upstart like the Dipty proper respect for his elders and betters? It is a bad thing for the country when the English Sahibs put low-caste men in authority."

"What better do they know? they are ignorant of the blessing of caste. English society is like the kingdom of Harbong, where greens and sweetmeats are sold alike at a pice a seer. They have no proper orders; the sweeper, they say, may sup with the priest, if he has only money enough," said Hurree, sententiously.

"But we needn't trouble ourselves about the Dipty so long as we can retain the favour of the English Magistrate Sahib," said Gangooly. "You will take heed, my brothers, that his honour's orders about secrets are remembered. You are not to go into the bazaar and sit down and gossip with folks about Afzul Khan being blamed for the robbery, or that the Dipty's orderly is coming to Dhupnagar to watch him. But if you wanted any news to give the villagers, I do not know that there would be any harm of speaking thus to them :—lo, you! what a great and good man is our magistrate, and how he respects our old headman, Gangooly! He treats our headman with as much courtesy as he does the Dipty Baboo, and trusts as much to his word as if he were the holy Hurrish Chunder himself, who never told a lie.—This much ye may say, my children, without doing harm."

"But surely we may tell the wives and friends of our families about the Muhammadan," said the watchmen; "there could be no wrong in that, O Mr Headman?"

"Nay, nay! the gods forbid that I should tie your tongues under the thatch of your own cottages!" responded the easy-going Gangooly, "for he who hides in his breast a secret from his friends, sits upon burning coals until he yield it up; I know that myself. I shall tell my own wife, and you may tell yours; but command them not to tom-tom it over the bazaar, for the orders of the Magistrate Sahib must be strictly obeyed. Beat up the pony, Lutchmun!"

Hurree and Lutchmun promised compliance; but it could hardly be wondered at that, in spite of Gangooly's interdict, the bazaar of Dhupnagar should be full of Afzul Khan's guilt before four-and-twenty hours had passed over, and that the Subadar's family were the only persons in the village who had not heard of what had transpired in the Gapshapganj court-house.

CHAPTER XII.

KRISHNA'S LETTERS.

KRISHNA sat in his room writing letters. Since his arrival he had not quitted his father's compound, and had confined himself closely to his own apartments, except when he went forth to bathe in the tank at early morning, or when he ascended to the top of the house to walk up and down its terraced roof for exercise after nightfall. He had spoken to none of the inmates save his father and old Bechoo, his attendant; and the young man's spirit was beginning to chafe at the solitary life. A hundred times a-day he would wish that he were up and doing something, however humble, for the regeneration of his countrymen, instead of purposelessly frittering away his time within four walls. Krishna had not as yet wavered in his purpose of becoming the deliverer of his country from idolatry and superstition. Something within seemed to tell him that he was not as other men were: that a great work was waiting for him in the world to do; and that fame and honours, brilliant as they were remote, were destined to crown his earthly career. Enthusiasm had in fact got the mastery over the young man's mind, and he owed it to the accident of education that his enthusiasm had been directed into a right channel. Had he not been sent to a Calcutta college, he might have laid aside his Brahminical cord and his caste as his uncle Shib Chunder had done when a young man, to become a Sunyasee or wandering mendicant, devoted to the service of Siva; but Krishna now would have scouted such an idea as ridiculous. He was sure that nothing could move *him*, but a firm belief in the True and the Right, and that his motives were of the purest and most disinterested character. And yet it is to be feared that the actuating principle of these feelings was ambition, an ambition not the less active that it was well disguised under the aspect of self-denial and generosity. And yet in all Krishna's visionary projects for the deliverance of his countrymen, self played a very important part. When he tried to fill his mind with the golden age which would dawn upon India when the idols were broken, superstition banished, and the people converted to the worship of the One, his thoughts persistently turned to what rewards, what honours, would be showered upon him who had wrought this great work. And he dreamed of a day when the name of Krishna Chandra Gossain would be spoken admiringly by every Indian tongue, and when men would make pilgrimages to Dhupnagar to look with respect upon the birthplace of so illustrious a character. But in proportion to the extravagance of such hopes, the fits of despondency which frequently overtook him, depressed his spirits; and at such times seclusion would begin to work the effects upon which Ramanath had calculated. Why, Krishna would then ask himself, should he thus voluntarily exile himself from the society of his family and his friends for a mere matter of belief which he might well keep to himself, and nobody be any the wiser? What call had he to become a martyr for Theism? And would his countrymen be any happier though they were all Theists to-morrow? Had knowledge made himself happy or the reverse? Then he would wish that he had never troubled his head about religion, that he could believe as devoutly in the Linga as Modhoo the porter did, or that he could accept the popular faith in his father's unquestioning spirit. Then he would ask himself, why should not this be so? He had merely to make a fashion of conforming to orthodox Hindooism, and he would be a rich, respected, and happy man during the rest of his life. Respected he might be, but would he respect himself? And what would the Brahmists say if he, who had been the boldest speculator, the most determined iconoclast among them, were to set up as the priest of an idol temple? No, no; he could never do it: he had made deliberate choice of the light, and would no longer abide in the darkness.

Then his pride would rise again at the thought that his belief, or his scepticism rather, had placed him far above the level of the vulgar masses; and his present position as a sufferer for a noble and unpopular cause, was not without its strong potion of vainglory for an ardent young mind. A glance at Krishna's correspondence will perhaps help us better to understand his state than any description would do. The first was written in Bengalee, and was superscribed, "To the fortunate Baboo Bholanath Thakoor, my friend, loved as my own life, I write as follows:—

"Though the promise I made to you at the Howrah station has been ever in my mind, it is only now that I am able to fulfil it. Need you ask why? Surely the heart of friendship can divine that it is because I have no good news to give you. Know, then, that my father has not cast me off, and that I am still living in his house, but apart from the family. But what of that? I cannot continue to stay here in idleness, and the time is at hand when I must break through the bonds of family love and go forth into the world to do the work. I need not tell your tender heart how hard it is for me thus to offend my father. I shall need all the strength that my prayers and yours can procure for me, to nerve me for the struggle. O Bholanath! would that I had you or some of our other friends by me to aid me with their counsel! for at times I feel the ground of my faith slipping from under my feet. If I were only out in the world where bodily temptations assail one, I think I could withstand them—at least I should wrestle with *them;* but my own mind is a far stronger tempter than I can get the better of. Sometimes an evil spirit asks me, Why throw away all your worldly advantages, your position as a twice-born Brahmin, your ancestral wealth, and your father's love, for an idea? At such times, Bholanath, I am sore bested; and but for prayer, and the thought of your sympathy and that of the brethren, I should assuredly fall away. Would that I were with you, Bholanath! I say again. Each day will be as a long year until I return to the society of you and our other friends. Think then of me, Bholanath, especially at prayer-time. What more can be said by your affectionate friend and fellow-Brahmist,

"KRISHNA CHANDRA GOSSAIN.

"But I must tell you of her,—not the wife to whom an untoward fate has linked me in name—though why should I complain of it, since that chiefly of earthly influences hath opened my eyes to the errors of Hindooism?—but of her to whom I have so long been secretly devoted. I have seen her again, Bholanath—seen her again face to face, as I did when she slew me with a single glance. Last night I was walking up and down my father's compound, when some irresistible influence led me to look upon the sacred spot where I had first beheld her. I wrapped my *chaddar* round my head so as to conceal my features, and stole quietly through the temple grounds until I reached the Lahories' ruined tank. The waters sparkled brightly in the moonlight, and the fire-flies' lamps glowed in the dark shade of the thick boughs which hang over the basin of the tank. It was such a night as our idolatrous countrymen might well have chosen for paying their homage to Kamdeo, the god of love. I leaned against a broken wall, well concealed by a thick clump of bamboos, and was unconsciously humming to myself a stanza of the Urdu song, which you may remember some of our Mussulman students used to sing :—

> 'Like soft wind's ripples upon beauty's stream,
> So fall thy tresses; and their dazzling gleam,
> More golden than the fountain of the sun,
> Sheds purer light than noontide's brightest beam.'

Just then I heard a rustling among the leaves, and Radha with her maid appeared on the other side of the tank. I crept forward, and from behind the shadow of an acacia-tree, I could see her quite distinctly as she came down to the water's edge and stood straight before me in the moonshine. If my pen could only describe the charms I saw, you would forgive me, Bholanath, for loving her. Radha's figure is fuller and more womanly than when I last saw her, but her face still wears that look of childish guilelessness which has been engraven upon my heart all these weary years. Once as she turned her face upwards, a yellow glow of moonlight fell upon her features, smiling upon her red lips, playing about her dainty nose, silvering her high square forehead, and sparkling in her large liquid eyes, while her black hair seemed almost blue as the soft moonbeams played upon it. Ah, Bholanath! it was a glance of heavenly beauty such as one only sees once in a life-time.

"'Kamdeo (Cupid) with the golden locks be propitious to thy handmaid,' said she, as she took from the attendant a small chip of wood, upon which a tiny wax-light was burning. 'Shall we say this is the Rajah of Ghatghar, my Sukheena?' she asked, as she gently launched the chip upon the bosom of the tank. 'Very well; a fair voyage to your highness. But see! what is this? I declare he is going to sink already! The Rajah's passion is soon cooled, my Sukheena;' and as she spoke, the chip was overturned by the weight of the taper, which had not been placed fair in the centre, and it disappeared among the waters with a hiss and a splutter.

"'Let this be old Ganga Prasad, the rich landholder of Gapshapganj, who wants me for his fourth wife,' she said, as she launched another. 'Well done, Ganga! you sail away steadily as if you were used to marry; but what is this?' Here a little fish sporting in the moonlight leaped up, oversetting the taper. 'So, so,' said Radha; 'Ganga is soon disposed of. If that is an omen, his suit will come to an unexpected end.'

"'Quick, Sukheena! quick with another!' she cried

hurriedly, as a breeze swept the surface of the tank. 'Let this be my own, my only, my nameless lover, for it is over no smooth waters that his bark must float.' As the third light was blown over the ripply surface, and as the tiny wavelets tossed it higher and higher, threatening every minute to swallow up the frail bark, Radha clapped her hands with childish delight. See, Sukheena!' she cried; 'watch how nobly it is sailing towards the other bank! Nothing can swamp the bark of true love, and our passion will guide us safely to love's haven, in spite of the many hindrances that come in its way. See, it touches the bank! I must catch it;' and as she spoke, the light-hearted maiden came running round to the side where I was concealed. She gave one shriek as she saw me, and turning quickly, bounded off to the house like a frightened antelope, while I made my escape as quietly as possible. Was it not strange that the third love-bark should come safely to shore through so many dangers? You will think me silly, Bholanath, but my heart instinctively told me that the maiden whispered my name as she launched the third taper."   " K. C. G."

Krishna's second letter was addressed to one of the leading reformers of the Calcutta Brahmo Somaj, and it was less frank in tone than the preceding. It was written in Bengalee also.

"BABOO KRISHNA CHANDRA GOSSAIN, TO THE MOST REVEREND AND HONOURED BABOO —— —— ——

"The only relief your former disciple finds in the

midst of his manifold afflictions is the thought of your sympathy and friendship, and that of the brethren. O my preserver and protector, let your prayers ascend to the Supreme Brahma for me! I am detained in parental bonds, and I lack the strength to break through them; although my condition here is far more harassing to the soul than the world's scorn, or hostility, or temptations could be. I am shut out here from all society except that of my books and my own thoughts; and the latter are my most deadly enemies. I have followed your counsels, and striven to conquer evil suggestions by prayer; but it is heartless work praying in this Black Age, when the mind is racked by doubts, and when no hand is put forth from heaven to raise the suppliant. But think not, my father, that I murmur at my lot, or that I mistrust the Supreme Brahma's care for those who truly seek to serve Him. I know that He is ordering all this affliction for my good; I only fear that there may be still some trial in store for me which I shall sink beneath. Advise me what to do. I would fain go out into the world to proclaim war against idolatry, and rescue our countrymen from the thraldom of caste; but you know how strong are the ties that bind a son to a father. Counsel me also in the matter of my wife. I was married to her when an infant, and we have never lived together. She is an insipid, narrow-minded woman, wholly sunk in superstition, and unable to see the beauty of our holy faith. I would be glad if our union could be dissolved, giving her, of course, an ample portion of my worldly wealth; but to do this I must have the sanction of our brethren. Can I trouble your kindness to put this matter before them in a quiet manner? I would be ashamed to force such an affair upon their notice, did I not feel that my usefulness is fettered, and my life embittered, by my relationship to this woman. Thenceforward I would live without wife or family to distract my attention from the service of the Supreme."

It can hardly be said that these letters set forth the whole of Krishna's mind without reserve. He had alluded to doubts and temptations, but he had not frankly acknowledged that his passion for Radha was the greatest trial that he had to encounter. The accidental meeting which he had described to his old class-fellow had fanned the smouldering flame into a blaze. His new faith now occupied but a secondary place in his thoughts, and when he did think of it, it was chiefly as the barrier between him and his love. The time which he had been wont to spend in prayer and religious meditation was now devoted to the composition of Sanscrit *slokas* in praise of Radha's beauty, or in scribbling love-sonnets in Bengalee. Night after night he paced up and down the house-top, watching Radha's windows until long after every light had been put out in the house of Lahory; and whenever a shadow passed between him and the light in Radha's apartments, his heart would begin to palpitate, and his frame to tremble, as he sought to trace the outlines of Radha's figure. O Krishna! could you have known that the shadow which seemed to you so lithe and slender was cast not by Radha's shapely form, but by the lean and withered skeleton who had been the maiden's nurse, how you would have loathed the foolish stupidity that made you go down on your knees and waft kisses across the darkness! But which of us has not made love to a shadow in our time as well as the priest's son?

Krishna sat at his table, embarrassed by a crowd of contending feelings. The letters were written, and lay sealed before him, but his mind was filled by a vague sense of misgiving, which made him wish that they were unwritten, and he felt irresolute about despatching them. Had he not been too frank with Bholanath? And yet if he could not confide in him, whom could he trust? What were his feelings and trials to the men of the Brahmo Somaj, who were too busy with their own affairs to waste their sympathy upon him? He remembered how he had vaunted his own firmness, how harshly he had judged the weakness of others; and he trembled at the thought of how men would scoff and sneer at his own instability. There were many of his fellow-Brahmists who sneered at him as a visionary, and turned into ridicule his great schemes for the regeneration of his country; but these men would jeer at him now as a weak-minded enthusiast, a dreamer who had never the courage to put his Utopian schemes into execution. But he would take care that they should not scoff at him; and he felt that he could almost persist in his design to become an apostle of Brahmism, if for no other purpose than that he might deprive his enemies of the pleasure of sneering at his recantation. He was conscious that he was not altogether loyal to his new faith, and this consciousness soon suggested a suspicion of the sentiments of his fellow-Brahmists towards him. He was sure that several heads of the society were jealous of his talents, and would be glad to hear that he had fallen off from the faith; but he would take care that their wishes were not gratified at his expense. No: he would at once go forth and begin the great work which was to regenerate his countrymen and raise himself to a higher niche in the temple of fame than any Hindoo had reached since the heroic ages. And warming in his enthusiasm, Krishna started to his feet and began to pace the room with short, impatient steps.

But why did he pause so often opposite that window which looked forth upon the village green? Over against him stood the house of Lahory, its huge pile of masonry seeming in the waning moonlight to be even more grey and ruinous than it actually was. A few lights glimmered here and there in the building. There was Kristo's reception-room, where he would be sitting and smoking with his poor relation and gossip, Jotendro, or with Radhakant, the Ghatghar Rajah's steward, who was said to encroach upon Three Shells' profession, and who was known to have more than once accommodated the needy head of the Lahory family. But it was those windows that looked towards the Gungaputra and Panch Pahar that riveted Krishna's attention, for they belonged to the zenana, where the lovely Radha was immured. How many times a day had Krishna studied that angle of Kristo Baboo's building! One might have thought that it was with the black moss-grown bricks, or the unpainted weather-beaten venetians, that he was in love, for these were all that he could feed his eyes upon. But the glance of love can penetrate deeper than the unaided vision of ordinary mortals, and a brick wall in Bengal is as little a barrier to the imagination as a bedroom blind in Britain. So Krishna looked and loved by day and night, feeding his feverish passion upon shadows and other such unsubstantial manifestations, but taking no direct steps to gain the maiden's affection. His love was a dream, and he was not sure in his present position that he would be pleased to have it turned into a waking reality.

As he stood looking out at the open windows, the cool night air came blowing in, chafing his hot temples, and rousing the restless spirit of impatience within him. The moon was driving rapidly downwards through fleeces of white gauzy clouds towards the western horizon, and the black shadow of the trees and houses was perceptibly lengthening. The light was so mellow and inviting as to woo one to come forth; and Krishna, after a few attempts to shake off the influence of the "potent night," wrapped a cloak

about his shoulders and stole forth from the house.
No one saw him; for Modhoo, the porter, was too sound
a sleeper to be roused by a footfall in the compound;
and Ramanath, his father, had long since finished
evening worship at the temple, and returned to his own
apartments. The temple door stood wide open; for
what thief in all the valley would be so impious as to
put forth a hand against aught belonging to the Linga
of Dhupnagar? Krishna regarded both temple and
Linga with utter abhorrence, but on this occasion his
thoughts were too tender for feeling angry even with an
idolatrous shrine. The temple, he even thought, looked
rather picturesque in the moonlight; and the *peepul*
tree growing up from the roof, and sending down tendrils all round about the building, was decidedly beautiful. But it was not to admire the temple that Krishna
had come out so late at night. Rather than waken
Modhoo he scrambled over the compound wall, and
stole stealthily across the village green, keeping well
under the shadow of the trees until he reached Kristo
Baboo's grounds. Kristo's compound was quite in
keeping with the ruinous condition of the family mansion. The grass was long and rank, bamboo and jungle
scrub were springing up all over the place, and the
tanks were almost choked up with silt and vegetable
decay. The compound wall was a mere heap of ruins,
over which Krishna could stride almost, as he made
for the old tank, where Radha had launched the love-
tapers. He concealed himself under the acacia-trees,

and hoped, perhaps, that he might again see Radha steal down to the water's edge. Surely since she loved him she might divine that he would be there. But Radha came not, and Krishna lingered until the silvery surface of the tank became changed to a sullen black, and darkness set in around him. He was cold and nervous, but still he could not go home until he had feasted his eyes upon the place where his idol was enshrined.

As he stood in the shade of a clump of bushes, looking up in rapt admiration towards the zenana windows, a venetian was thrown open, and Radha looked forth into the moonlight. The moon was just then setting behind Panch Pahar, and her beams came straight over the tree-tops, striking evenly upon the casement where the maiden stood. Her shoulders were bare, except where her rich, heavy hair, no longer confined by its plaits, fell down, and a tress or two, like the tendrils of a young vine, straggled over her bosom. Radha peered cautiously forth into the darkness, as she half concealed herself behind the *jill-mills*, and seemed to be looking for some one appearing among the shrubbery beneath. Krishna stood and gazed at the beautiful vision until he could contain himself no longer; and he rushed forward, throwing himself on his knees before her, and raising his clasped hands towards the window. Radha threw him a chaplet of flowers and hastily retreated, and he could hear the window shut and barred behind her. He remained for a minute entranced upon his knees, looking sometimes at the flowers, sometimes at the window where the vision had disappeared, as if half hoping she would again return; and then taking up the flowers he kissed them and placed the garland upon his temples. It was a wreath such as is worn on festival days, or at the worship of an idol, and a slight shudder passed through Krishna's frame as he thought that he was thus tampering with the accursed thing. But though it had been the symbol of all the heathen idolatries and abominations in Hindustan, Radha's hand had sanctified it to him; and as the chaplet pressed his temples, he felt a thrill in the thought that perchance but a few minutes before it had rested upon Radha's hair, and that the sweet odours of her person still clung to it, overpowering the natural perfume of the flowers.

Krishna now no longer doubted that his love was returned. He had received two clear intimations that the maiden loved him in secret; and what better assurance could man desire until he heard the sweet confession from her own lips? When she had launched the taper on the ruffled bosom of the tank, it was of course to see if their mutual love could outlive the storm which the customs of society, religion, and jealousy were raising about them. He had marked, too, how Radha rejoiced when the frail chip reached the opposite bank in safety. And if any lingering doubt could have remained that he was deceiving himself, was not this chaplet a certain token of love? The heavy odour of the flowers seemed to have intoxicated Krishna as he walked rapidly back towards the priest's house. A thousand thoughts seemed to be fighting in his brain for priority of expression, but nothing came of them, for his head was filled with the two great ideas of his love for Radha and his resolution to possess her. There was a great gulf between these two ideas, but Krishna's mind was then too excited to think of obstacles. It all seemed easy enough. What a fool he had been to distract his brains with idle speculations! to think of renouncing his caste and position, and to go forth into the world a beggar to beggar others! He might as well think of turning a mendicant devotee like his silly uncle Shib Chunder, and of trudging over the country, from shrine to shrine, supported by the alms of charity. In his father's house he might live in pleasure and affluence all his days with Radha as his wife, and no earthly cares to molest them. But then there was Chakwi—bah! what of her? A Hindoo's love is not limited to one woman, and Chakwi must make up her mind to see another wife brought into the house. How lucky it was that he had never given the girl any encouragement, and that her feelings could not be very seriously hurt by his marrying a second time! There was his faith also, his belief in the Supreme Brahma, his avowed enmity to orthodox idolatry. Well, what of that? Theism did not impose any obligations of martyrdom upon its followers; and he could keep his own belief to himself, and allow others to do the same.

No: his duty to his father and his family, which he had so shamefully neglected, clearly showed that he must dismiss such folly. It was a pretty religion, forsooth! that must needs break up family ties, and set the son at variance with the father. Providence had placed him in a certain condition, and had brought him up in a certain creed, and it would be little short of impiety in him to change his religion upon no surer ground than intellectual convictions. The Supreme Brahma might convert his countrymen when He saw fit, and it would only be arrogance in a mortal to attempt forestalling His work. And how did he know that his countrymen were fit for Theism? A grosser belief satisfied the masses, and it was very doubtful if a purely intellectual creed, colourless and symbol-less as Brahmism was, would take any hold upon them. Krishna felt that he had been too hasty, and that it was high time to retrace his steps. What hindered him from making his father happy by accompanying the old man to the temple tomorrow? It was, after all, but his duty.

In this reckless fashion Krishna indulged his fancy; but how different would have been his reflections if he could have seen what was passing within a few yards of him? Afzul Khan, the Muhammadan, had been lurking behind the bushes when Krishna had picked up the flowers, and had marked the impassioned attitude of the young Hindoo. Afzul ground his teeth, and handled his dagger; and it was by a strong exercise of self-control that he abstained from rushing forward and killing his rival upon the spot. Stealthily, as a cat watches its prey, he followed Krishna out of the Lahories' compound, until the Hindoo had passed the village green, and disappeared in the darkness of the temple precincts. Then he returned and took up his old position before Radha's window; but all the lights were extinguished, and only the feeble glimmer of a night-lamp showed where the maiden's bedchamber was.

"A plague upon the presumption of these Hindoo swine!" muttered Afzul angrily to himself: "are there no drabs in Dhupnagar that he must raise his ill-omened eyes to a *huri* of Paradise? I wonder how I kept my hands off him. The girl must be blind, to have mistaken yon loutish, puffy Bengalee for a tight *sowar* (cavalier) like me. By Allah! I thought I could have stabbed him when I saw him beslobber the garland with his filthy kisses; but I care not, provided he gets nothing more precious than a bunch of flowers. But I must keep my eyes on that fellow: he is the Kaffir priest's bookish son, and would be an acceptable suitor to the girl's friends. She comes not, and I am tired with watching. Confound the wanton! is it not honour enough to her that the son of Shamsuddeen Khan keeps guard while she slumbers? But I shall make her one of Islam ere all be done, and she shall see this impudent Hindoo, who has dared to lift his eyes to her face, and all her other heathen kindred, cast into scorching blasts and scalding water, and the shade of smoke in the Day of Separation. Amen! Blessed be the Prophet." And with a feeling of self-satisfaction at his own devoutness, Afzul went down the road to Walesbyganj, and began to knock at the door and bawl for Agha to admit him.

CHAPTER XIII.

HUSBAND AND WIFE.

THE cool night air which came blowing over the peaks of Panch Pahar, out of the pale, silver rift where the moon had just disappeared, brought no calmer thoughts to Krishna's fevered brain. He shrank from returning to the quiet of his own chamber, which seemed like a prison, and where his books, his papers, the very letters which he had written that afternoon, might rise up between him and his thoughts of Radha; so he walked rapidly up and down the grassy compound before the priest's house, revolving all sorts of projects for gratifying his passion, and smoothing down the obstacles which reason raised between them. How long his promenade lasted he knew not, and his reverie might have continued till daybreak but for a great speckled cobra which crawled across his path. The snake's red eyes sparkled in the darkness, his hood was angrily spread, and his head raised to strike, when Krishna noticed the reptile, and bounded rapidly backwards. Foiled in his first spring the cobra glided quietly away among the grass, and Krishna drew a long breath at the thought of how narrow an escape he had had. The shock recalled the young man to himself, and to the lateness of the hour; but how was he to get into the house? He found the door locked, and the noise that would waken so sound a sleeper as the porter would also alarm every soul in the house. He now felt for the first time that the wind was chill, and he did not like the prospect of passing the rest of the night upon the grass in such disagreeable company as the cobra he had just encountered. He knocked once or twice at the door, but Kumbakharna * was about as easily roused as Ramanath's porter. He looked up, but all the house was in darkness except the windows of his own apartment, where a lamp still burned. Krishna was young and active, and, like all his countrymen, an excellent climber. Seizing a projecting brick in one hand, and planting a foot firmly against the wall, he gave himself a great swing, until the other hand caught hold of the verandah railing. The rest was easy, and in another minute he had reached the window of his room. A nightlight shed a dim glimmer from a side-table, and on his writing-desk in the centre of the room stood a large oil-lamp, which was burning low down into the socket.

* Kumbakharna was the brother of the demon Ravana, king of Lanka. This monster slept six months at a time, and could only be roused by driving a herd of wild elephants over his body. He was slain by Rama of Ayodhya during his famous invasion of Lanka.

"I shall go to bed at once," said Krishna to himself; "my mind will be more composed to-morrow. How lucky I had not sent away these letters!" he muttered, as his eye fell upon the two unsealed epistles on the table, and a twinge of remorse passed through him; "I shall write others in a more cautious style to-morrow. O Radha! what is there that I would not do for thy love?"

The young man's passion again returned in all its former violence, and he strode up and down the room, muttering wildly to himself, and pausing now and then as he passed the window, from which he could see the house of Lahory looming large and black among the trees. He could not see Radha's room, but a faint reflection of light from the side where the zenana was, sufficed to feed his flame, and his mind was full of the image of his love as she stood in all her unadorned beauty looking forth into the night. Again he attempted to calm himself; and turning towards the bookcase, where his little library was kept, he was about to take down a volume when his glance fell upon Chakwi.

Yes, Chakwi, who sat in a chair fast asleep, with her head leaned back against the side of the bookcase. The duster which she still held in her hand told how she had been employed; and having sat down to sigh over her grief when her work was finished, she had fallen fast asleep. Her cheeks still bore traces of tears, and her face, even in sleep, wore an expression of subdued sadness. The contrast between this plain little woman and the vision of loveliness which he had just beheld, raised angry feelings in Krishna's mind. Unfortunate wretch that he was, to be linked to a creature that had no more beauty than a hen, and no more soul than the goose whose name she bore! What evil had ever he done, to be thus mis-mated? It was Hindooism that had done it—Hindooism that had cursed him with such a wife—ay, the very Hindooism with which he was now about to make a base peace, and to which he was going to sacrifice both his conscience and his honour. Krishna almost tottered under the sense of his own weakness, and he would have liked to fall upon his knees that instant and pray for strength against temptation.

"Sree Vishnu-jee!" muttered Krishna, forgetting his Theism; "what can have brought her here? It is a trick of the wanton to foist herself upon me; or could my father have thus advised her? What shall I do? Shall I rouse her and send her away, or shall I go to bed and take no notice of her?"

He sat down upon a chair opposite Chakwi and shifted the lamp so that the light fell full upon her face. After all, the girl was not bad-looking. Plain she was, but her face did not lack expression; and her figure, though inclined to dumpiness, was rounded and graceful.

"She is winsome enough in her own way," thought Krishna, "and might be lovable, too, under other circumstances. Poor girl! I wonder if she cares much about me now? I remember how fond she used to be when I would make love to her in a childish way about the time our marriage was celebrated. I used to think her both pretty and amiable in those days, and I daresay we might have been living happily enough as man and wife, had I not fallen in love with Radha. I wonder if I should waken her?"

He screwed up the lamp, and made a slight noise upon the table, but Chakwi still slept on.

"There is as much difference between her and Radha as there is between two orders of beings. A man might worship Radha with little danger of idolatry, for there must be some spark of divinity in one so beautiful. Chakwi, here, is a creature of earth; to mind the house and bear children is her sphere: but it seems to me almost sacrilege to associate such ideas with Radha. If she were mine, I would worship her with veiled face at a distance, until the goddess repaid the devotion of her votary by the beatific vision of her perfections. This creature has no soul, no sensibility."

A change came over Chakwi's face, and for a moment the girl looked absolutely beautiful. A smile played upon her lips, showing her pearly teeth, and a laughing dimple lurked in each of her smooth, round cheeks. "O Krishna! how could you have neglected me so long," she murmured, in her sleep; "but it will only make our love sweeter now—will it not, my husband?"

Krishna turned away his head and smothered a sigh

of pity. "Poor child!" he thought, "it is even worse than I had imagined; there was nothing but her love wanting to complete my misfortunes. I am not the only sufferer, then, from this accursed union. How happy she might have been if she had only got a husband of her own stamp! This union with Radha will make her still more miserable. Would to God I saw some way out of my perplexities!"

At that moment, as if in answer to his prayers, Chakwi opened her eyes and looked wildly about her. "What is this? where am I? how came I here?" cried she hastily, while crimson blood crowded to her dusky cheeks as her gaze fell upon her husband.

Seeing that Krishna made no answer, the girl began to tremble violently, and to cast uneasy glances towards the door. "I will go away," she said; "I did not know you were here. I must have fallen asleep in the evening when I came in to put your room straight;" and Chakwi rose and was moving away with faltering steps.

"Stay a little, Chakwi," said Krishna, in a kindly tone: "you have not spoken to me since I came home. Surely my wife is glad that I am come back again. Is it not so?"

"I am glad if you and my father are glad," said Chakwi, hesitatingly.

"That is but a cold welcome, Chakwi," said Krishna, half petulantly; "you are not afraid of your husband, girl, because he has turned Brahmist!"

"I should not be afraid of my husband whatever he

had turned," said Chakwi, in a decided tone: "but I am sorry that Krishna Gossain has forsaken his father's faith."

"That is as much as to say that I have never been a husband to you," retorted Krishna; "but, my poor girl, I can bear your reproaches. It was an evil destiny, Chakwi, that linked you and me together."

"And am I to blame for that?" asked Chakwi, indignantly. "Do you suppose that my father's daughter, if she had been left to her free will, would have laid down her love to be thus slighted? Evil destiny indeed! Have I ever placed myself in your way, or prevented you from choosing your own loves, or claimed aught of a wife's regards at your hand? I have done everything that woman could to please your dislike, except to die; and I shall do that next, and before long too, for my heart is nearly broken:" and the poor girl buried her face in her hands, and burst into a torrent of tears.

"Nay, but Chakwi, forgive me," said Krishna, unnerved at the sight of her grief; "I have not said anything to hurt you, and it is not right of you to distress me in my present condition. You know, Chakwi, that I am now an outcast from Hindoo society, and you, my dear one, would be treated in the same fashion if you were to call me husband, and so it is better for us both that we should remain just as we are, and see what time brings about; we may both be happier in the future than we have been in the past. Believe me, it was because I was unwilling that you should in any way suffer from your relationship to me, that I have not sent for you before this time."

"A wife has no caste but her husband's," sobbed Chakwi; "if you were to become a beggar, I would follow you, happier in your love, than if I were made consort to the Padshah of Delhi. But why should I say that? It is not my part to proffer my love to you, and it is not right that I should be here now. You may think that I have come on purpose to see you, but Mother Gunga is my witness that I had no such intention."

"Go then, Chakwi," said Krishna, releasing her, "for my mind is too troubled and too uncertain at present for me to know what I should say to you, or what I should leave unsaid. Believe me, I shall do what I think best for both our happinesses. Go, and do not be a stranger in my rooms any more."

So saying, he dismissed her with a kiss, and Chakwi went away to her room with a lighter heart than she had known for many a day. Krishna's demeanour had seemed to her more kind and grave than ever she had noticed it before, and she did not doubt that before long he would return her love. So she fell asleep and dreamed again the dream of blissful reconciliation with her husband which she had dreamed a little before under her husband's eye. Poor Chakwi! the only solace for the sorrows of her blighted young life was to be found among the confused joys of dreamland.

"Still deeper in the mire," muttered Krishna to himself, as he paced rapidly up and down his chamber; "where is all this to end? Just at the very moment when my heart was burning for love of Radha, comes this girl to torture me. And yet I could not speak unkindly to her, and the poor fool goes away puffed up to the skies with hopes that can never be realised. Well, after all, she is my wife; and even if I were married to Radha, she would still be my wife, and entitled to a share of my regard. I must speak more kindly to the poor child for Radha's sake as well as for my own, for it must be upon the ground of her love for me that I shall beg her to put up quietly with a second marriage;" and when he had sufficiently perplexed his brain by thinking over and over again upon the untoward condition of his love affairs, Krishna flung himself on his couch and at last found refuge in sleep.

The sun was high in the heavens before Krishna was astir next morning. After the excitement of the previous night, he felt as one who rises from a debauch: his temples were racked by headache; his veins throbbed with an irregular, feverish heat; his tongue was parched, and clave to the roof of his mouth; and his brain was dizzy, and incapable of thought. He was utterly miserable, but he could not well tell why. Was it because he had the assurance of Radha's affection? No, for this was what he had set his heart upon beyond all things on earth. Was it because he felt himself wavering in the faith, and because his zeal for the theistic creed was rapidly melting away? If it was this, he had not yet gone too far, and he could easily retrace his steps. But he could not tell whether he wished to break with Hindooism or with Theism that morning. He looked from the window, and saw the woody valleys of Panch Pahar, so green, and cool, and refreshing, that he wished he might go and live in the recesses of the forest, away from all these cares that were chafing him, like a Rishi of olden days. The Gungaputra came gliding slowly down the bottom of the valley, sweeping with its waters now the one side now the other, as the robes of a queen are tossed from side to side as she paces the palace hall; throwing up huge mounds of silt as it slowly doubles the corner of Milkiganj; then taking breath, as it were, and gathering strength for a dash upon the bathing-ghats of Dhupnagar; pausing at the Kalee point to undermine a little more of the crumbling rock upon which stands the deserted pagoda, looking as if it were almost ready to topple over into the stream; and, finally, hurrying with a swift ripple and an inviting murmur over the treacherous fords of Ghatghar, until it disappeared behind the Rajah's palace. The waters sparkled so limpidly and clearly in the sunshine that Krishna felt an uncontrollable desire to bathe in the river. Bathing in the Gungaputra is so much of a religious ceremony among orthodox Hindoos that Krishna had purposely abstained from doing it, performing his ablutions in a deserted tank that occupied a sequestered corner of the priest's compound. Oh why, of all the millions of his countrymen who had washed away their guilt in the holy waters of the Gungaputra, was he the only one who could not "from sin and dark pollution free, bathe in its blameless waters clear?" But still the river wooed him as it glided past, and eager to seek some respite from his thoughts, he started up, and calling upon Bechoo to attend him, walked briskly down the slope towards the water-side.

The walk, the free morning air, the twittering of the birds, the murmur of the trees, and the sweet smell of flowers, soon raised Krishna's spirits. It was the first time that he had been out of doors by day since his memorable return to Dhupnagar, and he felt like a captive who has regained his liberty after a weary confinement. The women coming home from the river, each with a pitcher of water gracefully balanced upon her head, looked askance at the handsome young man, and coquettishly drew their *sarrees* over their faces. Krishna had been so little about Dhupnagar for the last four or five years that few of the villagers would have known him, but for old Bechoo, who trotted at his heels. As he passed the gate of Walesbyganj, Afzul Khan, who was outside watching the grooming of his favourite mare, eyed him with a jealous scowl, and turning round whispered something, with a scornful laugh to Agha, who was sitting behind him smoking. Krishna noted this rudeness, but could only account for it as a piece of insolence peculiar to bigoted Muhammadans. As yet he had no conception that the Mussulman regarded him as a possible rival, or that a high-caste Brahmini maiden could be aught in the eyes of an unclean kine-killer. But Krishna knew not how little Afzul recked of the distinctions of religion or caste when his passions were to be gratified.

The bathing-ghat of a sacred river is one of the most curious and picturesque of Indian scenes. In the stream, and upon the banks, are groups of Hindoos of all ages and sexes. Here is a religious mendicant who has measured the road from Dhupnagar to the river upon his hands and knees for some sin, real or imaginary, and will continue to do so every day as long as his wretched life is spared. Mark how feebly, how abjectly, he creeps down to the water's edge, and how lightly he springs to his feet after the first plunge, as if his guilt had been all washed away. There stands a sorrowful crowd of mourners around the *charpai* (four-legged couch) of an old Brahmin who has been brought down to the river to die. Already the *domes* are gathering the wood and digging the pit for his funeral pyre, but the old man never flinches or removes his eye from the river. "To the water," he mutters — "to the water. He who dies fasting with his members immersed in the holy tide is never born again, and attains equality with Brahma. To the water with me, my sons." And cautiously looking round to see that no policeman is watching, the sons tenderly lift the old man and hold him with the lower part of his body immersed in the water until his latest breath is drawn.

Slim Hindoo maidens stand up to the waist in water, or dive boldly into the depths; others are wringing the moisture from their long black tresses, and casting arch coquettish glances at a knot of young bathers of the opposite sex, who ogle them in turn, and startle them by diving down and reappearing suddenly in the midst. Heedless of this folly, a stately Brahmin, with fair skin and lofty forehead, who has walked all the way from Gapshapganj to pay his morning's homage to the Gungaputra, stands in an ecstasy of devotion, his eyes fixed so steadily upon the crystal stream flowing rapidly past that he is lost to all sense of what is going on around him. Up and down the bank strut three or four young libertines, distinguished by their perfumed locks and foppish garments, whose only business seems to be to watch the gracefully-moulded forms of the girls as they come up from the river, their wet garments scarcely serving to conceal the charms of their persons. These young fellows belong to the dissolute household of the Ghatghar Rajah; and the decent villagers scarcely seek to dissemble their disgust at such conduct, and would gladly beat them away from the ghat with bamboos, if it were not for fear of the Rajah's vengeance.

As Krishna approached the ghat, all eyes were turned upon him in astonishment. A few of the loungers made way for him with a salaam, and stood with lengthened countenances to watch how one so strongly suspected of heresy would comport himself. The girls suddenly became grave as the whisper reached them, "'Tis Krishna, the priest's son." The young men on the bank assumed an air of inquisitive gravity, the mourners raised their eyes for an instant to look at him, and even the pious Brahmin ceases from his orisons to eye the impious man who had shaken off the old gods. Was ever such impiety seen, as for an unbeliever thus to pollute the holy river with his presence? What wonder would it be though the goddess in her wrath were to clutch him in her arms and drag him down for ever into her fathomless abysses? Yet it was a pity that so goodly a young man should have gone so far wrong; for he was a goodly young man, as everybody acknowledged, and as he waded into the centre of the current, and exposed his broad chest to its full force, the spirit of the stream might well have fallen in love with him as with the grandfather of Bishnu of old. " Will he do *puja* (worship)?" whispered each to the other as they saw him enter the water; but no *puja* did Krishna do. On the contrary, without prayer or prostration, he threw himself boldly into the middle of the current, and struck out stoutly against the stream. All Bengalees swim like water-dogs, and Krishna had all the skill, and more than the daring, of his countrymen. As he buffeted the stream his spirits rose with the exercise, the lassitude left him, and he felt like a new man by the time that he pulled up out of breath opposite Milkiganj. He was now out of eyeshot of the worshippers, and felt more at ease; and so he scampered out to the bank and began drying himself, although the exuberance of his animal spirits was such that he could scarcely keep himself from plunging again into the tide.

"No wonder though they worship the river!" he ejaculated in his enthusiasm; "who would not feel his heart stirred within him at the sight of so noble a stream? The fires of hell were but even now gnawing my heart, and after a plunge in the water I feel as if all pollution had departed from me. Of course I can account for the change upon physical grounds; but who can wonder that the ignorant should attribute their refreshment to divine properties in the river? In which of his works is the majesty of the Creator more apparent than in the endless flood that rolls before me? O Daughter of the Mountain!" added he, falling unconsciously into the language of his childhood's prayer, "I had rather be a dweller in thy waters than a monarch, the sound of whose war-steeds' bells scatter kings in consternation."

"Well done, sir!" cried a voice behind him; "may your prayers be grateful as *amrit* (ambrosia) to the gods! I wish I had my hands upon those blackguards and brokers who said that my old friend Ramanath's son had turned Christian; I would soon make them eat dirt. Give me your hand, Krishna, and let me welcome you back to Dhupnagar. I heard of the rough reception which these churls of Sudras gave you; but never mind them—these dogs can never forgive us for being of better caste than themselves. But I am glad that you have not fallen from the old faith, for who will remain a Hindoo, if the Brahmin becomes a *mlctcha* (a foreigner, an outcast)?"

And Kristo Baboo, for it was he who spoke, cordially grasped the young man's hand. The Baboo had been coming along the bank from visiting one of his tenants, when he overheard the idolatrous exclamation which Krishna had inadvertently let slip from him.

Krishna was too much surprised and confused to make a distinct reply, far less to correct the mistake into which the Baboo had naturally fallen. Besides, of all men, Kristo was the one before whom he was least anxious to parade his new religion; for not only was the Baboo a Hindoo of bigoted orthodoxy, but what was more, in Krishna's mind, he was the father of Radha. So Krishna muttered an inaudible reply, and in a louder tone hoped that the Baboo and all his family were well.

"Well! ay, as well as people can be who stand between a grasping Government and a beggarly tenantry. May Yama choke me if I don't think the landlords were better under the old Moghals than under the English rule, with all its fuss about justice and equity! Provided they got their money, the Moghals never asked how it was collected; but the last time I bambooed a ryot who was backward with his rent, the Magistrate Sahib made such an uproar that it cost me the building of a female school before I was *safa-karróed* (white-washed). But come along, Krishna, and give me your good company up the road to Dhupnagar."

And taking the young man's arm, the Baboo walked on, unburdening himself as he went of his many grievances, which were all reducible to two heads, his own impecuniosity, and the presumption of his more wealthy though lower-born neighbours. Upon this theme Kristo could talk by the hour; nor was Krishna sorry that he was not called upon to put in a word, for he felt that he ought to correct the Baboo's mistake about his orthodoxy, and yet he strangely lacked courage to begin. Was he the man, he kept asking himself, as he blushed up to his ears at the thought, who had burned to publish his faith in the faces of hostile thousands, and yet was afraid to confess it to one mild Hindoo, who at the most would only go away from him in disgust? But he was thankful Kristo's tongue never halted to give him an opportunity of saying anything about himself.

"Ay, ay, there they go! ride on, and may you never pause till you gallop over the brink of *Patala* (hell)!" cried Kristo, apostrophising Afzul Khan, as the young Muhammadan cantered past them on his way to the Ghatghar ford; "it is my two hundred acres of rice land that you have got your legs astride of. If the gods took the slightest interest in this world nowadays, they would throw down that kennel about the ears of these kine-killing dogs. If folks grow irreligious, the gods are mostly to blame for it themselves, for they don't do half the miracles that they used to do in the old times. I'm sure it wouldn't be much trouble to Siva to glorify himself by inflicting some notable calamity upon those accursed *mletchas* (foreigners) who took away my land, and it would be as good as the conversion of half the Gungaputra district. But for all that, I'm heartily glad, my son, that you have not gone astray among their new-fangled religions. It is all very well for these *kyasths* and *chamars* (writers and shoemakers) who have got no caste worth keeping, to make a merit of giving it up ; but the Gossains of Dhupnagar are not such crack-brained fanatics. I felt as glad, for my old friend Ramanath's sake, when I heard you at your prayers this morning, as if you had been my own son."

Again Krishna essayed to set the Baboo right, but still his courage failed him, and he endeavoured to make some commonplace remark about the genial weather and the favourable prospects of the *boru*, or winter crops. This set Kristo off into a tirade of invectives against his tenantry, who, though they were fattening upon his land, and making fortunes out of good harvests, would hardly pay a pice of rent until they were taken into court for arrears; while the Government Collector would neither want the land revenue nor allow him to put forth his hand to help himself to his own. This subject was quite sufficient to engross the Baboo's attention for the rest of the way; and he was still declaiming when they reached the temple gate.

Old Ramanath, sitting smoking in his usual place, beheld the two in company with great inward satisfaction, and chuckled to himself as he saw his plot in a fair way to be accomplished. He hastened down to the gate, and greeted Kristo and his son with the greatest cordiality, giving the latter his morning blessing, and entreating the Baboo to come up and rest in the shade of the temple porch. Krishna escaped to his own room, but he could see from the window that the seniors were carrying on a very agreeable conversation; and before Kristo Baboo took his leave, Ramanath had occasion to pay a visit to the house, and returned to the temple with a heavy weight in the corner of his waist-cloth. From which Krishna had little difficulty in concluding that a monetary transaction had been effected between the rich priest and the impecunious Baboo.

CHAPTER XIV.

A GIFT FROM THE GREEKS.

PROSUNNO, the lawyer, was hurrying through the bazaar in the early morning towards the house of Three Shells, the money-lender. Since he had fallen under Three Shells' displeasure, on the day when their attempt to excite the Brahmins against the priest's family had so signally failed, Prosunno had not ventured into the mahajan's presence—not that Three Shells had not frequently sent for him, but Prosunno had found it convenient to stay for a week at Gapshapganj, where he had many briefs in the Dipty's court, and to be otherwise engaged abroad when the money-lender required his presence. But the time had now come, Prosunno thought, when he might safely present himself before his patron. Three Shells' wrath must have cooled by this time; and the lawyer knew that the money-lender would have as much difficulty in dispensing with his services as he himself would have in parting with Three Shells' patronage. Each was mutually useful to the other, and there were secrets between them which could not be confided to the ears of a third person. So Prosunno had screwed up his courage to the point of facing the money-lender, all the more easily that he had something of importance to communicate; and he had set out at sunrise for the mahajan's house.

Even at that early hour the good folks of Dhupnagar were mostly astir. Some were hastening to the tanks to perform their ablutions and morning devotions, while others, more religiously disposed, were setting out for the Gungaputra to wash away the sins of the past four-and-twenty hours in its sacred waters. Many sat in the doors of their houses enjoying their hookhas, and looking too indolent and sleepy to return the lawyer's greetings. Active housewives were coming back from the tanks, each balancing a pitcher of water upon her head with one hand, while with the other she supported a child upon her side in the awkward Indian fashion. Some women were plastering the mud walls of their houses with cow-dung, which would serve as fuel to cook with when dried, and others were busy grinding rice for the breakfast with pestles kept in motion by the foot. Business had hardly commenced in Dhupnagar, for the tradesfolk were either dressing or bathing. Only greedy Ram Lall, the oilman, who never missed a chance of turning an anna, had opened shop, and was sitting among his jars looking out for a customer. The oilman greeted Prosunno with a salaam, which the lawyer, wishing to have the old man's good word with his son, the Dipty, ceremoniously returned.

Prosunno, finding the money-lender's porter astir, despatched him to inquire if his master was visible; and in a minute after, Gopee, the mahajan's clerk—an ugly, mis-shapen Bengalee, with no neck, and a face that seemed to be looking constantly askance at the sky—came forth and invited Prosunno into Three Shells' presence. Gopee was not permitted to enjoy a large share of his master's confidence. He kept the regular accounts between Three Shells and his clients, acted as his master's deputy in transacting small advances, collected interest, and kept a sharp look-out that the borrowers made away with none of the hypothecated property. But Three Shells kept many accounts that were not for Gopee's inspection, and it was one of the clerk's great grievances that the mahajan should have so many secrets which he could not succeed in penetrating. Gopee, however, concealed his curiosity under an affectation of indifference; and Three Shells generally spoke of him as a negligent lad, who took no interest in his work, although he could be careful enough when he pleased. Although Gopee's stated salary was a trifle, his perquisites were very considerable. No application for money to the master would succeed unless the man had been previously propitiated by a present. Out of every loan Gopee squeezed his *dasturi* (commission), and took a percentage upon every payment of interest that came through his hands.

When a borrower was unmindful of Gopee's interest, the clerk would pay him a visit, and hint that Three Shells was requiring his principal at an early date; or he would object to such and such property upon which money had been advanced being employed in such and such a way. A present would at once occur to the debtor as the readiest method of getting rid of the clerk; and Gopee would pocket the *bakshish*, and return home well satisfied with the results of his stratagem.

"Well, Gopee, what is doing, and how is the master's *mizaj* (temper) this morning?" asked Prosunno. "Is the worthy Three Shells in any better humour than when I saw him last?"

"The master is well contented," said Gopee, "and begs you to come to him immediately. He has asked frequently for you, Baboo, and said he was sorry you had gone to Gapshapganj without telling him, as there were some things he wanted done in the Dipty's court."

Prosunno was ushered through the money-lender's office into the little room beyond, where Three Shells sat busied with his papers. The mahajan's greeting was as cordial as if no difference had ever occurred between them.

"Why, Prosunno Baboo, what a stranger you are!" said Three Shells, jocosely; "you have not been away on pilgrimage to Benares, have you? I sent for you two or three times, but your servants always said you were from home."

"I was obliged to be at Gapshapganj, where I had several great rent cases to plead," answered Prosunno, in an apologetic tone, as he wondered in his own mind whether it was possible that the furious demon whom he had last seen could be identical with the smooth-tongued person who was sitting before him with half-closed eyes and bland countenance. Somehow Prosunno could not help thinking that the former expression was the one that sat most naturally upon the money-lender. "But I was not forgetful of your business, sir," he added. "I have made the inquiries you wished respecting that packet."

"Gopee," said the money-lender, raising his voice, "the quarterly interest upon the Nawab of Panch Pahar's bond is due to-day; go and give my respects to his highness, and say that you have come for payment. And, Gopee, you had better take the porter with you, for the Panch Pahar people are often readier with their cudgels than with their purses. Not that the prying scoundrel would be much worse for a good beating," he added in a lower tone.

"And now, Prosunno, what of the packet? where is it, and how did you hear of it?" asked Three Shells, eagerly, as soon as the clerk was out of hearing. "I hope you did not let out that I was interested about it in your inquiries."

"You see, sir," began Prosunno, "old Gangooly, the village headman, was attending the Dipty's court at Gapshapganj about the Gaogong robbery, and we both fell a-talking about the priest and his son Krishna Baboo. Gangooly has always fawned upon these Gossains, and he began to boast about his intimacy with old Ramanath. I had just been saying that the priest carried his head higher than his neck would well stretch, and that he counted the Brahmins of Dhupnagar as little better than his dogs.

"'Speak for yourself,' said the father of asses; 'I have known Ramanath Gossain for forty years, and I never heard him say an evil word against a good neighbour. But he is a wiser man than to choose his friends among you law kites. It was only last night that Ramanath sent for me to the temple and asked me to take charge of an important packet of papers; but you won't catch him putting such confidence in any of you lawyers.'

"'And what might these papers be about?' asked I, pretending to make light of them. 'Some serious matter, I warrant; the title-deeds of a *katha* * of jungle-land, or the rights of some tumble-down, clay hut.'

"'Nay,' said Gangooly; 'but they are papers of the utmost importance, and Ramanath said the packet was not to be opened until his death, and that the contents should then be dealt with according to the enclosed directions. I am to take the greatest care of them, and keep them among the village papers, and they are to be handed over to my successor if I should die in the

---

* A *katha*, the unit of Bengalee land measure, is equal to 320 square cubits. Twenty of these *kathas* make a *bigha*.

meantime. So I have put them in my great teak chest, and told my son, Gopal Chunder, to take as good care of the papers as if they were the *pottahs* (deeds) of his ancestral property; and Ramanath said, too, that I was not to gossip about them, so you must never mention the packet.'

"'And a most trustworthy person you are, babbling to me all this time,' said I; 'if you go on chattering, it will be no more of a secret in Dhupnagar before sunset than the rape of Sita.'

"'Nay, but,' said Gangooly, 'I have only told it to you, who are a discreet person, and to my own wife, who is as free from gossip as any woman in Dhupnagar. The gods forbid that I should be a tale-bearer, for, as the holy writings say, it is better to take a vow of silence than to make mischief by babbling.' Of course," concluded Prosunno, "he will go on in this way until he has told the whole town; but if you want to know what is in the packet, Gangooly can tell you no more about it than I can. Still some way might be devised, if you were very anxious."

"Not at all," said the mahajan, carelessly; "I only wanted to assure myself that Ramanath had not neglected a little matter about which we were talking. We had a monetary transaction together, and Ramanath wished to place some bonds in my hands as security; but I thought it would look better if they were deposited with a third party, as they relate to the temple lands. The bonds are assigned to me, if anything were to befall our excellent friend Ramanath, which I sincerely pray the gods to avert."

"The gods avert it!" echoed Prosunno, marvelling in his own mind what had occurred to make the mahajan all at once so friendly to the priest; "but still, sir, I think I could manage to get a look at the documents if you wished it. I could take an impression of the seal, and close the packet up again so neatly that no one would ever know it had been opened."

"I forbid you to think of such a thing!" cried Three Shells, angrily, "unless you wish to part with my patronage altogether. What! shall you or I presume to doubt the word of so holy a man as Ramanath Gossain? But what about the robbery you were talking of?"

"Two men broke into the ryot of Gaogong's house, and carried off a bag of two hundred rupees, which the ryot had borrowed from you the day before. The fellow kept his bed half dead with fright, and allowed the robbers to escape with their plunder."

"And I shall lose my money," said Three Shells, quietly; "well, it can't be helped, and I have a bill of sale upon his oxen. And what said the Dipty about the robbery? Has that mirror of wisdom and fountain of justice been able to find out the thieves?"

"Nay," said Prosunno, "he has got it into his head that young Afzul Khan, the Subadar's son, is the culprit, because one of the thieves spoke with a Hindustani accent. I took the liberty of representing to the Dipty that it was more likely Sonthals from above the passes; but he is too conceited in his own opinion to notice good advice."

"And you were a fool to do anything of the sort, Prosunno," said the money-lender, testily; "the Dipty knows better than you do. Is not that whelp of the Muhammadans a notorious *badmash*? Did he not beat me—*me*, with a bamboo when I went to crave my interest from him? Is he not a night-walker, and a gambler, and a drinker of *arrack* (native rum)? and who is more likely to commit robbery than such a fellow? You ought to know that as well as I do, Prosunno."

"What a fool I was not to have remembered the young man's bad character!" Prosunno readily answered. "Now that I think of it, I have not the slightest doubt but he is the robber."

"I should think not, Prosunno," said Three Shells, rubbing his hands; "the matter is plain enough to any one who has his wits about him. And what is the Dipty going to do?"

"Nothing at present, except to watch Afzul Khan's movements. Jaddoo, the Dipty's orderly, is coming privately to Dhupnagar for that purpose."

"Ah, it would be well that you should see this Jaddoo, Prosunno, and strengthen his suspicions against Afzul Khan," said the mahajan in an indifferent tone. "Tell him to keep his eyes closely upon the young fellow, and not to go about fancying he sees thieves in every honest townsman who is abroad of a night. And you may give him a couple of rupees as *bakshish* from me, for there is no one in Dhupnagar more interested in the capture of these robbers than I am, or has more danger to fear from them. A poor lonely man like me, that has generally money lying about, and that keeps only a few servants, is but too good a prey for such housebreakers."

Prosunno promised to attend to these orders, although he was astonished at the readiness with which the mahajan had caught up the suspicion against Afzul Khan. Hitherto Three Shells had persisted that Sonthal *dakaits* were the perpetrators of the numerous robberies that had been committed throughout the district, and had flown into a passion when any one dared to insinuate that the guilty parties might be found nearer home. "The thief thinks himself the only honest man in the world," the money-lender would say to such persons; "and let those who would cast suspicion upon a neighbour look that there is no *chor* grass upon their own waist-cloths."

But a still greater surprise was in store for Prosunno, when Three Shells went on to unfold his intention of dedicating to the shrine of Dhupnagar a golden vessel worth two thousand rupees, to be used in the worship of the Linga. He was pricked in his conscience, Three Shells said in explanation, heaving a deep sigh; for he had imagined evil against the guileless son of a Brahmin, and he was now desirous of anticipating the displeasure of the gods by this act of religious merit. "Alas!" said Three Shells, shaking his head in deprecation of Prosunno's praises, "I am a weak sinful man, only too prone to fall from the paths of religion, and to be ensnared by the desire of wealth. And what saith the 'Panchatantra'? 'Whose are the riches that are disposed of neither in alms nor in useful deeds—are they mine or thine?' It is the nature of money to corrupt the heart. If it were not that so many people would be distressed thereby, gladly would I gather all my substance together, and, repairing to Benares, spend the rest of my life in meditation and prayer within its holy walls. O, Prosunno! when we are well and strong, our religious duty rests lightly upon us as a festal garland; but when we are lying at the last gasp on the banks of the Gungaputra, each petty neglect will hang upon us like a fetter of iron to clog our souls in their ascent to Paradise."

"Ah, sir," said Prosunno, unconsciously pitching his voice in the sing-song snuffle that the money-lender had adopted, "would that I had your piety! But it is not every one that can afford to gratify the gods in the same way as you do. I hope that I myself am not so unmindful of my religious duties as some are. In my humble way I gave fifty rupees in silver to the Dhurma Thakoor's shrine at Gapshapganj, under whose holy protection I have placed myself, only a fortnight ago. May my offering find acceptance!"

"And when does the Dhurma Thakoor's rascally

priest intend to redeem the mortgage I hold upon his property?" asked Three Shells, sharply, in his natural voice; "I cannot afford to have so much money lying out all these years at only fifteen per cent. As good make him a present of it at once. I shall sell him out to the bricks and mortar before long."

Prosunno ventured to interpose that it was difficult to distrain temple property.

"But he has family lands of his own, then," snapped Three Shells; "we must have the debt transferred to them. Give him a little more tether, Prosunno—a little more tether, and I warrant he will go to the full length of the chain; and then, when we have his property fairly under our hands, we shall milk him, Prosunno, so long as the skin covers his bones."

"Certainly, sir," said Prosunno, chuckling at the idea of fleecing the priest of the Dhurma Thakoor, notwithstanding he himself was a devotee of the shrine; "I shall soon arrange all that to your satisfaction."

"And there are those papers about the houses at Bhutpore to be attended to," said Three Shells. "You must really try, Prosunno, to get some one to swear to the dead man's signature. Without witnesses, the money is as much lost as if it had been thrown into the Gungaputra."

"Oaths are up," said Prosunno, mournfully, "ever since the Magistrate Sahib transported Nando, the barber, for swearing about the sudden death of his father-in-law. I could hardly get a witness in Gapshapganj

last week when I was defending the Nawab of Panch
Pahar in a charge of deforcement. Old Hurrish, who
has done business for me since I began to practise, has
made a little fortune, and begins to cry out about his
conscience if I offer him less than ten rupees in a civil
case."

"Well, well, do your best," said Three Shells, benig-
nantly, "and you needn't make any secret about the
golden goblet that I am going to give to the temple.
The cup is coming up from Calcutta in a day or two,
and the townsfolk may as well hear of it from you as
from any other body. Not that I wish my gifts to be
blazoned abroad in the bazaar, for it is the favour of
the gods, not the praise of men, that I desire. The
hypocrite, O Prosunno, is as the crocodile, who, while
pretending to sleep on the sunny bank, slyly keeps a
watchful eye fastened upon his prey; but the truly
virtuous man who gets no credit for his good actions, is
dead even while he liveth. What would it profit the unworthy Tin Cowry, the mahajan, though his neighbours
should say, 'Lo! how religious a man, how charitable
to the poor, how pious to the gods!' if he felt that his
face was black before the shining ones? Nevertheless,
Prosunno, it would ill become me to say to a faithful
servant like you, tell this, and conceal that; so I leave
you free to say what you list about the matter, remembering ever that nothing tends so much to stir up good
works among men as the quiet, unostentatious example
of a neighbour."

Prosunno took his departure, lauding loudly the good fortune that had made him the means of conveying to his fellow-townsmen the first news of the mahajan's munificence. The lawyer's brains were in a state of hopeless perplexity as he came forth into the bazaar. He did not know what to think of his patron's altered demeanour; nor could he conjecture to what the change was due, or what would be the result so far as he himself was concerned. "Let me see," said Prosunno, standing up before a shop-door and thoughtfully scratching his head; "he has either begun to fear the gods, or he is shamming: that is safe so far. Well, if he has begun to fear the gods, he has committed some crime. But what could that crime be? He could hardly have murdered anybody here without my knowledge. And why should he trouble himself thus to dissemble before me? And why should he spend so much as two thousand rupees, when two hundred spent in the same way would make a saint of the greatest sinner in Dhupnagar? And why—but what is the use of raising questions that cannot be answered? Such a change from the swearing, murderous *rakshasa* (demon), that was ready to take my life the other day, to the sleek pietist who looks as if he would not sneeze without invoking the name of Rama—I can't believe it; surely I must be dreaming! Will any one slap me on the back that I may know if I am awake?"

Prosunno uttered this last ejaculation aloud, and was rolling his eyes vacantly about him as if in search of somebody to solve his doubts, when a smart blow with a bamboo quarter-staff across the shoulders sent him reeling among Ram Lall, the oilman's, pots and jars. Gathering himself angrily up, he checked the torrent of imprecations that rose to his lips when he saw that his assailant was the ex-trooper, who, swaggering along the bazaar in attendance on his young master, had heard the lawyer's exclamation, and had only been too glad to gratify his request.

"*Bakshish*, master lawyer, for the blow," said Agha, with a grin, as he held out his hand; "surely a gentleman like you would never bid a poor man work for nothing. If I did not lay on hard enough to satisfy you, have at you again with all my heart."

"You saw him, Ram Lall—you saw the Muhammadan knock me down," said Prosunno, appealing to the oilman; "you will swear to the assault when called upon."

"And you will swear, Afzul Baba, that you heard the fellow bid me," said Agha, laughing in the loud Afghan fashion, which more resembles the neighing of a horse than the cachinnations of a human being. "You are like the man that cried, 'Come, sweet Death!' when Death was beyond the mountain; but 'Begone, fell demon!' when Azrael looked in at the door. Let this be a warning to you not to cry out for being knocked down another time unless you wish to be taken at your word."

And the two Muhammadans went striding down the

street with their dragoon swagger, laughing like mischievous children at the lawyer's annoyance, and elbowing everybody out of the way with cool insolence. Quiet Hindoos crossed the street to avoid them, and such women as had any pretensions to prettiness covered up their faces, or shrank trembling into the doorways. They formed a curious contrast, the tall and slim, but muscular and well-formed youth, and the elderly trooper, whose back was bent and neck contorted by the wounds he had received from the Sikh lancers. But old as he was, Agha delighted in mischief as much as a schoolboy, and he was chuckling with glee at the success of his practical joke, utterly regardless of the offence he had given to the revengeful Bengalee lawyer.

Ram Lall did his best to soothe Prosunno, brushing the dust off his clothes, and trying to console him with the reflection that the rascals were only Muhammadans, and knew no better. But Prosunno was not to be appeased. He made a formal entry of the assault in his memorandum-book, and carefully minuted the evidence of Ram Lall and the other bystanders. All were indignant at the disgraceful treatment of a Brahmin by foul Mussulman *mletchas*, and said that it was enough to bring a judgment upon the aggressors. Brijo, the butterman, however, who was an inveterate joker, and had lately lost a plea by Prosunno's exertions on behalf of his adversary, deponed that he could swear to nothing but that he had heard the lawyer inviting somebody to strike him, and that he was just thinking of obliging him himself when the Afghan interposed to save him the trouble. To this Prosunno retorted that the speaker was a liar, and a broker, and the brother of a naughty sister; that his wife was a procuress of abortion; and that his grandfather had been guilty of incest; and Brijo responding by similar calumnies against the lawyer's relations, a wordy duel arose, and the neighbours speedily began to quarrel among themselves in their zealous attempts to reconcile the disputants. In the midst of the uproar, Prosunno, remembering that his professional dignity was compromised by taking part in such a squabble, and also that in case of blows he would be more likely as a neutral to be retained as counsel for one or other of the parties, stole quietly away to his own house.

"They are going to Rutton Pal, the spirit-seller's," said Prosunno, as he saw the Muhammadans at the end of the village; "but never mind, that young gentleman may go down the street of Dhupnagar with a policeman on each side of him before many cold weathers come and go. If I were his counsel on the trial he should hang for it. It might nearly be worth my pains to make friends with him, on the chance of getting the management of his defence. But I must go home and think over Three Shells' conversion."

CHAPTER XV.

A MORNING AT RUTTON PAL'S.

WE must now follow the two Muhammadans on their morning visit to Rutton Pal's spirit-shop, where neither Agha nor his young master was a stranger. The Mussulman soldier, habituated to the loose morals of a cantonment town, has less regard for the Prophet's prohibition of strong liquors than the Muhammadan civilian, whose faith in the Koran has not been shaken by contact with foreigners; and both Agha and Afzul would unblushingly take their seats under the thatched verandah before Rutton's shop, and quaff the abomination called rum under the eyes of all the respectable inhabitants of Dhupnagar. The Subadar was greatly distressed when he heard of this practice, and issued a stringent "garrison" order against resorting to Rutton's; but the "troops"—that is, Afzul and Agha—paid little attention to the old man's injunctions. As for Agha, he defended himself by urging the opinion of a Maulavi or Muhammadan doctor of divinity, who had assured him that the Prophet's prohibition—the peace of God be upon him and rest—did not apply to Indian *arrack* (rum), about which, not being brewed in Arabia, the Sent of Allah could have known nothing. But, had added the reverend casuist, as the practice of drinking even *arrack* partook of the semblance of transgression, he himself would take in hand the obtaining of a pardon for an annual consideration of a few rupees and a night's quarters whenever he should come the way of Walesbyganj. Fortified by this ghostly counsel, Agha went daily to Rutton's for his ration of spirits, and it only too frequently happened that his young master was disposed to bear him company.

Rutton Pal's shop stood at the end of the bazaar, near where the Gapshapganj road enters Dhupnagar. It was a large tumble-down house, or rather a collection of huts, full of all sorts of odd holes and corners, and wretched drinking-rooms lighted by narrow, iron-barred windows. Rutton not only sold spirits, but provided his customers with pipes of the still more intoxicating *ganja* and opium. The victims to the latter vice were easily distinguishable by their dull, leaden eyes almost buried in the sockets, their blanched and withered cheeks, and the careless, though careworn, aspects of their countenance. There were always three or four such debauchees squatted about Rutton's shop in a state of greater or less intoxication. To these poor wretches life was *kaif*, "the savouring of animal existence, the passive enjoyment of mere sense," as Captain Burton well renders it: a pleasant dream which would have been all happiness but for the recurrence of a waking nightmare, brought on by lack of the Lethean drug, and for the necessity of purchasing future pleasure by present toil. From being a resort for such persons, Rutton Pal's shop bore a bad character in Dhupnagar. Some drunken wretch with his head turned by the frenzy of *ganja* would occasionally rush forth into the street, armed with hook, or hatchet, or whatever other weapon came to hand, and, running amuck, would slay or wound such of the lieges as he encountered, until some one plucked up courage enough to shoot or cut him down. More than one robbery had been traced to Rutton's lodgers, among whom were numbered very doubtful characters of both sexes; and the respectable villagers often complained that so bad a house was tolerated by the authorities. But there was some cousinship between Rutton and old Ram Lall, the oilman, whose son the Dipty may have remembered the relationship when complaints came up before him. But though the Dhupnagar Brahmins inveighed loudly against Rutton and his calling, not a few of them quietly availed themselves of the private *entrée* to his premises. The fact was that in Dhupnagar, as in too many other Hindoo villages, the high-caste Brahmins were among Rutton Pal's best customers, and their patronage was all the more lucrative that they paid for secrecy as well as for the strong liquors which they drank; and Rutton Pal, like a judicious man, was never known to betray a patron.

Rutton, a bull-headed, frog-necked Hindoo, whose obese and greasy person was the fitting envelope of a bloated and slippery moral nature, placed a low stool for the two soldiers in a shady corner of the verandah, for he knew them to be customers who did not court concealment. Rutton Pal was less obsequious than his countrymen generally are, for he had a monopoly of the means of vice in the village, and his patrons cared little for politeness provided they were promptly served. But he greeted the two Muhammadans with a respectful salutation, for they were not only liberal paymasters, but violent and hot-tempered fellows, who were ever as ready to bestow a buffet as to settle a score. So the spirit-seller abandoned his other guests to the care of an assistant, and hastened in person to set a measure of liquor beside the troopers, and to fill a pair of his largest hookhas for their use. After sipping a little *arrack*, the two began to smoke in silence, Afzul lolling carelessly against the wall, and Agha sttting with his cynical face turned intently upwards, as if he were immersed in a deep study of the blackened joists and rafters which supported the roof of Rutton Pal's verandah. The Sikh lancer's stroke at Aliwal had distorted the muscles of Agha's neck so that the axis of his face formed a constant angle of forty-five degrees with the level of his right shoulder;

and a scar upon his left cheek—inflicted by private Ameer Jan of Walesby's Horse with a knife-hilt, in a debate concerning the respective merits of the clans of the Khyber Pass and of the Eusufzye valley—had writhed his mouth into a perpetual sneer, to which his innate ill-nature had given forcible expression. As he smoked, the older trooper drank draught after draught of the *arrack*, until his little eyes were beginning to twinkle with a fiery redness; nor did he, like Afzul, wash down each libation with a mouthful of cold water, as is the manner of oriental topers.

"And how fares your suit for the daughter of the infidel?" asked Agha, suddenly laying down his hookha, and turning his head stiffly in the direction of his young master.

"Bravely," replied Afzul, with a laugh; "my love comes about as much speed as the nightingale's wooing of the rose-tree. She came to the window last night and looked out into the moonlight, but her eyes never rested upon the slave of love, though she saw clearly that I was there. She carelessly dropped a sprig of *champak* blossoms just at my feet, and then turned coldly away to her room."

"And what idiotcy may a *champak* sprig portend?" said Agha, with a contemptuous whiff.

"May Allah make it clear! What know I about flowers? What was her tongue given her for, unless to speak? and there was no one to hear."

"I knew a man in the clan of the Wuzeer Kheyls,"

said Agha, musingly, and speaking rather to himself than to Afzul, "who could speak the language of flowers, and tell what the birds said to each other when they chirped among the boughs. When any man got a flower from a maiden, he went to this Wuzeerie, Karim Khan, to find out what it signified; and Karim would tell them the meaning in a rhyme, pat enough, I warrant you. Oh, he was a mad fellow, continually going about through the country maundering to himself and making verses. He once fell into the hands of a tribe with whom the Wuzeeries had a blood-feud, and the clansmen, of course, were going to kill him. But Karim took his lute and sang to them of the deeds of their forefathers, which so stirred up the spirits of their young men, that they snatched up their swords and ran ten miles into the Sikh territory to burn a couple of villages; and, what was more, they escorted Karim back in honour to his own clan, with a present of the two best cows taken in the foray."

"Wonderful man! I wish we had him here to fiddle old Kristo Baboo out of his daughter. Couldn't you send for him, Agha?"

"But he came to grief among the same people soon after," Agha continued. "He thought his music might stanch the blood-feud between them and his own clan, and so he made up a fine new song and set out to sing it in the enemy's village. But his pains were not so well paid this time, for they called him a meddling spy, and broke his lute across his sconce, until the poor wretch forgot his lay through fright, and was as mute as a parrot with its tongue cut out. So, when they saw that, they knocked out his brains with an axe, which was, on the whole, a wrong thing to do, for those who make verses are fools, and Allah himself guides people to whom he has not given sense enough to guide themselves. And you have never yet spoken to the infidel woman?"

"I have never had a chance," said Afzul, gloomily. "How can I speak to her with twenty feet of brick wall between us, unless I wished all who dwell in the Baboo's house to hear my love-speeches? May Shaitan confound all Hindoo fathers who lock up their daughters on an upper flat! If I could only get to the girl's ear, I warrant she would listen to me fast enough, for I know by her looks that she loves me. But one may wait some half-score of years without ever getting a chance of speaking to her."

"And by that time she will be an old woman, or the bed-fellow of some filthy Hindoo. Give her up, Miah, and your father and I will marry you to two or three Muslim damsels, who have more beauty in their little fingers than this Bengalee wench has in her whole body. Give her up: it is a shame for a Muhammadan and a trooper to bother his head about such a slave. I have seen a fairer sold in Cabul for half the price of an Afghan gelding."

"No, never, by Allah!" cried Afzul, jumping to his

feet, and striking his fist passionately against a pillar of Rutton Pal's verandah. "I would sooner see all your Muslim damsels in Jehannum. I never loved, and never will love, woman as I love this Hindoo girl; and I'll have her yet, though I should carry her off with the sword's point against all her kinsmen. I tell you, Agha, I shall die without this Radha."

"Exactly what you used to say about the Milkiganj girl," said Agha, with a sneer, as he drained out his liquor and knocked upon the floor with the pitcher for a fresh supply; "and you continued to be madly in love with her for whole six weeks after you carried her off. Then you quarrelled with her the sixth—was it the sixth or the seventh week?—and the week after you were only too glad to get rid of her when your father sent her back with money to her people. It would be just the same if you had this one."

"No; by the soul of the Prophet and the tombs of the Blessed at Kerbela, I would love this girl to my latest day, and never another woman!"

"Oh, ay, of course you would," grinned Agha; "how often have you sworn the same to others when you were away with the regiment? But, Miah, you may just as well fall in love with the moon as with this high-caste Brahmani. Why, man, what would the Hindoo dog her father say if you went and asked him for his daughter? I trow he would soon call for quarter-staves and have you beaten from his house."

"And I should cut him down before a slave could

lift a hand to obey him!" cried Afzul, furiously; "now, Agha, give me good counsel for once; you are always advising when no one wishes you. What would you do about this girl if you were in my place?"

"If I were in your place, I would not bother my head about her," responded Agha, contemptuously. "Who am I that I should make myself the slave of a *sari* (female garment)? Bah! wait till you have lived as long in the world as I have, and you will see clearly the mischief and wickedness that lie under black eyes and soft cheeks. I once brought home a Persian girl with me from Turkistan when I went there with the Amir's troops before I came to serve the English Sahibs. I was as proud of her as a hen with one chicken, and was constantly bragging of how much more beautiful she was than the swarthy wives of my own clansmen. I thought nothing of going forty miles to plunder a necklace or some other pretty trinket to adorn her. Well, there was one night that my brother and I and half-a-dozen other horsemen went down into the Khyber to stop a company of rich merchants coming from Jellalabad to Peshawur; but the weather was stormy and the *kafila* (caravan) did not start. So when we grew tired of riding backwards and forwards among the blinding snow-drift, we galloped home again empty-handed, and cold and hungry. I had been thinking all the way, how the warm welcome at home would make up to me for my cheerless ride; and whom should I find with my wanton of a wife but Sekandar Khan, the chief of my village. I shot Sekandar through the shoulder as he fled, but my nerves failed me when I turned round to kill Souda. I raised my sword to strike her; but as she knelt before me, with her little head thrown back, her soft tresses, which were fairer and more silky than those of any maid in the valley, hanging down to the ground, and her soft hands clasped about my wrist, I thought how often that head had been pillowed on my bosom, and grew as weak as a girl. I tried several times to strike her, but my arm was witched by the piteous look of her pale face, and I fled from the house and passed the night in rushing wildly about among the drifty glens. I was not a whit stronger next day; and when my brother and kinsfolk told me that I must either wipe out the disgrace by killing my wife or flee the country, I thought it would be much easier for me to go away. I rode that night to Loodiana upon the chief's best charger, having burned down his houses and killed his two brothers, who were the only males of his family I could fall in with, before I set out. After all, poor Souda had a worse fate than if I had killed her, for Sekandar took her home to his house, and she is now the slave of his other three younger wives, and does all the drudgery of the family. Allah the merciful, what is fated is fated!"

"And what in the name of Eblis have I to do with your long-winded stories? I don't wonder at your wife taking up with another man, for she could never have cared for an old wolf of the Khyber like you. You in love! I could as well imagine a frog catching cold. A pretty Mejnun you must have made to this Turkistani Leila! But come, Agha, my brother, do advise me what I am to do."

"Well," replied Agha, as he drowned his matrimonial reminiscences in a huge gulp of spirits, "if you *will* have the maiden, it must be by foul means, for fair ones won't work; and what is more, they must be by safe means, for there would be no use in carrying off the girl one week, to be thrown into prison and banished across black water the next. Am I right?"

Afzul, busy with his hookha, nodded assent.

"Then we must carry her quietly off some night, and keep her out of the way until the *tufan* (storm) blow over; and then, when her caste is fairly broken, her Hindoo relations will disown her, and will be too much ashamed to make an uproar about her."

"Excellently suggested, Agha. But how am I to keep suspicion off myself? These Hindoo dogs would get me arrested at once," doubtfully remarked the young man.

"Umph," said Agha, "we must guard against that, and fasten the suspicion upon some other quarter. Ah, I know a plan," he added, after a moment's reflection; "suppose we dress ourselves like Sonthal bandits, and break into the house with spear and torch. The Bengalees would be frightened to follow us in the direction of the passes, and we may easily conceal ourselves in the jungle until we can place the girl in some secure concealment. Won't that do?"

"Capitally," said Afzul, rubbing his hands in glee; "the Nawab of Panch Pahar is a true man, and would never betray one of the Faithful to the Bengalees. I shall keep the girl in his house until the danger is past, and I can take her with safety to my father's. And we can give out, Agha, that I am gone to Pultunpore on a visit to the regiment."

A fresh measure of liquor was ordered in to aid them in maturing their lawless enterprise; and the more they discussed it, the less difficult did it seem. Afzul was only too glad to catch at any suggestion that promised him the realisation of his passion; and with the unthinking rashness of youth, he was prepared to brave any danger that stood between him and his love. As for the Khyberee, he took a natural delight in mischief, provided there was a dash of romance or daring in the transgression. Agha's ethics had been formed in a somewhat arbitrary school among the wild frontier tribes. He would have deemed it a heinous sin to pilfer his purse from a sleeping man, or to rob a poor ryot of his cow; but there was no turpitude in robbing with the strong hand, or in driving off a herd of cattle from a rich landholder. Laws designed for the protection of property were in Agha's eyes rather a disgrace than an honour to a nation, for they presupposed impotence or cowardice on the part of the possessor, and tended to the encouragement of these base qualities, and to the destruction of whatever was free and manly and noble. Nor had Afzul's mind entirely escaped the contagion of these ideas. The Khyberee's tales had produced upon his imagination an effect analogous to that which is wrought upon the uneducated youth of England by the lower jets of sensational literature. No undergraduate of St Giles' or Whitechapel ever perused his pennyworth of blood and murder with a keener relish than that with which Afzul listened to Agha's trans-frontier experiences. And what was that they were now proposing to undertake but the fulfilment of his boyish dreams of carrying off a bride, the captive of his spear, as the warriors of old had been wont to woo? and the difficulties and dangers that beset the adventure were only additional enticements to him to put his fortune to the touch.

They drank off the remains of their liquor and strode back through the bazaar towards Walesbyganj — not quite so steadily, perhaps, as they had come—jostling the quiet townsfolk out of their path, and terrifying the shopkeepers by their loud talk and fierce gestures. The troopers saw and enjoyed the nervous demeanour of the Dhupnagar villagers; and their natural insolence was designedly exaggerated for the purpose of frightening the people still further. Wickedness and arrogance were inbred in a Muhammadan, argued the Bengalees; but these two were more vicious and oppressive than all the Mussulman tyrants put together, from the days of Muhammad the idol-breaker to the time of Nawab Suraj-ud-daulah.

"See how unblushingly they walk through the

streets to Rutton Pal, the spirit-seller's!" remarked Protap, the accountant, who was himself not altogether unsuspected of being one of Rutton's private patrons. "It was perfectly intolerable that men whose hands were red with the blood of sacred kine should be allowed thus to annoy the town's-folk," observed Dwarkanath, the village schoolmaster; "and if the headman would only do his duty, some order would be taken with these blusterers to keep them from putting honest folk in peril of their bodies."

But old Gangooly shook his head, and averred that it was a foolish thing to rouse a sleeping tiger; it would be time enough to cry out when anybody was beaten. Though the *nim* tree were watered with syrup, its leaves would still be bitter: so would a Mussulman be always a tyrant wherever he dwelt. His, Gangooly's, advice to his townsmen was to take care of themselves, for the Magistrate Sahib Eversley was friendly to the old Subadar; and the gods forbid that the villagers of Dhupnagar should blacken his honour's face by complaints of his honour's favourites. But since Afzul had fallen under suspicion of the robberies, the abuse of the villagers had grown more unmeasured, and the peaceful counsels of Gangooly less effectual; and though the Dhupnagar Hindoos might have to put up with Afzul's domineering ways while the young man stood well in the magistrate's favour, matters were very different now that he was in disgrace. Thanks to Gangooly's talking propensities, and the gossip of the two watchmen, there was not a house in Dhupnagar, except Walesbyganj, where the charge hanging over Afzul remained a secret. And so, as he and Agha went home from Rutton's that day the Hindoos regarded them with sulky looks and scowls of hardly-concealed defiance, although each was prudent enough to avoid any provocation that would break the wand of peace upon his own person.

No sooner had the Muhammadans departed from Rutton's than Jaddoo, the Dipty's orderly, crawled out from behind an old deal box in a corner of the verandah, and began to rub and chafe his legs and arms, which were cramped by lying so long coiled up in a snake-like posture. Jaddoo's face wore an air of triumph, indicating his appreciation of the news which he had overheard. Here was a discovery, not exactly what either he or his master had expected, but still a plot which would be quite sufficient to secure a conviction against the Muhammadan. Rutton Pal came gloomily in to take away the stools and jugs, and Jaddoo in his delight gratified the spirit-seller with a rupee in return for the means of eavesdropping which Rutton had afforded him.

Rutton took the coin and rang it upon the floor. "I didn't want to see either your face or your money, Master Orderly," said he, securing the coin in his waist-cloth. "It is the first time that ever Rutton, the son of Gopal, sold a patron or a neighbour, and he hopes it will be the last. If anything befall the

Muhammadan, your dirty *takka* (rupee) will scantily repay me for the loss of their custom."

"You might chance to be put to a greater inconvenience, brother Rutton, than the loss of a customer," said Jaddoo, with a grin, "if his honour the Dipty and I were to order a search of your premises. You will take care that no one hears of my being in your house, if you wish to keep my favour."

Rutton changed countenance at this threat, and bowed the great man's great man submissively out by the back door. Jaddoo sauntered away carelessly in the direction of the bazaar, and spent the day chatting and smoking with his acquaintances, and enjoying the hospitality which everybody readily proffered to one who enjoyed so large a share of the Dipty's confidence. Jaddoo, however, took good care to say nothing of the business which brought him to Dhupnagar, although more than half the village could easily guess his errand. His honour, the Dipty, had given him a few days' leave, Jaddoo said when questioned; and where could he spend his holidays better than among his friends and relations? As for business, he had enough of that at the Gapshapganj Court, where he could not avoid it; and he knew a better way of employing his leisure than by meddling with their police matters. And though the shopkeepers knew that Jaddoo's statements were all a *banao* (hatch-up), they did not care to call them in question, but sought rather by bribes and flattery to secure Jaddoo's influence with the Dipty on behalf of their little lawsuits and grievances. And the first day of his sojourn in Dhupnagar, Jaddoo fingered so many largesses from persons who wished to purchase his favour, that he began to think there were more unpleasant tasks in the life of an orderly than such "special duty" as had fallen to his lot.

Jaddoo had little difficulty in making up his mind that it would be prudent for him to keep the discovery which he had just made a little longer to himself. "For," he argued, "if I report what I have heard to the Dipty, he will think it quite sufficient ground for placing the matter in the hands of the regular police. But I am much better here, going about, my own master, with plenty of money for *karaj* (expenses) in my pocket, where nothing costs me a pice, and where everybody worships my feet. No, no; I don't get such a case every day, and must make it spin out. So I had better report to the Dipty that I have got no evidence as yet, but that I am daily expecting to fall in with a clue."

CHAPTER XVI.

BEJOY, THE GHATAK.

ONE morning all Dhupnagar became alive to the important fact that Bejoy, the *ghatak*, had been sent for by Ramanath Gossain, and there was nobody so simple as not to know what this foreshadowed. It was Bejoy's business to arrange all the Brahmins' marriages in the place, to settle the question of dowry and nuptial expenses between the high contracting parties, and generally to keep a list of all the marriageable boys and girls in Dhupnagar, with their prospects, their pedigrees, their personal attractions, and every other quality desirable in a husband or wife. Bejoy was a most useful man in the village, and the depositary of many grave domestic secrets; but no one had ever known him violate a client's confidence. Bejoy was an important man in the community, and he sometimes presumed upon his importance to take liberties, which in the case of any other person would have been rewarded with a bamboo or a slipper. If a Brahmin was so far forgetful of his duty as to allow his daughter to grow up into girlhood without having chosen a husband for her, Bejoy would put on his best clothes, refresh his memory from his list of unmarried boys, wait upon the negligent parent, and gravely remonstrate with him upon his want of natural affection. Bejoy could expatiate by the hour upon the impropriety of allowing girls to attain womanhood before they were settled in life, of the dangers which might thence result to the reputation of the family, of the grief with which the souls of deceased ancestors saw the chance of posterity thus cut off; and then he would artfully shift his theme to the good qualities of such and such a family, their pure Brahminical descent, their comfortable circumstances, and the amiable character and good looks of the oldest unmarried son. If the father was reluctant, and hinted at his inability to make a suitable settlement, Bejoy would assume another tone, would talk of the religious obligations which bound a parent to provide for his family's welfare, quote scripture by the page to convince the poor man of his sinful conduct, and end by pretending to take his departure in pious horror at his host's godless and unnatural conduct. But paterfamilias cannot afford to have his character blackened to all his neighbours, and his domestic affairs perhaps brought before the village council; so he calls Bejoy back, with much concern that any offence should have been given him; and the *ghatak's* kind interest is repaid with a fee, and a half-permission may be wormed out of paterfamilias to make inquiries regarding the boy and his family—just for mere curiosity, in a private way, and without liability to either party, upon Bejoy's word. So Bejoy goes away to the other family and tells the converse of his former story, is fee'd and feasted, and perhaps empowered to conclude a definite alliance; and then he goes home and books the match, calculates the net fees which it will bring, and casts his eye down the list in search of another eligible couple. Many a match is entered in Bejoy's books of which the families concerned can have little anticipation. Have the Fates, for instance, ever decreed the marriage of little Dossee, who was born on Saturday, with Khetter, who is now beginning to walk in leading-strings, and to lisp the names of his father and mother? I cannot say; but they are already coupled in Bejoy's ledger, and unless the Fates call death or disease to their assistance, the *ghatak* stands a fair chance of carrying out his own project.

I have often thought that the *ghatak* is an institution which some of us good Christians might well condescend to borrow from heathenism. Start not, my most respectable reader! I am not going to say that our British marriages are not the most perfect, the most happy, the most disinterested, the most pure—with this—— which you may fill up with any other superlative that expresses your views of what a marriage ought to be—I repeat, the most perfect, the most happy, &c., unions possible in this iniquitous world, where, nowadays, the decrease of marrying sons, the alarming increase of marriageable daughters, the competition for women of property, the upstart of new capitalists, the poverty of eligible aspirants, the ineligibility of rich candidates, the influence of society, that Board of Trade which looks so sharply after our domestic weights and measures, and many other awkward and untoward circumstances, are, I am assured upon good authority, every day threatening to bring business upon the matrimonial exchange to a complete dead-lock. But excellent as our matrimonial system is, I am not at all sure that it might not be mended. We do not sell our shares and stocks ourselves; indeed, some of us who think not little of our own cleverness, would make but a sorry bargain if we went into the City for that purpose; and why should we buy and sell our own flesh and blood when Bejoy, the *ghatak*, would do it so much better for us? Consider what humiliations my friend, Mrs Fisher, has undergone during these nine years since her eldest daughter became marriageable; how she has bowed and flattered, smiled and fibbed, gone out in evening dress when her rheumatism ought to have kept her at home, neglected her husband, and allowed her household to go to rack and ruin; and yet in spite of the exertions of that devoted mother, we all say that Miss Fisher is no more likely to get a husband than her old aunt, Miss Witherington. Ah, my good lady, they order these things better in Bengal. Had your daughter's name been in Bejoy's list, I believe Helena would have been settled years ago; at least *you* would have been spared no end of trouble and mortification. And how much more pleasant would it be for poor Tom Westerall if he could only make love by proxy to that raddled, bony Miss Silverley, who is forty at the least, but who has a fortune that would clear off all Tom's creditors, and set him on his legs again with the world —poor Tom! who has carried a faded little photograph of penniless Maggie Gordon, his sister's Scotch governess, in his pocket-book for the last ten years, until the likeness has become quite dog's-eared and dirty! Send for Bejoy, Tom, and if the lies must be told, don't tell them yourself; and then if she will have you, marry her, in heaven's name, pay off your debts, and deal as kindly with her as you possibly can. But there is so much to be said in favour of the *ghatak* that I shall keep the subject until some time when material is more scanty. Our French neighbours have their *bureaux de confiance;* but the French are a vain nation, unhappily inclined to make light of serious subjects; and my friend, Captain Slack, late of the Bengal Junglywallah Cavalry, who spends much of his time in the Parisian capital, as a change from Boulogne, has cautioned me that these institutions are seriously abused by *mauvais sujets* of both sexes. The Bengalees are, however, a serious and sober race, who view domestic institutions in as sacred a light as the greatest Pharisee who ever boasted of Great Britain as his birthplace possibly could do; and we may safely enough take a lesson from them. How I longed last Sunday, while escorting my friend Mrs Fisher from church, when that excellent lady made the remark *apropos* of the sermon —man's first disobedience and its fruit, had been the preacher's theme—" How little trouble our first parents must have had in marrying their sons and daughters," —it was the poor lady's highest conception of primeval bliss, and a very natural one too,—how I longed, I say, to recommend her to adopt the Bengalee *ghatak*, and thereby set an example to other British matrons, for which a grateful posterity would bless her name!

But enough of Mrs Grundy; and really after her and her ways the primitive savagery of the City of Sunshine is a sort of relief. The villagers were at no loss to guess what was on foot when Ramanath Gossain sent for Bejoy, the *ghatak*. Bejoy lost no time in obeying the summons, although he had an old grudge against the priest, for Ramanath had not only married his second wife, but had also arranged his son's unfortunate match with Chakwi without Bejoy's intervention. Bejoy was, however, delighted to forget all this in the prospect of securing so good a client as the priest, and he put on his best clothes, assumed a pretentious expression of professional gravity, and hastened to the temple to make his bow to the priest. Ramanath was sitting on his usual seat in the temple porch; his hookha had gone out unnoticed in his abstraction, and his head was bent upon his breast in a reverie, when a rustling of primly-starched cotton garments, and a heavy perfume of musk and sandal-wood, aroused him to the fact that Bejoy was salaaming before him. Bejoy's duties led him not unfrequently into female circles, and a little foppishness was excusable, and even requisite, in his profession.

"Salutation, Bejoy," said Ramanath, cordially, as he motioned the *ghatak* to a seat and proffered him the hookha. "Why, man, it is as good as an offering of incense to the gods, when you come to the temple. I suppose you can't guess why I have sent for you?"

"Though I am no reader of riddles, I yet think I may venture," replied Bejoy, with a smirk. "I have long said to myself, 'What a wonder it is that a lusty, hearty man like his worship, the priest, who can so well afford an establishment, should be content with one wife!' I warrant now you will want a young girl to nurse you in your old age. The Rajah of Ghatghar has a sister who is just turned of twelve, an Apsara * of loveliness: her face is round as the full moon, her waist slender as a cuckoo's throat, her ankles——"

"Nay, nay, friend Bejoy," interrupted Ramanath, with a laugh, "say no more of her charms, or I shall be as foolish as to fall in love with her at my time of life. I have been married enough for this world, and if I had wanted another I would have wooed one for myself—no offence to you, however, my good friend."

Bejoy made a grimace and a bow. He had known this well enough, but he thought Ramanath would

* The celestial females who dance in paradise before the god Indra.

feel pleased to be complimented upon his youth, and he had made the mistake on purpose. And certainly there was no accent of anger in the priest's voice as he continued:—

"No, Bejoy, it is my son Krishna who wants to make a fool of himself. You can't put an old heart in a young body; and I don't mind telling you, who are a discreet man, in confidence, that there is little love lost between him and Chakwi; and a pity it is, for she is a good girl. But the lad has set his heart upon Kristo Baboo's daughter, and I have thought it best to let him have his own way. So I am going to put the case in your hands, and if you manage it well, I promise you it will be the best match for you that was ever made in Dhupnagar."

Bejoy grinned and rubbed his hands, and then burst forth into a torrent of blessings upon the priest's wealth and liberality, and vowed that if he did not make up the marriage before a month was over, he would never attempt another in Dhupnagar. The case was a difficult one; but Bejoy, like the barrister who is delighted at being entrusted with a *cause célèbre*, was duly sensible of the importance which he acquired in undertaking it, and was determined to stake his professional reputation upon the issue. Kristo Baboo's daughter had long been a standing reproach against Bejoy in his own eyes. Radha's father could not have been more chagrined at his daughter's ill-fortune than was Bejoy, who looked upon a maiden so well-born and so beautiful, but yet unmarried, as a professional disgrace to himself. But be it told to Bejoy's credit that Radha's spinsterhood was no fault of his. The *ghatak* had proposed all manner of matches, both likely and unlikely, until Kristo Baboo had lost patience, and had told Bejoy not to trouble him farther upon that subject, though he acknowledged the *ghatak's* concern for his daughter's welfare by a heavier largess than he could well afford. So far-seeing a man as Bejoy had of course observed how suitable a match Krishna, the priest's son, would be for Kristo Baboo's daughter; but the Gossains had never been clients of his, and Bejoy had no faith in any marriages that were not of his own making. But now the case was altered, and Bejoy felt as if he should like to begin work that very minute.

But the priest had to moderate his ardour. There were many things that must be taken into account before a formal proposal could be made to the Lahories. The young man might not impossibly raise some scruples about a second marriage, although he was madly in love with the girl, for he had picked up a lot of whimsical notions among the English Sahibs at Calcutta. Bejoy shrugged his shoulders contemptuously at the idea of any man having scruples about marrying a girl of such beauty and of so high a caste as Radha. Moreover, Ramanath must not have the *izzat* (reputation) of his family compromised by exposing his son to a chance of being rejected by the

Lahories. Bejoy rubbed his hands impatiently, as much as to say that Ramanath might trust him to take care of that. So Bejoy must go to work cautiously, and sound Kristo upon the subject, before he gave the Baboo to understand that he had any powers to treat with him; and above all he must keep the villagers from getting wind of the matter, until it was definitely settled; and he could hint to Kristo, added Ramanath in a dignified way, that the marriage expenses need not be any drawback, for though Ramanath Gossain need not pay a pice to get the best Lahory in Bengal for his son, yet he would take care in a neighbourly way that his old friend Kristo should be put to no loss by the marriage, and that there would be no want of funds to provide a ceremonial suited to the rank of both families.

"*Bas* (enough), *bas*," cried Bejoy, jumping to his feet—" say no more, sir; the marriage is made!" and it was all the priest could do to prevent him from rushing across to the house of Lahory, and broaching the matter to Kristo Baboo that very minute.

It was astonishing how many of the villagers were congregated about the green after the news went out that Bejoy, the *ghatak*, had been sent for to the temple. The shadow of a jackass had fallen between Dwarkanath and his pupils while they were busy at lessons, and the pious schoolmaster could not possibly proceed with his work after such a portent. Shama Churn, the grain-dealer, left his shop to meet an imaginary merchant, whom he had engaged to see upon the village green, the Rialto of Dhupnagar. And what could have brought Prosunno, the lawyer, and Protap, the accountant, there at that moment? Some pressing business, no doubt. Protap's house was hard by, and Prosunno had recollected himself that he must talk with Gangooly, the village headman, who was of course quoting proverbs in the centre of the group. Each seemed to imagine that he himself, and no other, had a right to be there at that time; and when a new-comer sauntered up to the party, he had to put up with a host of cynical queries as to what *he* could be doing there just then. And then the great topic of the day would be introduced. It was no doubt on Krishna's behalf that Bejoy's services had been called in; but who was the girl? Protap, the accountant, who would gladly have given his own unmarried daughter to the priest's son, but who knew also that Krishna would never seek her, pitied the poor thing, whoever she was, and said that a woman might as well marry a *mletcha* (barbarian) or an Englishman as a Hindoo who had no religion.

Old Gangooly must have his joke, that a man who had been once burned should again plunge his hand into the fire, and was sharply rebuked by Dwarkanath, the schoolmaster, who had three wives himself, and who detected an irreverent allusion to the sacred institution of polygamy in the headman's remark. Shama Churn was mentally calculating the expenses which would be incurred by people of the Gossains' quality, and how much grain would be required to feed the Brahmins, and whether it would not be worth his pains to be a little more regular in his devotions at the temple, in order to get the contract. Nitye, the village doctor, was understood to say that no good could come of marrying a man who used European medicines; they tainted the blood, and his children would consequently be predisposed to leprosy and cholera. To which Gangooly responded that they would be all the better patients to him then; but the old charlatan shook his head, and said that physic did little good to a dead man, and English doctors were worse than Hindoo devils, for the latter might be driven away by charms; but when a man took medicine from the former, he made a covenant with Yama, the god of death. And Prosunno, the lawyer, speaking from the brief he held for Three Shells, said that the Gossains were excellent people—most excellent and honourable people; that an alliance with them would be an honour to any one in the place; and that he was surprised—nay, grieved even—that people should have allowed their tongues to cast aspersions upon Krishna's orthodoxy, when that good young man was bearing so clear a testimony to his *Swadharma* * by taking to himself a second wife. Whereupon the elders stared at Prosunno in amazement and held their peace; but that ornament

* *Swadharma* is the creed in which one has been born and brought up.

of the legal profession never lost control over a muscle of his countenance.

When Bejoy, the *ghatak*, made his appearance, there was a general movement to meet him; but that gentleman was too full of the importance of his mission and of professional responsibility to pay much heed to their greetings. He came stepping daintily up, his well-polished shoes creaking jauntily beneath him, and his stiffly-starched *chaddar* thrown with studied carelessness over his shoulder. His face was half turned aside, his eyes fixed upon the ground; and his face wore an air of pensive contemplation, as if it would say, " See here, how I am drudging for the happiness of you and your families! It is little wonder though we *ghataks* be melancholy men. Ah! if you only knew the toil, the care, the anxiety it gives us to arrange your domestic affairs, you would be more grateful to your benefactors." With a courteous wave of his hand and a sad smile, Bejoy acknowledged the salutations of his townsfolk, and declining, with a solemn shake of the head, Gangooly's laughing invitation to come and revive his friends with a smell of him, he passed along the green until almost in front of the house of Lahory, while all eyes anxiously watched his progress. It may be that Kristo Baboo was not without his share of the popular curiosity, for that worthy gentleman, who was standing at his own door, started when he saw Bejoy coming towards him, and went hurriedly inside. But Bejoy had no intention of troubling Kristo at that time. He walked slowly across the green until he came to the road which led along the village, and turning to the left, passed on, apparently engrossed in thought, until he reached his own house, and was hid from the anxious view of the Dhupnagar public.

"Well, well," said Gangooly, "if he makes a marriage it can't be in the dark, and we shall doubtless hear of it in time. And Bejoy, the *ghatak*, is none the worse that he does not gossip about other people's business. One loose tongue will make more mischief in a minute than twenty can mend in a month. What think ye would be the consequences if *I* were to chatter about every matter that came before me as your headman?" The village elders, who had good reason to distrust Gangooly's commendations of his own prudence, shrugged their shoulders, and went their several ways. There were divers conjectures put forth in the bazaar that day regarding Bejoy's mission. Some had it that Ramanath, provoked by his son's heresy, had made up his mind to disinherit Krishna, and to marry another wife in the hope of having male issue. Others were sure that Bejoy had been commissioned to bring a European madam from Calcutta as a wife to the young man, and hence it was no wonder though the *ghatak* did not like to speak about so disgraceful a job; they wondered that so respectable a man as Bejoy would have had anything to do with these Gossains and their dirty work. Chand, the barber, who was the great authority upon the Brahminical side of all public questions, was astonished that people could fabricate such stories. He had been most credibly informed that Bejoy's visit to the priest was nothing more than a mere friendly call. Of course, when so clever a fellow as Bejoy got his hands upon a man, there was no saying what would occur, and it was just possible that a marriage *might* come of it; but any such announcement would be premature at present. However, there were more things of which the folks of Dhupnagar might assure themselves, and they were these—that the Gossains would only ally themselves with a family of the very best caste; and that if there was a bridal, it would be the grandest affair of the kind Dhupnagar had witnessed for many a day. Bonoo, the broker, who was the organ of the opposition, inveighed loudly against the corruptions of Dhupnagar Brahminism; they would hardly bestow a glance upon a person of lower caste than themselves, and they were ever ready to excommunicate any poor man who intermarried with a Sudra; but they had no scruple about smoking and drinking with a rich heathen and a beef-eater like Krishna, the priest's son; surely the latter days of the Black Age were come, when the twice-born caste thus forgot themselves. Moreover, Bonoo warned the townsfolk to keep a sharp eye upon the priest and his family; they had already introduced heresy into the village, and the gods only knew what they might do next. Whereupon Chand, the barber, the conservative exponent, expressed himself in withering scorn of the opinions of Bonoo, the radical, and wondered that no judgment befell a man who had ventured to open his mouth in disparagement of the holy caste; but what could be expected of such an insignificant, ill-conditioned fellow, who got his information at second-hand from the cow-dung wives in the bazaar? The undaunted Bonoo stoutly replied that his opponent was an old crow and a father of fools, that he followed the Brahmins as a kite follows a sick bullock, in the hope of picking something up from off them, and that he knew nothing about the matter in question. Then, of course, Chand would abuse Bonoo, and Bonoo vilify Chand, until the townsmen took sides and a clamour arose. But why detail the progress of the controversy? Is Bengal the only country where Chand and Bonoo bespatter one another for the public amusement and their own profit?

There were not many people the wiser that evening, when Bejoy slipped out at his back door after dusk, and took his way through the deserted lanes of Dhupnagar to the house of Lahory. Was it entirely a lucky accident that the *ghatak* found Kristo Baboo just about to sit down to supper, upon which more than ordinary care had been taken; or had the Baboo divined that Bejoy might possibly look in upon him? This point I cannot pretend to settle; but it is certain that Bejoy received a warm welcome, and being a man of good caste he was instantly set down to share the Baboo's meal. The rice was served up smoking hot and boiled to perfection; the curry and *chillies* were so hot that you could hardly hold them in your mouth, and yet so sweet that you scarcely felt the heat; the mango fish were deliciously sour, and almost floating in melted butter; there was also mango *phul*, or the fruit of the mango-tree beaten into custard; piles of sweetmeats; and, to crown the whole, a couple of bottles of "European water," which we English call by the name of soda, the last of a dozen which Kristo had received in a present from a Calcutta friend. The production of this wonderful liquor denoted the importance which the Baboo attached to Bejoy's visit, for it was only to great personages, like the Rajah of Ghatghar, and Preonath, the "Dipty" magistrate, that a similar attention had been shown. So Kristo and the *ghatak* gorged themselves upon the good things, and fed each other with the choicest delicacies, until the servants came to remove the dinner-carpet, and brought in the Baboo's massive silver hookha, when both, fairly surfeited, leant back upon their respective cushions, and waited there in patient endurance of the pleasure of repletion, too indolent to speak or even to think, until they had privacy for the discussion of business. Then began the contest, the *ghatak*, on his part, endeavouring to probe Kristo's real feelings regarding his daughter's marriage, without committing his client to a definite proposal, and the Baboo doing his best to appear indifferent to the subject. They talked of all the gossip of the village, and how frequent robberies were becoming, and how young Afzul Khan was likely to get into trouble about them, and how many thousand rupees the Rajah of Ghatghar had squandered among the English Sahibs at the last Pultunpore races.

"May Siva blast him and his whole generation!" growled Kristo, at the mention of Afzul Khan. "When his father robbed me of my land, I always said these Muhammadan dogs would come to the gallows. Ill-gotten land never thrives with such people, Bejoy; and I should not wonder though the Government were to take back the grant from them, now that they are become Thags and Dakaits."

"You speak the truth, Baboo," said Bejoy. "There is little good in these Muhammadans. They have no order or decency in their marriages. I have heard that they will take a slave-girl for their head wife, if she is pretty, as readily as a woman of their highest caste."

"If they would be content with their wives," cried Kristo, indignantly, "it would not matter so much; but I tell you, Bejoy, there is not an unmarried woman or a widow in the district safe from that young blackguard. You have heard, of course, how he behaved to the ryot of Milkiganj's daughter?"

"It must be a serious thought to you, sir, to have an unmarried daughter of such beauty in your house while this lawless young Mussulman is at large," said Bejoy, making a bolt at the opening thus presented to him. "If I might make a respectful representation, I would advise that you should allow me to seek out a good husband for her. It is time, Baboo, that your daughter were well mated."

"He won't be at large long, or I'm much mistaken," said Kristo, taking no notice of the *ghatak's* insinuation. "The Magistrate Sahibs have got their eyes upon him, and I trust they may soon send him to the Andamans—or, better still, hang him."

"The over-ripe mango loses its bloom, Baboo," persisted Bejoy. "Your daughter is fast approaching maturity. It is neither prudent nor natural to delay longer. The townsfolk murmur about it, and no wonder."

"Murmur! Plague choke them!" said Kristo, angrily. "What have Sudras like them to do with me and my daughter? I have no doubt they would like well enough that I should go into the bazaar and pick out some of their pariah shopkeepers as a husband to my girl. I would tenfold sooner follow her corpse to the banks of the Gungaputra. Those who come after me may well say that Kristo Lahory lessened the family property, but they shall never taunt me with tainting the blood. Better that the family should end in a pure virgin than endure as a mongrel strain to grieve the souls of our departed ancestors."

"There is no need to go into the bazaar, sir," said Bejoy. "Your daughter has blood and beauty to make her a match for the best Brahmin in Bengal. If you were not so difficult to please, I could soon make an excellent match for her."

"Oh, ay! and where, in the name of Kali, am I to get money to pay her dowry and provide for the marriage expenses?" cried Kristo, in an impatient tone. "Am I to take to the highway with that blackguard of a Muhammadan, and plunder purses to dower my daughter? or am I to send her away like a beggar with my poor mother's bracelets and nose-rings, and burn half-a-dozen oil-lamps upon the verandah in honour of the occasion? When I brought home my wife, Bejoy, the road from the Pagoda Tope to the village was lighted with more than two thousand lanterns upon each side; and when the one end of the procession had entered the village, the other was not come in sight of the valley. That was something like a bridal; the expenses did not cost my father a pice less than half a lakh of rupees."

"And what would you say, Baboo, if as gay a bridal could be provided for your daughter, without putting you an anna out of pocket?" said Bejoy, triumphantly. This was going to the full stretch of his commission; but Bejoy, like every skilful practitioner, was fond of carrying his point by a bold stroke.

"Say! Why, I should say such a thing might be possible if one of the immortals came to woo her, as they came to Damayanti, the wife of Nala," cried Kristo, in a tone of angry incredulousness. "It does not cost *them* much to get up a *tamasha* (show); and if it is any of them that has made you his *ghatak*, he may have my daughter with my blessing, though he had an elephant's head like Ganesha, or were as ugly as Yama, the god of death."

"Such jesting is unseemly," said Bejoy, with a look of grave reproach. "You surely do not think that I would venture to trifle with a person of your consequence. May my face be black before you if ever you find Bejoy taking such a liberty! I was only remarking that with your kind permission and good fortune, I might be able to find a suitable husband for your daughter, and a way of providing for a proper marriage ceremonial, without putting you to any expense."

"Then it is some low-caste fellow who wants her," said Kristo. "It won't do, *ghatak*. The gods forbid that Kristo Lahory should sell Brahmin's blood to a churl though he were lord of ten provinces! Nobody would make such an offer unless there was something wrong about him. I tell you I shall never be the person to lower the caste of Lahory."

"Bejoy never took a fee from a churl in his days," said that gentleman, with an offended air. "I have been a *ghatak* in Dhupnagar for twenty years, and I never yet arranged a match that Manu himself might not have blessed for being equal. The husband I suggested comes of as good a caste as your own."

"Is it Ramanath Gossain, or his son Krishna?" said Kristo, in a low stammering voice, and with a flushed face. "Is it of either of them you would speak, Bejoy?"

"I certainly am not empowered to make an offer upon the part of these worthy Baboos; but since you have suggested it, I think that the young man might be a most advantageous match," returned Bejoy, fully fathering the idea upon his host. "It would give me most sincere pleasure to arrange a marriage between your families, and I do not think there would be much difficulty in bringing it about. Ramanath is as generous as he is rich, and from what he said to me this morning, I am sure he would be willing to take all the outlay upon his own shoulders, in a neighbourly way, if his son were marrying again to his satisfaction."

Kristo smoked away in silence, but his face was flushed and his pulse beat quickly. A marriage with the Gossains would end the reproach to his family, and they were so wealthy that they would never miss the money required to release him from his creditors. But then there was the disgrace of allowing Radha to leave his house a portionless bride. Well, when he considered the matter, he would have fewer scruples in being obliged to his old neighbour Ramanath than to any other person. But he must take care not to show the other party that he was so eager for the match, nor to allow the dignity of his family to suffer in the negotiations. So he returned no immediate answer, but smoked on, debating in his own mind the *pros* and *cons* of the proposition, especially as it affected his own pecuniary interest and the opinion of the public. With regard to his daughter's happiness, it is due to Kristo's character as a high-minded Hindoo parent, to state that he never bestowed a thought upon so trivial a subject.

"What about this young fellow's religion?" he asked, at length. "It is only a short time ago since the village *panchayat* was going to try him as a Christian and a kine-killer. You would not have me give my daughter to such a man, *ghatak?*"

"Who would heed what brokers and *badmashes* (blackguards) say?" asked Bejoy, scornfully. "The better a man's character is, the more they abuse it. Why, there is not a better Hindoo, or a stricter Brahmin, or a man that reverences the gods more, in Dhupnagar, than Krishna Gossain."

"So much the better for him, Bejoy," said Kristo; "but for all that, I do not see that he can marry my daughter. Krishna has a wife already, and I am not going to give Radha to be the slave of the *saukan saut* (rival wife)."

"Far be it from your bondsman to think of such a thing!" cried Bejoy, readily. "The gods forbid that I should offer the second place in any man's household to your daughter! Besides, Krishna hates his present wife, and has long fixed his eyes upon your daughter."

"Well, Bejoy, you are a good and trustworthy man,

and I should be sorry to stand in the way of your earning a fee in this business," said Kristo, with affected carelessness; "but remember that the dignity of me and my daughter suffer not in your hands. A clear and distinct offer must come from their side, and it must be solicited as a favour from me rather than proffered as a benefit to us. They are a good family, the Gossains; but a marriage with them is no honour to the Lahories. You will come again soon, friend Bejoy, and give me the pleasure of your gossip. I would have made you a present, but may Kuveru (the god of wealth) sweep away any rupee that is in my house until my rents come in. However, we may be more prosperous one day, when your kind interest shall not be forgotten."

"It is not necessary," said Bejoy. "It is pleasure enough for me to be serviceable to such excellent people without payment. I am not like the dirty *ghatak* of Gapshapganj, who fixes his fee of fifteen per cent before he will cross his own threshold. Nevertheless, you may depend upon me doing all that man can do to bring this affair to an auspicious termination."

"Sri Krishnaji! but this is a lucky hap," muttered Kristo to himself after the *ghatak* had departed. "Ramanath could pay my debts and redeem my land without knowing himself a pice the poorer; and I warrant him do it too, for he is a right generous neighbour, if the matter goes right. And then I can adopt one of my grandchildren, and keep the property from these kites of cousins. I shall give a silver *lota* to your Linga, O Siva! if this affair come right. What will the folk say about it? By the by, I shall have to keep it quiet until my lawsuit with Keshub of Bhutpore is over, or that rascally Dipty would give a decree against me for very spite. Impudence, indeed, for the son of an oil-seller to pretend to my daughter! I wonder his presumption does not bring a judgment upon him!"

CHAPTER XVII.

KRISHNA AGONISTES.

POOR KRISHNA! he was now to learn how frail are the best of good intentions. If, as folk say, the road to a certain place is paved with these, what a slippery pathway it must be, to be sure! and the descent to Avernus will be easy indeed. Your reprobate takes a header sheer over, and goes down with a rough come-tumble, accompanied by so much "hideous ruin and combustion," setting so many stones rolling in his descent, and altogether making so unpleasant an uproar, and presenting such a disagreeable spectacle, that everybody who sees him is quite shocked, and moralises primly over the downfall of the wicked. But the poor man who is always making good resolutions and never keeping them, whose conduct is the very reverse of his intentions, has ventured upon an easier but not less dangerous slide. Down he goes, gradually and gently at first, but, in spite of the pleasant incline, he is nervous and begins to pull up. Again he is off; this time with more confidence, and we see him gracefully nodding and bowing to the gentlemen and ladies, his friends, who crowd round to cheer and applaud the bold skater. A few more pauses and the slide has become so smooth that really he hardly knows whether he is at rest or in motion. He does not see the posts with the placard "Dangerous!" He does not hear the warning hollas of the bystanders. A crash and a splash, and he is wallowing in the dirt, the mud, and the *débris*, the *negra belletta* of Styx; and the world has a more harsh judgment to pronounce upon him than it had upon his neighbour. Poor Krishna! who thought that he was standing so firmly all this time, had slipped his foot, and was somewhat hurt, but more humiliated. Was this the man who had been to perform such feats, to cut such figures, before he bound on his skates? Tumbling at the first step upon the ice, and everybody laughing at him too. Krishna laughed bitterly at himself when he remembered the temptations he was to overcome, the stripes and the imprisonment he was cheerfully to undergo on behalf of his opinions; and here he was, before a sword had been drawn or a standard unfurled, bought over to the enemy's cause. Where now was that strength of character upon which he had prided himself—that self-confidence which had led him to take up a loftier standpoint than his fellows? What availed it now that he had evinced his intellectual superiority over the Calcutta students, since his intellect was no match for base, brute passion? Was he not worse now than Preonath, the "Dipty," whose servile adherence to Hindoo orthodoxy he had so often scoffed at? Why, even his old companion Premchand Dass, who had turned Christian, and whom Krishna had been wont to taunt with having exchanged one superstition for another, was more to be envied than he was. Premchand had at least remained consistent to his faith, while he——. But I doubt much whether Krishna's mental humiliation oppressed him so much as the dread of public ridicule — the sneers of the Brahmins and the scorn of his fellow-Brahmists. They could not help knowing everything about it, for the Brahmins would be sure to tom-tom the recantation of so distinguished a heretic all over the country. The 'Bengalee Baboo,' the organ of the orthodox party, would hail his return to Hindooism with patronising sneers; while the 'Cossitollah Reflector' would make his defection the subject of indignant leaders, full of invectives against himself and all his connections for six months to come. O God!—or gods rather—the poor youth would groan; what sins had he committed in his present or former births that he should be thus bound and delivered over to himself for punishment and torture?

It did not require a long siege to bring Krishna to capitulation. Day after day found the poor youth waging a vain battle with himself, now by prayer and good resolves beating back the enemy, but only to

yield the vantage-ground again under the pressure of
passion and selfishness. Could his friends have come
to his rescue, or could he have possessed himself with
an enthusiasm for his faith, he might have been saved.
But how far will the enthusiasm produced by a purely
intellectual belief, such as that of the Brahmic Theists,
carry a man? Who ever laid down his life for a theory
of Causation? Would Comte have gone to the guillo-
tine in defence of Positivism? or Mr Darwin—I mean
no disrespect to that great thinker—allow himself to
be led to the stake in St Paul's Churchyard for the
sake of his 'Origin of Species'? A certain amount of
opposition and persecution will make a martyr of any
man for any conceivable opinion; and I have no doubt
that, had Ramanath adopted this course with his son,
Krishna would have borne an illustrious testimony to
the principles of Brahmism. If the priest had risen in
wrath and turned him out of doors, Krishna would
have gone to Calcutta and given himself all the airs
of a martyr; or if the father had attempted by petty
persecutions, by continual worrying, by threats, and
by sneers, to bring him back to the paths of orthodoxy,
I daresay Krishna would have hugged the rack and
the thumb-screws, would have faced the priest's anger
unflinchingly, answered argument by argument, and
remained in the end a more enthusiastic Brahmist
than before. But Ramanath did nothing of the kind:
he left the young man to himself, and treated his
religious aberrations as a genial father would deal

with his son's boyish folly — his mental wild oats,
which he would be all the steadier for having sown;
and he did his best to stir up the youth's self-interest
and passions, which the old priest well knew would
plead more powerfully on behalf of Hindooism than
any language of his could. Krishna was perfectly un-
prepared for this mode of attack. He had come home
to be martyred, and was on the whole rather disappointed that nobody took any notice of him. He had
no small share of vanity, which would have fed upon
persecution; but what right had they thus to treat
him as a child? If the mob in Calcutta had stoned
Kheddarnath Chatterjee when he was baptised as a
Christian, surely *he* was as well worthy of lapidation.
The Brahmins of Padrepore had beaten young Hem
Chunder Mitter within an inch of his life for breaking
his caste and declaring himself a Theist; and had not *he*
too torn off his Brahmin's cord and thrown down the
gauntlet to the gods of his people? Did they think
that he who had been held up to honour as the most
promising student in college, had been made so much
of by all the great natives in Calcutta, whose conversion had been considered so great a triumph for the
Brahmists—did these wretched barbarians of Dhupnagar think *him* too insignificant to be noticed, or did
they realise what might be the consequences to Hindooism of *his* apostasy? In fact, Krishna felt quite
angry with the latitudinarianism of his townsfolk, and
began to think that there would be but small benefit

in teaching them a new faith when they cared so very little for their present creed.

Then to these feelings of pique and disappointment, and a half-formed suspicion that he had been led somewhat far away by his self-conceit, were added his passion for Radha and his interest in standing fast by the old faith. If he abjured his caste and his creed, Radha could never be his; and what had he to look forward to but a life of misery without her—a life of poverty, scorn, and hardships? Well, he was prepared for this; but the bright spot beyond, the life of well-earned ease and honour that was to succeed his troubles, was not that another of his delusions? What hope could he have to see so gigantic a system as Hindooism overthrown in his lifetime? and so long as Hindooism prevailed, he must continue to be an outcast and object of popular persecution. Then consider what misery he would cause to his friends by an ill-advised profession of his enlightened opinions,—to his poor father, who had been so good-natured, so indulgent, and whose old age would be rendered lonely and miserable by the desertion of the only child left to him—to Radha, whom he loved—to poor innocent Chakwi, who loved him, and whom fate had, so unfortunately for them both, mated with him. Why should he be the cause of grief to all these innocent people? For what was it that he was thus bent upon ruining himself and distressing his relations? For a belief; but how well grounded was that belief? Had he never doubts and misgivings? was he as happy as those who had a more sure, though a grosser, faith? was his purely intellectual *cultus* as calculated to make the masses happy as the old emotional worship of the country? On the whole, Krishna began to fear that he had been following a phantasm which had led him away until he was lost in the jungle. So when Ramanath made a direct attack upon Krishna's citadel, the fortress was carried by an easy assault, the garrison having been starved out by cutting off the supplies of vanity, and disheartened for want of allies. The old priest came and sat down beside his son, took the young man's hands in his own, and in tones of parental kindness told him that he was making proposals for Kristo Baboo's daughter. He had done very wrong, the priest meekly confessed, in contracting the marriage with Chakwi, and in attempting to coerce his son's affections, and the best reparation he could make for it now would be to secure for his son a girl whom he truly loved. As for Chakwi, it was an awkward affair, and the priest was very sorry; but his son was a good-hearted man who would feel for the poor, gentle girl, and do his best to show her some appearance of husbandly regard. And then he began to talk of the marriage, and to grumble good-humouredly over the expenses that they would have to be at in providing a ceremony worthy of so grand a lady as Radha. They must have the house decorated anew, although really her own home was not so luxurious that the girl had any reason to be fastidious. There were some folk who would not be over well pleased when they heard of Krishna's good fortune. Our friend Preonath, the Dipty, for instance; an ill-conditioned tyke, my son, whom learning had made proud without making him a gentleman: a fellow who, forsooth, was ashamed of his old father, Ram Lall, the oil-seller, an honester man than ever stood in the Dipty's slippers. That young profligate, the Rajah of Ghatghar, too, would fain have been a suitor; but Ramanath Gossain's son did not need to salaam to any of these great people, and could hold his own against the best of them. No, no; Krishna might perhaps count rupee about with his highness; and pretty highness he was too—a broken-down debauchee before there was a rough hair upon his face; and his son could, at any rate, get through this world without sitting upon a bench to be deaved by the chattering of lying lawyers and policemen for three hundred rupees a-month.

Krishna sat in silent thoughtfulness, allowing his father to rattle away in this manner. The old priest talked against time, hardly pausing to take breath, for he knew that if he allowed his son to speak for himself, and a controversy arose, his cause was lost. But Krishna was then in no humour for arguing. His brain was in a whirl; and the only idea he could lay hold of, was a feeling of doubt whether he was the same Krishna Chandra Gossain, the boldest, the most ardent of Brahmic converts, the fiery "Iconoclast" of the 'Cossitollah Reflector,' the man who had proclaimed war without quarter against the idolatry and superstition of his countrymen,—he wondered whether it was the same person who was sitting there so calmly and hearing all these things. The priest, it is true, had never mentioned religion, taking for granted, as it appeared, that Krishna's enthusiasm had cooled down; but the Hindoo marriage with all its idolatrous rites— nay, the bigamous union itself—would be a public profession of his recantation. He knew all this, but still he held his peace. The thought of Radha was a spell upon his tongue; and he sat there giving a silent assent to all that his father said; and when the old man had finished and hurried out of the room rubbing his hands in great good-humour, Krishna allowed him to go away without a word of expostulation.

It was all over then, and he felt wonderfully relieved. To be sure, his honour was shattered, his good faith bartered for the possession of a woman, his name become a disgrace to all his Calcutta friends and associates; but still he was less miserable than he had been when tossed about, the prey of contending passions, seeking to do the right, yet choosing to do the wrong. The Rubicon was passed, and the dangers that had been like to daunt him upon the other side were fast melting away in the bright vistas opening up before him. Love as well as gold can deaden the sense of disgrace; with Radha as his wife he would be independent of the sneers of the Brahmists. He could spend all his days in ease and pleasure in the valley of Dhupnagar, and need never go near the city again with its racket and turmoil, its chattering and hollow inhabitants, its insincerity, its censoriousness, and its empty conventionalities. Here he might lead a life as happy as that of his free Arigian forefathers in the early pastoral days, before lust and priestly ambition and the love of money had inaugurated the Black Age. The Brahmists would of course revile him; but what mattered it what the Brahmists said? He felt he was beginning to hate the Brahmists; idle speculative visionaries they were, the most of them; or else officious, meddling busybodies, who, having no definite faith of their own, took a mischievous delight in unsettling other people's ideas. Who were they that they should attempt to overthrow so venerable, so æsthetic a ritual as that of Hindooism? What warrant had they for the position they took up? They had no revelation, no scripture, nothing but the faint and uncertain light of human speculation to guide them. They abused the Christians; but what, after all, was the Brahmist system but Christianity without Christ? their ethics, their forms of worship, the whole structure of their religion, were they not taken from a system that they professed to despise? And what would be the end of the Brahmic movement? They might go on smoothly enough so long as they had a man of powerful intellect and saintly character like Keshub Chunder Sen to guide them; but what would become of them after his death? They would be split up into half-a-dozen different sects, each fighting with the other and bringing their principles into utter discredit; or they must become Christians, or perchance relapse into Hindooism. It was only a partial and uncertain movement; and Krishna began to reason himself into an assurance that he was very fortunate in getting out of it before he was too deeply compromised to retreat.

Krishna's first act, however, did not speak much for the sincerity of this conviction. He wrote to his Calcutta friend Bholanath Thakoor, a cautious, diplomatic letter, intended to forestall the news of his recantation, and modify its effect upon the members of the Brahmo Somaj. Poor Krishna, who had hitherto been so honourable and ingenuous, was serving a rapid apprenticeship to duplicity. But we had better let his letter speak for itself:—

From BABOO KRISHNA CHANDRA GOSSAIN of Dhupnagar, to BABOO BHOLANATH THAKOOR of Calcutta.

"MY DEAREST FRIEND,—Your letter was welcome to me as the dewy moonbeams to the love-parched *chakar*. Like a ray of sunshine gleaming through prison-bars to gladden the hearts of the captives, your cheering counsel came to refresh my soul. O Bholanath, how much I need your company! In my father's house I am as much a prisoner as if I were a bound convict in Alipore jail. I have no one to talk to, no one to whom I can open my heart, no one of whom I can ask advice. I am shunned here as if I were a leper, or as if I carried the cholera about in my waist-cloth. Yet it is little loss to me upon the whole, for I can have but little fellowship with people who are so far sunk in ignorance and superstition.

"I may confide to you that solitude and constant meditation have wrought a considerable change in my opinions. Think not, Bholanath, that my faith in the Supreme Brahma has ever for an instant wavered, or that I am falling back into our old errors. What I mistrust is my own ability to battle with Hindooism, and the expediency of provoking a contest while our party is still in its infancy, while our views are not fully matured, and while the position of the enemy is still so strong. A few years longer, and education will have prepared a fitting soil for the reception of our good seed. At present we hazard our cause by exposing it to defeat. You remember, Bholanath, how we used to talk in our youthful ardour about going forth as missionaries to rescue our countrymen from their delusions. It was a dream, a generous ideal, but still a dream. When Brahma thinks that the time has come to enlighten his countrymen, he can by a single flash of his glorious truth before their eyes turn millions from their idolatry. As for me, who am I that I should attempt to take God's work out of His own hands? I find myself placed here by Brahma in a certain sphere with certain duties to perform, and with certain rights belonging to me. What does it profit me if I neglect these duties, that I attempt a great work, not knowing whether Brahma will require it at my hands? Suppose I, by my teaching and my testimony, turned a few Hindoos from idolatry, but still broke my poor father's heart and distressed all my kind relations, would I have satisfaction—would my conscience approve my conduct to me? How could I preach the sacred obligations of filial affection when I have slighted them myself? You will reproach me for all this, and say that I am striking a truce with error. My answer is, that I am not, and shall never be, reconciled to Hindooism; but that while I loathe idolatry myself, I hesitate to unhinge men's minds from their *swadharma* (own religion), until I can present them with a more objective creed than our own philosophical system.

"I must also tell you that I am likely soon to be married to the maiden whom I have so long loved, of whom you have heard me so often speak. My head is so full of coming bliss that I hardly know what I am writing. Do not reproach me for contracting a bigamous union; Chakwi has never been my wife but in name. The marriage will of course be celebrated according to Hindoo fashion. That I cannot help, for no other form of marriage is known here among us, and I shall assent to the idolatrous rites with a mental reservation. I tell you this in confidence, as I do not wish it to be mentioned at present. But every man has his enemies; and if you should hear a rumour among the Brahmists that Krishna Chandra Gossain has abandoned the paths of Theism and gone back to the ways of error, I need not ask my friend to contradict the report, and to assure them that my faith in the Supreme Brahma was never more steadfast than at present. I know that your affection will do all that is needful and all that I could wish. Greet all our brethren for me, and assure our reverend leader that my lips are longing to kiss his feet.—From your brother in Brahma,

"KRISHNA CHANDRA GOSSAIN."

As Krishna read over this letter he could not conceal from himself that he had hardly stated his case frankly. But what good would it do him to enter into particular details to persons who were not likely either to realise or sympathise with his position? He had done his best to prepossess his friend Bholanath in his favour, and to take the sting out of slander; and that was really all that he wanted. As for stating his mind clearly, he had better wait until he knew it clearly himself, for he was in such a whirl that he was never two days of the same opinion. But why not open his heart to his trusted friend Bholanath, and confess to him at once that he had succumbed to temptation, that he had sold his conscience for a fair bride, and that he was really more miserable now when he had a certain prospect of obtaining Radha, than ever he had been while his love seemed hopeless? Krishna felt that this was a subject on which he had better be reticent. His Calcutta friend could not be expected to enter into all the feelings and motives which regulated his conduct; besides, good friend as Bholanath was, it was not impossible that he might indulge in a little natural triumph over the backsliding of one who had always boasted himself to be a more zealous reformer than his fellows.

The sequel showed that Krishna, judging probably from what he himself would have done under the same circumstances, had not miscalculated his friend's disposition. No sooner had Baboo Bholanath Thakoor mastered the above epistle than he hurried off to the leaders of the Brahmo Somaj, and disclosed to them the startling intelligence that Krishna Baboo, the hope of the sect, their most distinguished disciple, the convert in whom of all others their firmest confidence had been placed, was on the point of relapsing into Hindooism, and of sealing his recantation by marrying an idolatrix from the family of Lahory. This was terrible news to the reformers, and a meeting was specially summoned to consider the case. Bholanath, proud of being the cause of all this commotion—for Bholanath was one of those small Baboos who are always glad to take advantage of any chance of notoriety—read and re-read his letter, commented upon its contents, and explained all the circumstances of Krishna and his family, until the heads of the sect were glad to silence

him. Then began such a clatter of tongues as is to
be heard nowhere outside a Bengalee meeting. Some
would have the Brahmo Somaj to wash its hands of
the young Gossain, and to publish his name in the
'Cossitollah Reflector' as an apostate from the faith;
others thought that the matter should be kept quiet, as
it would only give their enemies an occasion for triumphing over them; a third party considered the Hindoos should be informed how far Krishna stood committed to the principles of the Somaj, and how he had
on one occasion breakfasted upon beefsteaks cut from
the sacred rumps of kine in company with certain of
his fellow-students at Spence's Hotel; a fourth counselled moderation, and argued that Krishna should not
be condemned unheard, that an expostulatory epistle
should be addressed to him, and that he should be exhorted and encouraged to withstand temptation; and
a fifth made the happy suggestion that some influential
member of the Somaj should be despatched to succour the young man in his hour of need, and save the
Brahmists from the reproach of a perversion. This
proposal was instantly caught up by all present,
opinions differing only as to the person who might
most suitably be intrusted with the mission. When
the spiritual welfare of so interesting a youth as Krishna
was in question, everybody was willing to take a trip
to Dhupnagar at the expense of the Society, and to
spend a few weeks among the green fields and shady
woods of that pleasant valley—an agreeable change

from the sweltering heat and dusty streets of Calcutta. There were so many volunteers that the heads of the Somaj were puzzled how to avoid the odium of making a selection. Bholanath urged his intimacy with Krishna as a claim to the preferment; but half a score of voices pronounced him to be a *chokhra* (boy), and a parasite of the young Gossain, and probably no better a Brahmist than his companion. So Bholanath shrank away into his original insignificance, and left the others to fight for the prize. Kali Baboo said that the Gossains were of his acquaintance, that he had great influence with the young man, and that he was quite confident in his own ability to steady Krishna's wavering faith. To which the others replied that Kali Baboo was a professional busybody, a wallower and a coiler in other people's affairs, a neglector of his own business, a broker, and the brother of a lascivious sister. While Kali was retorting at the top of his lungs, Siva Prasad Baboo put forth his pretensions, and was instantly attacked as an unsound Brahmist, a man who had a sneaking kindness for the Theism of the Vedas, who followed the Nyaya school of philosophy; a man who ought never to have joined the progressive Brahmists, but to have allied himself to the temporisers with error of the Adi Somaj: a proper mentor for a young man indeed! The turmoil had reached its height when the heads of the congregation announced that the choice of the Society had fallen upon their esteemed brother Mr Romesh Chunder Roy.

Baboo Romesh Chunder Roy—I beg his pardon, Mr R. C. Roy, for this is a point upon which my good friend is extremely sensitive—was the latest and most distinguished acquisition of the Brahmo Somaj, and the heads of the Society were naturally anxious to do him honour. Mr Roy had been educated in England; and having but lately returned to his native country, he was still regarded as a lion by his friends, who were confident that one of so much authority and experience would have no difficulty in leading Krishna back to the Brahmic fold. Mr Roy had himself begun life not far from Krishna's own village, his father being a small landholder near the town of Bhutpore. The young Romesh had attended the Anglo-vernacular school at Bhutpore, where he displayed such proficiency in acquiring English that Mr Eversley, the collector, took notice of the lad, and urged the father to send him to a Calcutta college. The father's ambition for his son would have been satisfied with a clerkship in the local courts, but the magistrate's word was not to be gainsaid; and so one fine morning young Romesh trudged away from the Gungaputra valley with a few books upon his back, his father's silver-mounted hookha, the family palladium, in one hand; a pair of new patent-leather shoes, which he was on no account to put on until he reached Calcutta, dangling from the end of a staff, carried over his other shoulder; and a small store of rupees, for which his father had mortgaged the best bullock to old Mahesh, the Bhutpore usurer, knit into a corner of his waist-cloth. The old man accompanied Romesh to the Pagoda Tope, which crowns the southern ridge of the Gungaputra valley; and his mother, and little sisters and brothers, and a bevy of neighbours, pursued him with good wishes and prayers for his welfare as long as he was within earshot. Romesh was sorry enough when the old man gave him his blessing and hurried away, that the boy might not be dispirited by the sight of his grief: but Romesh's heart was light, and the world was before him; and so he trudged cheerily onwards until he came to the line of railway, where, not without considerable misgivings, he embarked upon the *ag-ghari*, the wonderful fire-coach, which is swift as the car of Indra, god of the firmament, and much more useful to mortals. True to his father's cautions to be careful of his money, Romesh spent half a day in higgling for an abatement of the fare at the railway station, and threatening to walk all the way to Calcutta if he could not have a ticket at his own price, much to the amusement of the "knowing" clerks, who indulged in many a joke at the prudent simplicity of the "jungly" youth.

But Romesh's "jungly" simplicity was soon rubbed off in Calcutta. His little stock of money was speedily exhausted, and his wits were often sorely tried to get a living; but he made many friends, and as he kept those that he did make, he was never altogether reduced to starvation. In those days Romesh was the most orthodox of Hindoos. No one shouted louder or pulled more lustily at the Padrepore car festival; no one was more devout at the Durga Puja, and none more loud in professing horror at caste laxity, at intercourse with the beef-eating English, and at the progress of heterodoxy. In due time Romesh obtained a scholarship which a benevolent Anglo-Indian had founded for the purpose of enabling deserving students to obtain an English education; and in spite of his former declarations of antipathy to the English, in spite of the remonstrances of his friends, who gave him up for lost, both body and soul, the young adventurer crossed Black Water and ate roast-beef in its native climate. At the commencement of the voyage Romesh was sore troubled in body, and inclined to think that the judgments of his country's gods had overtaken him for his presumption in venturing upon Ocean, and for his impiety in eating forbidden meats; but in a few days the painful sensations lessened, and his spirits rose so, that before he had been a week at sea he found himself—such is the rapidity with which we harden in guilt—actually eating beefsteaks as if he had been used to them from infancy, and as if Brahma had not created the cow to be a sacred animal and the mother of the gods at the same time as he had formed the Brahmin race.

In Calcutta, Romesh had been but a poor half-starved student, who felt himself highly honoured when an English Sahib took the slightest notice of him; but in London, Mr R. C. Roy found himself a personage of no small consequence. The "enlightened Hindoo" was not then so familiar an object to the British public as he is at present, and Romesh was speedily caught in the toils of a host of lion-hunters. Ladies of title received him in their drawing-rooms; public men who had, or wished to have, an Indian connection, sought him out, and asked him to dinner. He was received by the Secretary of State for India, and he was even toasted as an Indian prince at a corporation dinner. Romesh accepted all these attentions with great affability, and comported himself with a dignity suited to the exalted society in which he was now moving. He would have been condescendingly civil to Mr Lyttleman, the joint-magistrate of the Gungaputra district, then on furlough, when he encountered that official at Lady Gotham's reception, had not Mr Lyttleman, chagrined doubtless at finding himself completely eclipsed by a native, turned away with great rudeness, and remarked to his wife in an audible tone that the impertinence of these confounded Bengalee Baboos was growing really intolerable, and that the Government *ought* to do something to put them down. On another occasion, at Lord Blackmore's, who was looking out for an Indian Presidency, Romesh was placed next Sir George Blitzen at dinner, as a compliment to the ex-commander-in-chief of the Indian forces,—in consequence of which ill-advised allocation, a severe attack of gout, brought on by Sir George's indignation at the proximity of a "blasphemed nigger," very nearly deprived the British army of one of its brightest ornaments. It was whispered, however, that there were fair Anglo-Saxon damsels who did not share in the narrow prejudices of these Anglo-Indians, and who would have gladly been bride to the young Romesh Chunder. But there was a "Mrs Roy" already in his father's house, who had been married to him when they both were infants, and whose face he had not seen for many a weary year, and Romesh prudently refrained from inspiring hopes of matrimony into the bosoms of his fair admirers.

The time at length came when R. C. Roy, Esquire, of the Outer Temple, barrister-at-law, and Bachelor of Laws of the University of Cockaigne, was free to return to his native country. It cannot be said that the feelings with which he contemplated revisiting the scenes of his youth were those that might have been expected to animate so warm a patriot. In his 'Champak Leaves,' which was published about this time, with a dedication to his honoured patron, the most noble the Marquis of Gotham, Mr Roy had informed the public that, though

> "Distant far in western isles
> I bask in Beauty's radiant smiles,
> My heart still haunts the lonely piles
>   That frown o'er Ganga's stream.
> My country's woes, 'neath alien sway,
> Uncheered by freedom's faintest ray,
> Are still my bitter thoughts by day—
>   By night my troubled dream."

But in spite of this sentiment, Mr Roy would gladly have remained in England, to be fed and petted by an appreciative public, rather than return to his former insignificance in Bengal; but his scholarship was at an end. He had no prospect of employment, and so he was compelled by force to take shipping for Calcutta. The news of his coming had of course preceded him. The 'Bengalee Baboo' had chronicled his academical triumphs, and transcribed wonderful paragraphs from the English newspapers concerning the doings of their distinguished countryman. The editor had lauded 'Champak Leaves' to the skies as a work destined to mark an epoch in English poetry, and wondered at the little-mindedness of the Laureate who could wear the bays that more properly belonged to worthier temples. They were all proud of their countryman's success, and now that he was soon again to be among them, the 'Bengalee Baboo' conjured him by all that was venerable and sacred in their ancient religion, not to add another name to the perfidious list of those who had apostatised from the faith of their forefathers. On the other hand, the 'Cossitollah Reflector' invited Mr Roy to cast in his lot with the little band of reformers who were struggling so nobly for the spiritual emancipation of India, in spite of the persecutions and sneers of society, and undeterred by the ignorant opposition of corrupt and illiberal journals.

We may be sure that Romesh's father, the old ryot, with his wife and family, packed closely inside a third-class *ticca-ghari* (hackney-carriage), was down at Garden Reach when the steamer came up the river bearing back his illustrious son to his native shores. But who could that great man be whom so many Baboos had rushed forward to greet, and who was whisked away to the city in a grand carriage, before the worthy folk had time to disentangle their ravelled senses? It must surely be a new Lord Sahib come to rule the country, or a Commissioner Bahadoor at least, that grand personage in the flowing robes. But where was their son, their Romesh who had left them ten years ago, with a pair of new patent-leather shoes in his hand and fifty rupees in his waist-cloth? And so they drove sadly back to the town, wondering whether Belatte (Europe) had so much altered their son that they had allowed him to pass unrecognised. Poor folks! little wonder though Romesh's own mother did not recognise her son in the barrister's wig and gown and the law hood of the Cockaigne University, which he had donned to give dignity to his debarkation. We must not ask too curiously whether Mr Roy saw that rickety carriage drawn by two miserable, half-starved horses, and whether he had caught a glimpse of his parents' faces as he was driven rapidly past them. It was an unseasonable time and an awkward place for a display of filial affection, when so many of the Calcutta aristocracy had come down to meet him. But we hope that he made up for his parents' disappointment when he met them some hours afterwards at the humble lodging of his college days.

So Mr Roy settled down at the Calcutta Bar, and his authority upon England and the English was held in the highest respect by his native countrymen. He still retained his English dress and English habits, and did not seek to dissemble his contempt for his untravelled countrymen. His affectation would have been intolerable but for his good-humour, which nothing could ruffle, and for his conceit, upon which no rebuff could make any impression. After some slight hesitation, during which he had been weighing his chances with either party, Mr Roy had joined the Brahmo Somaj, more especially as his old rival, Gobind Chunder Mitter, who had also been to England, and had come back a barrister, was a most zealous supporter of the opposite party; and thus it happened that Mr Roy had been selected by the heads of the Brahmo Somaj as the person whose arguments were likely to have most weight with Krishna, the priest's son.

END OF THE FIRST VOLUME.

PRINTED BY WILLIAM BLACKWOOD AND SONS

www.ingramcontent.com/pod-product-compliance
Lightning Source LLC
Chambersburg PA
CBHW031902220426
43663CB00006B/737